PENGUIN BOOKS

ON AND OFF THE FIELD

Ed Smith read history at Peterhouse, Cambridge. When still at Cambridge he made his debut for Kent, batting first as an opener, then at number three. His first book, a comparative study of cricket and baseball called *Playing Hard Ball*, was published to acclaim in 2002. As well as playing professional cricket, Smith reviews for the Books pages of the *Sunday Telegraph* and writes sports articles for *The Times*.

D1585567

On and Off the Field

ED SMITH

PENGUIN BOOKS

In memory of Eric Scarbrough (1910–2000),

a good Yorkshireman

PENGUIN BOOKS

Published by the Penguin Group
Penguin Books Ltd, 80 Strand, London WC2R 0RL, England
Penguin Group (USA) Inc., 375 Hudson Street, New York, New York 10014, USA
Penguin Group (Canada), 10 Alcorn Avenue, Toronto, Ontario, Canada M4V 3B2
(a division of Pearson Penguin Canada Inc.)
Penguin Ireland, 25 St Stephen's Green, Dublin 2, Ireland
(a division of Penguin Books Ltd)
Penguin Group (Australia), 250 Camberwell Road, Camberwell, Victoria 3124, Australia
(a division of Pearson Australia Group Pty Ltd)
Penguin Books India Pvt Ltd, 11 Community Centre, Panchsheel Park, New Delhi – 110 017, India
Penguin Group (NZ), cnr Airborne and Rosedale Roads, Albany, Auckland 1310, New Zealand
(a division of Pearson New Zealand Ltd)
Penguin Books (South Africa) (Pty) Ltd, 24 Sturdee Avenue, Rosebank 2196, South Africa

Penguin Books Ltd, Registered Offices: 80 Strand, London WC2R 0RL, England

www.penguin.com

First published by Viking 2004
Published in Penguin Books 2005
4

Copyright © Ed Smith, 2004
All rights reserved

The moral right of the author has been asserted

Typeset by Rowland Phototypesetting Ltd, Bury St Edmunds, Suffolk
Printed in England by Clays Ltd, St Ives plc

Except in the United States of America, this book is sold subject
to the condition that it shall not, by way of trade or otherwise, be lent,
re-sold, hired out, or otherwise circulated without the publisher's
prior consent in any form of binding or cover other than that in
which it is published and without a similar condition including this
condition being imposed on the subsequent purchaser

Contents

Acknowledgements

My thanks go to: Tony Lacey and Zelda Turner at Penguin, who worked hard to make my life easier; Chris Stone and Ian Brayshaw for throwing a thousand balls at me; Dave Fulton and Rob Key for spotting something was wrong with my batting in May; Martin Trew for watching Kent so closely; Laura Winthrop, Adam Janisch and Jonathan Shapiro, who all, at different times, said to me, 'I hope you're writing this down in your diary, not just telling me about it'; Sarah Wooldridge at IMG for her good advice; Michael Prodger at the *Sunday Telegraph*, who always sends me interesting books to review; Becky Quintavalle, who was an excellent agent without taking 15 per cent; the Loudon family, who made me feel so at home in my new house; my parents, who never change, whether I am in good form or bad; John Blundell at the Institute of Economic Affairs, who was an invaluable help throughout; Robin Martin-Jenkins for being a great companion in India; Keith Blackmore of *The Times* for initially sending me to Harvard, where I was brilliantly looked after by David and Tink Davis, Geoffrey Movius and the Master of Quincy House; and the lucky girl who brought me five hundreds out of five.

Picture Credits

Anthony Roberts: pictures 1, 2, 6, 19, 20, 21; Getty Images: 7, 9, 14, 15; David Dawson: 3, 4, 5; Empics: 10, 13; Reuters: 17, 18; Terry Mahoney: 8; Hugh Routledge: 12.

Preface

When I agreed to write this diary a year ago, I wondered whether it would help my cricket. Would it be a burden or an escape, an extra worry or a way of exorcizing demons, an unnecessary contortion or a natural part of my life as a cricketer? I didn't know what its themes would be, still less its narrative trajectory of success and failure.

Now, having just finished reading the whole thing through for the first time, I can see recurrent preoccupations that weren't obvious at the time: how to alleviate pressure; how to structure your life in order to perform at your best; how to balance the madness of competitive drive with growing up and seeing sport more in the round.

That is now, writing this preface in November 2003. Back in November 2002 – themes unknown, season unlived – I wrote the introduction. It had two purposes. The first was to encourage Penguin Books to give me an advance. The second was to provide a private blueprint, a mission statement to myself for what I ought to be writing in my diary – runs or noughts, win or lose.

Whenever I doubted I was being true to why I wanted to write this book, I re-read that introduction. It appears after this preface. I haven't changed a word.

E.T.S.
Harvard
Cambridge, Mass.

November 2003

Introduction

I hate to name-drop, but this book was Steve Waugh's idea. It was almost the first thing he said to me, while we were lying down, stretching our hamstrings, before his first game for Kent in August 2002. 'You wrote a book about cricket and baseball, right? Next you should write a diary of the English season. Definitely. Tell the truth as much as you can. I'd buy it.'

I thought about it many times over the next few months, but then talked myself out of it. How would my team mates react to being described and analysed? The outsider's journalistic zoom lens is one thing; it is quite another when one of your own is taking the notes and drawing the conclusions. Beneath the bravado, most sportsmen are extremely sensitive; even the smallest criticisms can be taken as betrayal.

So much for them; what about me? What if I had a terrible season, and the book became a story of failure? Even if I played well, would I give too much away about myself? A preparedness to be vulnerable may be admirable and even attractive as a human quality, but it is scarcely normal in a professional sportsman. Simply allowing yourself to be known, letting the guard down, is a risk in any competitive world. It gives ammunition. 'When people ask you what aspects of your game you are working on,' Colin Cowdrey told me once, 'say, "Oh everything, thank you."' But writing a diary with the guard still up is a waste of time. How much to say, how much to trust, how much to give? These questions keep coming back.

But none of the questions ever stopped me from having the same feeling of excitement I got every time the idea came into my head. It is the story I have always most wanted to tell. In fact, I had been a diarist of my life as a county cricketer right from the start, in 1996, when I made three debuts in one summer: for Cambridge, for Kent and then for Young England. But instead of writing it, I had spoken it – often to my family, but to friends and girlfriends too. They got to know the characters and the stories and the inside track. Some Kent cricketers would be surprised how big an impression they have made in the most unlikely places. After a long and bleak day for Kent in the field, my mother – who teaches art and rarely watches sport – might say to me, 'What did Keysey have to say about today?' She had come to learn that Rob Key has a wisecrack for every occasion, and a gloom-lifting sense of irony. Funny, too, that people are more interested in hearing about honest and abrasive team mates than pious or party-line ones. The dissenting notes strike many more chords among non-cricket lovers.

When I started playing cricket professionally, I used to avoid talking about it to my 'civilian' friends. Surely they wouldn't be interested in dressing-room life and its daily round of affectionate but brutal rough-and-tumble? And, anyway, shouldn't I be getting a break from all that cricket? But lots of my friends *do* like hearing about life inside a professional sports team – I suspect because in the arguments and affections of the dressing room they see the tensions of their own working lives expanded and given fuller voice. Most professions keep a tighter lid on both discord and celebration than we do. Their lives are more masked. In contrast, the life of a professional sportsman may be far from civilized, but it is often dramatic, and drama makes for good conversation.

If I learned that people liked to hear about Kent, I found that I also liked to talk about it. Not all the time, of course. Every October for the last five years, soon after packing up my cricket kit following Kent's final game, I have gone to America, where I usually stay with completely non-cricketing friends. Their first question is, 'How did the cricket go this year?' That is the last time they mention it, which is fine by me. But that is October, after six months of living every minute of a cricket season. March to September is a very different story. Every day is a step on the journey, a journey in which everything is provisional. The game and the team are so much a part of my life that it is hard to imagine how I keep myself occupied during the winter.

Even in the middle of the season, I try to get little breaks from the relentlessness of county cricket – an afternoon in London, a walk by the sea, a film or a book. Switching off consciously thinking about cricket is a survival strategy – it stops you going mad. But beneath the surface, the game is always there in your subconscious, this vast mass of unfinished business: politics unresolved, conversations unfinished, errors regretted, praise withheld. When you are playing badly, it kills. When you are playing well, you could always be playing better. If you are playing very well, why isn't anyone noticing? That is what you say goodbye to – if you've any sense at all – in October. After all that hanging in there and holding on, you let go for a while. God, it feels good.

This, though, is the story of the hanging in there and the holding on, the self-doubt and the frustration, the rows and the friendship. Cricketers spend more time with each other than they do with their wives, girlfriends, parents or best friends. More time out there in the middle, engaged with the opposition; more time in the dressing room, with just ourselves to sustain our competitiveness. And guess what? It's the quiet spells that are the problem, the quiet spells with no battle to paper over the cracks and focus the mind. If I have one piece of advice to someone starting out, it would be 'Go quiet in the quiet spells . . .' Because I never did.

November 2002

December 2002

New Year's Eve and the last day of my off-season. No, I have not been called up to play for England in the fifth Test at Sydney, nor will I be playing for anyone else tomorrow. Kent's pre-season does not start until March, and the season proper begins in late April. But for me, in some subliminal way, cricket starts now. On 7 January I fly to India, and from India onwards it is business as usual. In other words, cricket as usual.

That does not mean I have completely forgotten about cricket for the last three months. We'll get the work-ethic worthiness out of the way up front: I do three or four days of fitness training per week pretty much all year round, and I stretch every day. In the winter I also plan which aspects of my game I'm going to work on, and I fantasize about successes in the new season. But cricket doesn't live with me in quite the way it does from January to the end of September. Life comes before cricket. For the rest of the year it is the other way around.

Though I would happily trade them in return for playing for England, I enjoy my three months off. I write a bit – *The Times* just sent me to Boston to cover the Harvard–Yale American Football game – but not too much. I go on holiday – it was so warm and sunny in Cornwall this December that I almost went swimming in the sea – but not for long. But the holidays and the writing are such fun partly because I don't ask too much of them. They are all part of my non-cricket world, vital as a restorative balance, but to some extent still defined by what they are not: cricket. Without the cricket, I would feel much more pressure to achieve in the rest of my life. I wouldn't be able to relax so much and hibernate so deeply. It is still having the dream – the dream of making it as big as I always wanted to make it – that allows you to indulge before the next big push.

The next big push starts on 7 January in Bombay, where I will train twice a day and practise playing on dusty, spinning wickets against local Indian bowlers. It will be about a hundred times less comfortable than my last three months. I can't wait.

But for now, I am in a train, going to London for a New Year's party, listening to two skinheads, one of whom is on his mobile talking to his drug dealer in rhyming slang: 'Listen, mate, have you got the Jack-and-Jills or not?'

At Sevenoaks, some public schoolboys get on carrying a crate of lager and hooting a lot. ' 'Appy New Year, guv'nor!' says one. Given how hard they are trying to emulate the style of the drug-dealing skinhead who is buying pills, they would be disappointed to know how quickly they gave away their wealth and privilege. The rest of the journey is a prolonged stare-off between the Pills and the Carlsberg.

In London, it is a good party, with old friends, but I feel a bit restless. The others seem busy, idealistic and involved with their jobs. I have been out of action long enough, resting and thinking. Now I could do with a challenge. If you are prone to reflection, that is the best thing about sport: it is real and primal and it jolts you out of too much introspection.

At midnight, I speak to my girlfriend in South Carolina, still five hours from her New Year. That's another problem when you are itinerant: the phone. Sometimes it's even harder than the cricket.

January 2003

8 January 2003

Bombay has changed its name to Mumbai, but the airport has stayed the same. It's three in the morning, and even in the middle of the night it is utterly chaotic. A hideous water-fountain announces your arrival in immigration clearance; then the queues and the heat begin. The air is sticky, the queues shambolic, the passengers hot and tired. Large British-Indian families, parents placating their exhausted kids with promises of sleep and goodies, are inching towards the passport booths. In contrast to the exasperated parents, I am feeling awake, perky and – indulging the privilege of the well-rested solo passenger – amused by the chaos. I am delighted to be back.

Two years ago, on my one previous visit to India, I was with Kent's left-arm spinner, Min Patel, who was born in Bombay. 'Let me tell you one thing about India,' he said as we started our descent into the city. 'If you can't hang on to your patience and your courtesy, you'll go mad here within minutes.' Without Min to translate, bargain and negotiate on my behalf it might be more of a challenge this time.

When the taxi-company employees lead me to my cab, I find the driver fast asleep behind the wheel, which is not at all unusual here. What is surprising is that his colleagues can't wake him up. He's not dozing, but deep sleeping. I mean: we cannot rouse him. They assure me all will be fine, that he is a tip-top driver, and then they disappear. My driver eventually wakes, reaches for his bottle of water, splashes himself, groans, and turns on the ignition. 'Cricket Club of India,' I say. Indecipherable reply. 'CCI? Near Marine Drive?' Groan. 'OK.' I am not convinced, but we are off. The corners are fine, because turning the wheel requires effort and hence being awake. But on the straight roads, my driver's eyes close sleepily. 'Are you awake?' Eyes open. 'Oh yes, very awake, sir.'

Driving in India is an experience at the best of times. The only consistent rule is: don't hesitate; and the roundabouts have built-up edges to stop people driving straight over them. But this trip is even more perilous than usual. I am relieved to get to the CCI and find my room. Room service, however, closed hours ago, so I am grateful for the box of chocolates and half-bottle of mineral water I brought off the plane. Tap water is absolutely off limits here; and you are advised not to drink any bottled water unless it is sealed. I even close my mouth in the shower and use bottled water to brush my teeth. I will try not to waste too much tonight – the remaining 200 ml has to last me through a hot night.

9 January

What am I doing here? The standard winter away for the English pro trying to work on his game is playing club cricket in Australia or South Africa. Typically that means Sydney, Cape Town or Perth. Toughening up in the southern hemisphere. Playing hard on and off the field – sun, sand, surf, swearing – that kind of thing.

I spent three spells in Perth, Western Australia, and learnt a lot. If you can handle the Pommie-bashing Aussie put-downs, there are few easier places to adapt to than Australia. It is instantly recognizable as part of the Anglo-American world. And to observe the best attitude to sport – positive, uncluttered, expressive, competitive – Australia is the place to go.

India, of course, could not be more different, and very few English cricketers have come here for winter practice, partly because the structure of Indian cricket does not easily accommodate overseas pros, partly because there is less money around, and partly because people are apprehensive about the subcontinent.

But the plus points are enormous. Dusty, turning Indian wickets provide great practice for batting against spin; people will bowl at you all day long simply because they love the game; and the Indian school of batsmanship – Gavaskar, Tendulkar, Dravid – has produced some of the best players in recent history. They must be doing something right – very right. And yet we don't talk about them as models as much as we do the Australians. The wristy, masterful Indian batting style seems too exotic to emulate. The best way to learn from something is to immerse yourself in it, and that is what I am doing in India.

The last and equally important reasons to come here are the lasting friendships and because India is a beguiling, irresistible country.

I stay at the Cricket Club of India, an exclusive ex-colonial enclave in the middle of south Bombay. A swimming pool, tennis, squash, badminton courts, four restaurants, lovely guest rooms, a cricket stadium. Hardly India at the sharp end, I admit, but India all the same.

Originally, it was going to be a practice trip just for me and Robin Martin-Jenkins, the Sussex all-rounder. But, quite by chance, five English county spinners are also out here attending a spin camp run by several ex-Indian Test greats, including Bishen Bedi. When I wander down for breakfast, the organizer rushes up to me. 'Hello, Ed, I am director of the World Cricket Academy – we are running this spin camp and we need batsmen. Do join us from this afternoon onwards.' He points out to the middle, where I can see that Robin (who got here a few days earlier) is already batting.

Plenty of bowlers, some kind of organized structure, nets a mere hundred yards from my room – it looks like I have landed on my feet.

10 January

This is like the good old days. I wake up, have a quick breakfast, then put my pads on and walk in to the nets to find bowlers keen to keep going until I've had enough.

Why 'the good old days'? Because every young professional cricketer has heard the old pros talk about the good old days. 'You've got no idea, Ed,' they sigh during sprint practice in early March. 'Back in the good old days, you would never have seen the senior pros do anything like this. They just strolled out of the pavilion with their pads on, had a bat, went in for lunch, then played golf. That was their pre-season. I just bowled at them all day.

'And now it's my turn, and look . . . [disdainful wave of the hand towards fitness apparatus] . . . sprinting, jogging, all-in-it-together, team bonding, psycho-babble, equal net time for junior pros . . .'

They just can't believe their bad luck.

I'm anything but an old pro, but it is certainly nice to be able to practise on your own terms and concentrate on your own batting without distraction. Right now I am working on two things, both central. My preliminary foot movements (what I do before the ball has been bowled) and my pick-up, or back-lift (the upswing of my bat before the downswing, i.e. the shot itself).

Back-lift and preliminary movements are connected, all part of the most important thing of all – rhythm. Change one, and the other will change too, and you might lose your rhythm. So think carefully before tinkering.

One of the biggest mistakes I ever made was in the winter of 1999–2000, when I changed my foot movements radically, reducing them from two preliminary 'trigger' movements to one. I also tried to move later, nearer the moment at which I decided which shot to play. Sounds good – simpler, streamlined, less that can go wrong. In fact, I became rushed, and found myself late getting into position and late in my downswing. I only put it right in the middle of the 2000 season.

I am not trying anything like that now, quite the opposite. I am trying to get my preliminary movements done a little earlier in order to give me more time to play the shot. This is something Michael Vaughan has done brilliantly over the past year. I am not changing it much, just a fraction. Alongside a tiny adjustment to my pick-up, they will be the only basic technical changes I make this winter.

So if you see me sitting down after a net – helmet off, pads still on, sweating, pensive – it is possible that I am in fact thinking about batting and not just resting. Aside from games themselves – real battle – one of my favourite things about being a sportsman is total absorption in practice. It doesn't always happen. But when it does – and you really concentrate on trying to enact something practically you have figured out mentally beforehand – for those precious moments little else comes into your head.

It takes time to come out of that intense state. That's often what the pros are doing when they are sitting on the ground, not doing much after their net – they are coming out of introspective practice mode. I did plenty of it today. Think, practise, think, practise. Too much theory can ruin anyone's batting. But a little, in January, can help.

12 January

Boundaries do not get much more marked or symbolic than on the far side of the Bombay Gymkhana. This side of the rope, everything, from the far sight screen to the pavilion, is the Bombay Gymkhana club. Along with the CCI, the Bombay Gym is the grandest private club in the city. Its swimming pool, tennis courts, nets, cricket square and numerous bars, restaurants and verandas are spotlessly maintained. You are never far from an easy chair or a gin-and-tonic in the Bombay Gym. Nor is it an *arriviste* establishment: it was the preferred polo field of the British social élite of the early 1900s.

The other side of the sight screen – literally just beyond the boundary rope – is the public cricket field, the Maidan. The Maidan is a chaotic carnival of cricket: no ropes, no pavilions, no boundaries, no apparent administrative system; just lots and lots of cricket. It is several times bigger than the Bombay Gym, but into that space they have squeezed seventeen cricket pitches to the Bombay Gym's solitary square. The pitches not only overlap; the *infields* overlap, so square leg has to walk in past cover point in the adjacent game. The opening bowler in one Maidan game had a curious 'S'-shaped run-up. I eventually worked out that he had to kink his run-up to avoid a large drain.

In the early decades of the twentieth century, the emerging Indian cricketing community petitioned for more space. They wrote to Lord Harris – former Kent cricket legend, then governor of Bombay – hoping he might be a kindred spirit. Surely thousands of cricket lovers had a right to use more of the precious Bombay Gym turf at the expense of only a handful of polo players? Harris disagreed and upheld the polo privileges.

These days, of course, the contrast is not between polo and cricket, but between two versions of cricket. The Bombay Gym has officers and groundsmen and uniformed attendants and countless distinctions of rank and importance. The Maidan simply has hundreds of cricketers. A photograph hangs in the Bombay Gym of Armanath and Jardine shaking hands before the first Test match on Indian soil, played at the Gym. To the Maidan belong more recent stars: Sachin Tendulkar honed his improbably brilliant batsmanship on its ragged pitches.

Early this morning, before my own game, I read about that famous first-ever Indian test. The match was watched by 100,000, sitting in temporary stands or perched on nearby roofs and trees. About 100 watched our game. But I felt more excited than I normally do before non-representative warm-up games. I was glad for the historical resonance.

Most pros hate playing games that don't matter. Success doesn't count, their negative voice tells them, but failure still hurts. Worse, if the bowler is an amateur, as he probably will be, the outcome could be embarrassing.

But pick-up games can be good practice, not just as batting practice, but as mental practice too.

I used to give myself easy 'out' clauses when I played friendly games. What did it matter? I would experiment, play a few good shots, get out, then console myself that (a) I was 'hitting the ball well', and (b) I would raise my game when it mattered.

About two years ago I started to take a different approach.

Though I would still try out new shots and grow aspects of my game, I would never take the pressure off myself in practice games. I reasoned that the correct mental state for match play was difficult to re-create in nets, so any friendly game was a precious opportunity to rehearse going through the steps of building a big innings. The better I knew the journey, the easier it would be when it really did matter.

That year, 2001, I got a hundred – in India, in fact – in my first game of the calendar year, I got plenty of runs in pre-season, and had a good season proper. Last year, I got 222 in my first game of the calendar year – in Perth, Australia – then got three hundreds in five pre-season innings, and went on to have my best season.

So getting a hundred in my first game of the year has become a tiny superstition of mine. It didn't happen this year. I got six, before chipping an off-spinner to midwicket. Hitting the ball well? Hell, it really doesn't matter. I can say that now with no guilt. I prepared mentally for today exactly as I would have for a first-class game. I was in the right psychological state. I will be better off for it. I didn't get any runs. So what. They will come. Not because I will 'raise my game', but because the runs do come if you stay in that right, balanced state of mind.

And it was nice to play at the Bombay Gym, scene of India's first Test in 1934, and my first failure of 2003.

15 January

Two years ago exactly, after my net practice at the Bombay Academy, a man in his mid-fifties with an intense stare and a passionate, almost maniacal love of cricket offered his opinions about my game. 'You can play,' he began, 'and believe me, I can pick them. You will play for England in the next eighteen months, two years at the most. But you've got to start using long-handled bats. You're six foot two, and you're stooping over a short handle. Use a long handle.'

You get lots of advice as a professional cricketer, and much of it should be ignored. But there was something about this man who ran the Bombay Academy – his conviction, warmth and transparent love of the game – which demanded attention.

I said I would think about it. 'Don't think about it. Do it. I know these things. I can pick them. You'll play for England soon. But get those long-handled bats.'

It was Vasoo Paranjape. I tried long handles, preferred them, and had two good years. I am running out of time, though, for him to be right about me being picked for England inside two years. I got to know Vasoo's son, Jatin, who played for Bombay and India, and have often remembered Vasoo's complete self-certainty that I would play for England. I know about Indian charm, but this seemed different.

Vasoo tells you things. It is funny how the modern trend is towards consulting rather than teaching, a knock-about chat between teacher and taught, an exchange between equals. And yet it is often the teachers and mentors who pass on clear, simple axioms that make the difference – the ones who tell you things. It is the injunctions we remember, not the chatty debates. If you're going to tell people what to do, of course, you'd better get it right. But the best teachers do get it right and they aren't afraid to tell you.

This year, Vasoo has been watching me at the CCI. He walks around the net while I bat, watching from behind the stumps, from the side, from mid off, from behind the bowler's arm. Today he spoke for the first time.

VP: How many first-class double-hundreds have you scored?
ES: None.
VP: None! None! That is ridiculous. None! I have watched carefully for days now. I can't see what's stopping you. It is ridiculous. Do you want to do well or not?
ES: Of course, I desperately want to do well.
VP: Well, why no doubles then? I'm not interested in hundreds, still less seventies. You should go double, then another double, then – all right, I'll let you off – a hundred and seventy.

Then you'll get picked for England and score hundreds for them.

ES: I'll try.

VP: I'm not interested in trying. I'm interested in doubles, doubles – DOUBLES.

[My smile turned into a laugh.]

VP: I don't know what you're laughing about. If I don't see you scoring doubles for Kent and then playing well for England against South Africa I will be furious. Doubles, OK, *doubles*.

And with that he walked off to watch someone else bat from all angles, to tell them what to do.

20 January

The phone in my room rings at 7.15 a.m. That's 1.45 a.m. in England. Perhaps my girlfriend, who is a post-graduate at Cambridge, has been out and couldn't wait until the morning to speak to me? I prepare to answer the phone, adorably sleepily.

'Are you awake? Well, you must be now. Meet me downstairs in five minutes and we'll say hello properly.'

If that sounds like a nice surprise, I should add that the voice is not that of a willowy 24-year-old female, but a rugged 48-year-old cricketer from New Zealand. It is John Wright, ex-Kiwi opener and captain, my old coach at Kent and now coach of India.

We have breakfast in the café by the swimming pool, me drinking as much coffee as possible, John re-hydrating after running to the CCI from the Taj Hotel.

I look for signs of deep stress in him. India is the most cricket-mad country in the world, and coaching them, particularly as a foreigner, is tough at the best of times. These are not the best of times. With the World Cup in South Africa only twenty days away, India have just been humbled by New Zealand in their last warm-up tournament. But, amazingly, John looks younger, fitter and more optimisitic than he did at the end of his time at Kent.

Genial, charming, very tough and hugely talkative, John coached Kent for four years. He brought us great passion, commitment and a world-record number of team talks. 'You're a words person, Ed,' he would say. 'Should I make my team talks shorter?'

He was intensely critical of us and yet one of the best people to share a drink with. But he would be the first to admit that he was never quite able to make the batters – his primary charges – click. The long, heart-felt chats didn't result in long, match-winning innings.

At first, he thought I was just the player he was looking for: an opener (as he had been), young, keen to learn, ambitious, someone to tutor. I used to travel with him to away games. He was – and is – great company. We got on straight away.

But I too fell short. Journalists and sports psychologists talk a lot about ambition. No one ever talks about the dangers of too much ambition. Excessive ambition can cause impatience and crucial lapses in judgement. You're too keen to 'do what it takes'. So you say the right thing, even when it's the wrong thing. Looking for an opening batsman to eliminate risk and bat all day, even if he's only got an ugly 60 at the close? 'Yes, that's me, sir!' But it wasn't. I listened and changed too much, and I lost my own voice as a player.

But even now, when I have real moments of clarity as a batter and feel close to understanding my game, I can hear John Wright saying the exact words that I am thinking. Maybe all the self-analysis and self-criticism he encouraged had a kind of delayed return.

When John was coach at Kent (1997–2000), he twice had to tell me I was dropped. The second time I had been reinstated for only one game and played on one of the worst pitches ever. No sequence of failures, just one game and out. He rang me on a mobile from the motorway. I was at home on my own, half looking forward to the call, half dreading it.

You know straight away from the voice. Kind is out; tough is in. His voice was ultra-nice. 'I'm fucked,' I thought. And I was. I was desperate to play, desperate to succeed, too hungry, in fact, for my own good. I had to get back, had to turn it round, I wouldn't let myself fail. The phone kept cutting out. 'Jesus . . . I'm . . . sorry . . . don't . . . what to say . . . shit . . . let me pull over . . .' So he stood there, late one summer night, standing by the side of some strip of motorway, holding a mobile phone while trying to explain to a 22-year-old what had gone wrong – trying to get it right.

That was as bad as it had ever got for me as a player. Would it have been easier if it had all been done with complete professionalism and less emotion? The phone call would have been easier, certainly. But his obvious involvement was oddly inspiring. I was still worth bothering about.

I never felt I'd completely lost his faith, and I suspected that he really did want me to prove him wrong. I remember another phone call to my mobile, early one Sunday morning, when I was still out of the first team. 'Where are you?' I was in London. 'Christ, I won't keep you then. I just want you to know you'll get there in the end. I know you will.' That's usually a lie. It wasn't with John Wright.

That's a lot of history. Three years on, where do you start? Remember that phone call on the M20? Remember saying we'd have a meal before my first Test match? Pass the marmalade, please? In truth, it was easy, as it always has been when we've bumped into each other. We could have talked all day, laughing and disagreeing, going over the same old ground but enjoying it all the same.

Perhaps the people who count are not only the ones who help you in the obvious sense, but also the ones who stay with you when they have moved on and, by staying with you, add to the scope of your existence.

21 *January*

When is it too late to correct a case of mistaken identity? If someone is quite determined that you are a different person, is there ever a point at which the best course is simply to agree, draw things to a hasty conclusion, and slide off with everyone's pride intact?

I thought about trying that policy today when Raj Singh, President of the CCI and a great personality of Indian cricket, mistook me for Robin Martin-Jenkins. From a distance, we do look a little alike, and, anyway, having made plenty of social gaffes myself, my sympathy has long since passed from the forgotten to the forgetter.

Raj bumped into me outside the CCI pavilion, and quickly introduced me to a Mr Bindra from the Punjab. 'Meet Robin Martin-Jenkins, the Sussex all-rounder.'

'Sorry, I'm actually . . .'

'He's the son of Christopher Martin-Jenkins, who writes for *The Times* . . .'

'I'm Ed . . .'

'Robin's so modest he'd never let on, but he's a good chance of playing for England soon . . .'

'I had lunch with your father,' put in Mr Bindra, 'only a few months ago. Do send him my best wishes.'

I decided to keep quiet. Raj Singh has been extremely generous to both Robin and me, and the last thing I wanted to do was make him feel guilty about mistaking us. But finally he cottoned on.

'Hang on a minute, you're not Robin at all. You're Ed Smith. Right, meet Mr Bindra . . .' And so we started again.

A chance meeting, an easy mistake, but an unusual outcome.

'Both you and Robin should come up to the Mohali stadium in the Punjab,' Mr Bindra added. 'We'll put you up, lay on net bowlers, sort out a gym and organize a bowling machine. You must be bored of Bombay by now.'

'Excellent, that's settled,' said Raj. 'Both you and Robin should come to my office in fifteen minutes.'

We did, and we agreed to the trip and flew the next day. India is like that.

Where is the Punjab?

23 January

The Punjab borders Pakistan in the north-west of India. We are heading for the state's capital, Chandigarh, which is a three-hour train ride from Delhi. Three hours, that is, unless it's foggy. Today is very foggy.

Foggy and cold. When I was told in Bombay that it might be cold 'up north', I assumed a touch of Indian exaggeration. When we flew into Delhi last night, it was too late to find out – we got a cab straight to the well-heated hotel.

We found out this morning. The hotel insisted that we get up at five to 'beat the traffic'. We therefore arrived at the train station ninety minutes too early. It was three degrees above freezing, and I had only the clothes I had been wearing in the 90-degree heat of Bombay. I cannot remember ever being colder. But discomfort fades, shame endures. In my shivering state I accepted Robin's offer of a Sussex First Eleven sweater. 'Tis done. I am a turn-coat. Seeing me with Sussex martlets on my chest really would have confused Raj.

Trains are part of everyone's idea of India. Since my guidebook described Chandigarh as 'beautifully positioned in the foothills of the Himalayas', I imagined a romantic ascent through idyllic hillside villages. Instead we crawled for six hours along flat plains in thick fog. Maybe the Himalayas would emerge when the clouds lifted.

In other respects the train didn't disappoint. Though we were in something called First Class, it was absolutely packed. Hindi music played throughout. Coffee, bread and omelettes were brought to my seat. The toilet was an immaculately maintained room consisting of a sink and a hole in the floor. I looked into the hole and saw clearly the train tracks below. They were not passing very quickly.

We were met at the station and chauffeured to the impressive new Mohali stadium. The white neo-classical colonnade is enormous, the atrium is grand enough for a prince. The bedrooms, though, were cold enough for a monastery. It will be home for the week. 'Please, sirs, have lunch, your net bowlers will be here at three this afternoon.'

The fog has lifted. The nets are hard and true. The net bowlers are keen to bowl all afternoon. Now where are those Himalayas?

25 *January*

Today I had a Eureka moment. Something has been bothering me about my batting for years: my off-side bat swing. My off drives, I think, have been slightly out for five years. They've been bugging me ever since 1997, when I was nineteen and scored 1,100 runs, averaging 40-odd in my first full season.

How can something be wrong for five years? Why can't you just put it right? Ironically, most problems in your batting are side effects resulting from trying to cure a different fault. In my case, after 1997, the theory was that if I stopped getting caught behind the wicket I would get even more runs. The captain, coach, and senior players all agreed. That would be my winter's work. 'If you stop nicking it,' one adviser put it, 'you'll never get out.'

It worked. I got out caught much less frequently in 1998 than in 1997. But I got out much more often in every other way. Worse, I became ordinary. No one watching me in 1998 would have said I was at all special. I fought hard and hung around, but I had completely lost my fluency. It didn't look like me. 'All' I had done was to close my grip a touch and lower my back-lift. But back-lift is connected to footwork, and footwork to rhythm, and rhythm to everything. I had solved a small thing and lost the big things.

For two and a half years my form came and went. I had spells of scoring heavily and then I clicked out of sync again. I got nearly a thousand runs at an average of 40 in 1999, but I never felt consistently fluent. I was always searching, rarely expressing myself.

I got it back in the middle of 2000, not long after that terrible phone call from John Wright. From July 2000 I started to bat more like I had in 1997. When I got 175 against Durham, it was better than 1997.

Since mid-2000 – and I am touching wood – my form has been consistent. I have rarely averaged less than 40 for long. But averages are overrated as gauges. More importantly (apart from a two-game spell last season), I have felt secure at the crease. Of course, it could have been much better. I could have converted lots more starts into hundreds. I could go on for hours about lapses of concentration and squandered opportunities. That, I'm afraid, is the batter's lot.

And yet, even in the last two and half years, despite being in good rhythm, I have often felt one notch out when I drive on the off side. Even when I hit it well, it doesn't feel quite like it did in 1997. Does it matter? Maybe not that much. Is it worth making more big changes? Certainly not. Would I like to click it back into place without losing anything else? Definitely.

I think I did today. Last night, in my room, I watched Michael Vaughan batting against Australia on TV. He is much more of an off-side player than me, but I noticed how he cocked his wrists quite early in his swing and yet kept his back-lift quite compact. In other words, it wasn't a long, loose, full swing of the bat, which would be prone to giving catches behind the wicket. But he was still able to play perfect cover drives just by releasing his wrists.

Today, batting against the bowling machine, I was searching for the right compact pick-up. I couldn't quite get it.

I doubt anyone noticed. Any professional batsman batting against a bowling machine at 70 or 80 m.p.h. hits most balls well enough. If you weren't watching carefully, you'd think he was batting well. The predictability of the bowling machine – it lands the ball in almost exactly the same spot every time – allows you to get away with small errors, and still time the ball well. So while I was hitting

70 per cent well, I was privately thinking, 'What am I doing wrong?'

Then I got it right. The bat was coming down straighter for longer, following through more fully and easily. It's so much about feel rather than mechanics. And I was starting to get that right feel. Timing a cricket ball, when you get it just right, is a sensual experience.

Over the last five years, I have become a much better on-side player. Now I was hitting off drives like I had as a nineteen-year-old – and without any great changes, just a slight cocking of the wrists. I was like a kid with a new toy. 'Just a dozen more . . . six more . . . ten more . . .' I could have stayed all day. It was worth the air fare to Bombay just to have today's net session.

If I can play as well on the off side as the on side, I will force the bowlers to bowl straighter and towards my strengths. It might make all the difference. I was already imagining two cover drives in the first game of the season, followed by two clips through midwicket.

Then Robin finished in the bowler's net and we swapped places. My first ball against real bowlers, bowled by a smiling, gangly, eighteen-year-old Indian, was a bouncer. It hit me firmly in the ribs.

Bounced out in India? Right, I'm not letting that happen again. Get stuck in. The new cover drive will have to wait.

February 2003

2 February

Two days ago I flew back from India. Yesterday I split up with my girlfriend in Cambridge. Today I moved house to Wye. It is all happening. My new house is a small Victorian gatehouse that is being let to me by the parents of one of my Kent colleagues. Their house, only a few hundred yards away, is usually clearly visible from my front door. Except for now – it is five thirty in the afternoon – because it is *dark*. Pitch black. I'd forgotten how damp, dark and thoroughly gloomy England can be in February. Five thirty! That's three hours to dinner; six hours until I go to sleep. There is a limit to how many boxes I can cheerfully unpack in one day.

I haven't yet broken the plastic seal on the brand new fridge, let alone filled it with food. There are no paintings on the walls, no sofa, no TV, no lamps, no reading lights. I have a simple choice of lighting arrangements: one, overhead light bulb switched on; two, complete darkness. My back hurts from craning over cardboard boxes.

One thing working well is my CD player. Its tiny green and red lights have become like a redemptive shrine in the corner of the sitting room. Nick Hornby wrote that he found it hard to find the right soundtrack for his divorce. The two great break-up albums, Bob Dylan's *Blood on the Tracks* and Bruce Springsteen's *Tunnel of Love*, having been mined extensively in peacetime, had little left in reserve when he needed them most.

I have the same problem now. I've settled on Neil Diamond's *Solitary Man* and Puccini's *Madam Butterfly*. For the first time in years, music feels not nice but essential.

Wye is very pretty during the few precious hours of daylight winter allows us. It is in the heart of rural east Kent – which in February is a spare, sometimes haunting mixture of downs and valleys. It is so different from Tunbridge Wells, Sevenoaks and Tonbridge, where I grew up in the west of the county. Fewer city suits, more tractors, fewer people, more cows.

I have already discovered three things Wye has going for it. An agricultural college, affiliated to the University of London, set in a beautiful cloistered abbey; a lovely parish church (I sometimes like sitting in unfussy, old churches, but rarely attend services); and a really excellent pub called the New Flying Horse. I must confess this is the best news of all.

The last time I tried living on my own on this side of Kent was four years ago. That was the 1999 season, my first year after university, and I never got the hang of the solitude. After three years at Cambridge, in which everything was on my doorstep, suddenly on my own in Canterbury I kept wondering when something was going to happen. Not much did.

It should be different this time – I know the rest of the team much better now, and I feel part of a broader community. I also have this laptop; and when I am launched on a book, I am rarely bored.

More immediate problems are finding my woolliest sweater (for now), and a sheet and some blankets (for later). The bedding won't matter much, though, unless they deliver my bed before the end of office hours (forty-five minutes remain).

23 February

Today I listened to a radio interview with a science professor who likes to compose music in his spare time. 'As a scientist,' he explained, 'I spend my working day having to prove everything I say, use reason, provide evidence. So composing music is a perfect way for me to experience a world where things don't necessarily develop in logical steps or along clear thinking lines.'

Music was the emotional counterpoint to his professional rigour.

I feel the same about writing and cricket. They exist in opposite spheres. Writing, for me anyway, grows out of reflection. Cricket is an opportunity to stop reflecting and be present in an activity. The writer in me doesn't stop asking why or hold back from uncomfortable truths. Uncomfortable truths are precisely his business. The writer strand is always trying to work out what makes me tick and what motivates others.

Where the writer is interested in yesterday, the cricketer is interested in tomorrow. Analysis is necessary for the cricketer, but only up to a point – then you've just got to go out there and do it. The cricketer also knows that, no matter why his team mates are the way they are, they're probably not going to change, so he might as well not worry too much.

All that is not unique to cricket, of course. It goes for any performer – musician, sportsman or actor. Edmund Morris put it well in *Dutch*, his biography of Ronald Reagan:

Understand that actors remember forward, not backward. Yesterday's take is in the can: tomorrow's lines must be got by heart. Writers are different. Their stock in trade is past experience (particularly past rejections), and their whole instinct is to turn it to literary account – make art out of life, as the cliché goes.

And here's one the sports psychologists won't like: the cricketer in me understands the power of denial. Blanking out failure. Sportsmen do it all the time. Like it never happened. Their self-belief is not hampered by a selective memory; it is dependent upon it. After hammering myself for years by going over every error I've made, I'm now starting to understand why other players don't. Of course you've got to learn from your mistakes. But sometimes, and this is the bit sports psychologists never admit, ruthless self-examination of your own failings serves merely to summon a monster that you then cannot slay. There are times to figure out why, and there are times to take a shower, have a drink and come back tomorrow.

25 *February*

Tonight I went to the annual *Sunday Telegraph* Books party. Exactly five years ago, as an undergraduate about to write my first *Sunday Telegraph* book review, I apprehensively went to the same party, wondering what literary London would be like.

Back in 1998, as I watched the novelists, columnists and news-paper editors meet and greet each other with clubbable familiarity, I retreated into a slightly surly shyness. I knew no one and it seemed that everyone else knew everyone. The first surmise was true, but the second untrue.

In truth, a very few familiar faces and a preparedness to make an effort can easily get you through an evening with strangers. If that surly twenty-year-old undergraduate had watched me at tonight's party, he might have made the mistake of thinking I was a London insider. I'm not. All I did was talk to the half dozen or so people I knew and say hello to a few I didn't know. That's all most people do. So much of social life is a kind of confidence trick: almost everyone is more lost than they look.

The same could be said about a cricket dressing room. When I first came into the team, I marvelled at the easy banter and casual warmth. How deep the bonds seemed between the senior players, how warm the shared stories, how numerous the adventures they had all been on together.

They are, in a way. But sporting society is like all society. It looks closer-knit than it is. What I didn't understand as a debutant was how much is not said between senior players, how much is off limits, how many sensitive areas are ring-fenced. A shared history does not always mean shared opinions, or even mutual respect. The past is there, and there to be enjoyed. But much of it also hurts and divides and will never be righted or atoned.

Near the end of the *Sunday Telegraph* party, I felt someone push past me on his way to a large open window. He looked like a man tired of too many fawning faces, in need of fresh air and a moment's reflection. I realized it was the novelist Vikram Seth.

Educated in India, England, and California, Vikram is multi-lingual, beguilingly charming, a poet, librettist, novelist and Chinese calligrapher. It has been a quietly brilliant career. I have bumped into him in Western Australia, London and New York – the last time three years ago.

'How is the cricket?' he asked me tonight. The last time I saw Vikram I was practising like a madman, jogging every day, talking sports psycho-babble and playing moderately. By trying to be all too professional as a cricketer, I had 'gone under' and lost my personality as a player.

I explained that I had played much better in the last two years. Recently I had found a better balance in my life and a healthier sense of proportion and perspective. Writing had helped me take a break from thinking full-time about cricket. Having two forms of self-expression hadn't diminished my main career; it had helped it.

'The word "amateur" is such an abused term,' Vikram said. 'It derives from "to love". And yet now it is synonymous with sloppiness and inattentiveness. Don't we all need to keep loving what we do?'

Yes, to keep loving what we do – not to go under, to keep a freshness – that is the trick.

March 2003

18 March

This year's fitness test is today at 10 a.m. Eight times round the athletics track in less than thirteen minutes, or else re-tests, then more re-tests, then maybe fines or suspensions.

In my first year at Kent, when the only time I would run voluntarily would be to get cigarettes before the shop closed, I was scared of being shown up. Over the next few years, with many more miles under my belt, I looked forward to the fitness test as an opportunity to show how fit I was. Now I am ambivalent about the whole thing – not because I am less ambitious, but because I am certain that there is scarcely any correlation between being a good jogger and a good cricketer.

If you come from the hard-work school of coaching, the first thing you say is, 'We're going to get fitter.' Fitness is easy to measure – the times come down, the muscles get bigger, the boys look sharper – so the coach can say, 'Our fitness levels have gone up. The work will pay dividends. Soon the cricket will follow.'

But does it? There is no doubt that cricketers perform better when they are in good condition to play. Endurance work can help bowlers to bowl long spells; Pilates and yoga may enable them to spend less time injured; sprint training, by increasing fast twitch muscle fibre, helps some batters and fielders move quicker. Working at physical fitness can also help self-esteem and personal discipline. To that extent, I am a convert.

But let's be honest. How many professional cricketers have sometimes gone to the gym when they might have benefited more from doing extra fielding practice? And was it physical vanity, rather than professional drive, that motivated their weights training? How many of us have sometimes gone for a jog shortly before the pre-season fitness test, rather than gone sprint training at the track? The first will help us look good at pre-season, the second might get us a run-out in the first game. And how many of us have sometimes trained out of boredom rather than to become better cricketers? And do we remember the players – they're out there – who said, 'I'm going to get so fit I'll definitely play for England,' and then got worse?

So what's my philosophy? Physical conditioning is one of the few areas of cricket preparation which qualify as a science. It can help. So listen to the fitness coaches, definitely. But as you listen, always ask yourself this question, 'How will this make me a better cricketer?'

One coach used to say to me, 'If players really wanted to play for England, they'd double their fitness levels.' Hmm. 'But what if their fitness levels are optimal already?' I asked. 'Then they'd be doubly optimal if they doubled them.' It's easy to get sucked into that non-logic, especially if you're trying to get noticed.

I passed quite easily, by the way, about a third of the way down the list.

From the track, we drove straight to Buckmore Park, a scout retreat, for three days' 'team bonding'. Now that, much more than 'fitness test', is a phrase that sinks my spirits.

Buckmore Park, just off the M2, not one of Kent's lovelier corners, is a centre for outdoor pursuits, embracing a sprawling series of aircraft-hangar buildings. It is very popular, apparently, among Boy Scouts, for whom my iron bunk bed was obviously designed. There are three of us in each cell, one shower between six, and one communal area which trebles as a dining room, meeting hall and stage for the evening soirées. My room mates are Jamie Hewitt and Alamgir Sheriyar. We are told to hand in car keys, switch off our mobiles, and focus our minds on climbing walls, shooting rifles, swimming lengths and building team spirit.

Simon Willis, the second-team coach, is laughing. 'Not quite your kind of place, Eddie.' No, it is more like an open prison minus the openness.

But I can never sustain depression for long on team-bonding outward-bound trips. There really are only two options: get stuck in and laugh later, or stay aloof and be miserable. And besides, we've got the rest of our lives for comfort and indulgence.

A pillow would be nice though.

19 March

Will historians be able to tell us when it began? And who started it? Team bonding, team building, team values, core covenants, signing up, buying in, signing off, shared commitments, norming-performing-storming, white boards with red arrows, flow charts, Venn diagrams, photocopied sheets, plenary sessions, brainstorming, acrostics, abstract nouns, pooling ideas.

It pre-dates my career, which began in 1996, and has been going strong ever since. There is now a whole industry for team psycho chit-chat. The team builders have built themselves a tidy little nest. Once it was 'Go West' and find fortune; now it is 'Go Woolly'.

This is the usual format. Someone who isn't a cricketer – perhaps an ex-army officer or a professional 'team builder' – comes into the team for a couple of days and 'helps' us to learn how to win. 'I have worked with x number of winning teams,' they say. 'All x of them shared the following characteristics [add abstract nouns of choice]. Ergo, if this team has the same abstract qualities, then you too will be a winning team. QED.'

But let's make it real, they say. Let's make it snappy and put some juice in it and bring it into the real world of actions not words. Let's link the abstract nouns to the cricket pitch. Their three favourite topics here are process, measurability, precedent.

Let's take them in turn. Process. We all agree that you cannot determine the outcome of a sports match beforehand. So what can we control? The process, they say. Practice, preparation, pre-match routine. If we get them right, we will be in the right state to win more games than the opposition. I agree. But the team builders talk about preparation as though it is a large pot of resources into which the team can make deposits by hard work and practice. We can then draw upon this winning pot of resources in the heat of battle: the more deposits of practice-units, the better. Scientific stuff. But it doesn't work like that. Quite often more (or aimless) practice makes teams play worse, not better. They leave their best stuff on the training ground. Sport is no more just than life; the deserving do not prevail.

Measurability. There's no point talking about teamwork in the abstract, teams builders say. We've got to measure it so that we can check how well we are doing it. So what do good teams do well? They practise; they spend time together; they support each other; they tell the truth. So let's make sure we practise *x* amount; go out for *y* number of team meals and so on. Then we will be able to monitor how our team building is going. In 1999, Kent made a commitment to take fifty practice catches each every day, even if it was snowing. That would make us better catchers surely. As it turned out, we dropped Justin Langer on 10 in the first game (he went on to get 200) and it didn't get much better from there. We also agreed never to say 'bad luck' to each other. The theory was that 'bad lucks' would foster weakness and excuse-making. In reality, banning it was simply inhuman. The same year we committed to have a team drink together one evening every week. All eleven of us. Every week. Good teams do that, apparently, even when they don't want to. No, they don't. They want to spend more time together than bad teams; but they don't force the issue. It is organic, not imposed from above.

Precedent. The Chicago Bulls have this document on their locker-room wall (add abstract nouns of choice – work ethic, honesty, trust, desire, etc.); the All Blacks have this document; the New York Yankees have this one; Arsenal have that. What's the common thread here? All the winning teams commit to a winning formula before the season. Well, I'm sure they do. But so do all the losing ones. Because pretty much every team has got a mission statement or a core covenant these days – from the Warsop Warblers to the Mickey Mouse Munchers – even the teams that break out into open warfare and then get relegated. Especially those ones, perhaps.

Chronology is not causality. The evidence of a mission statement and the fact of success do not mean that the mission statement caused the success. I am often asked in the dressing room about the practical uses of a degree in history. A grasp of causality is one thing. Understanding why things happen is central to success in any sphere, and I have yet to see any link between mission statements and winning.

If I am sounding cynical, in fact I am not. I find it almost impossible to disagree with much of what the team builders say. Last year, Kent's list of abstract nouns was: Quality, Commitment, Pride, Attitude, Responsibility, Team, Honesty, Humility. Some of my favourites. I share the goal one hundred per cent. It is the method I question.

I believe you build team spirit – to borrow from Wordsworth – by the small, unremembered acts of kindness and of love. The tap on the shoulder that says more than words; staying on in the bar when you are bored and tired but one of your team mates is down and lonely; not giving pub-talk advice to players who are out of form; sitting and watching from the balcony when you are out – not because you have been told to but because you are sharing the journey of the guys out there; being normal around people who are losing it – denying the problem exists simply through your faith in them; being all out there, not semi-detached, when you are batting in a partnership – it's in the eyes, not the words; never letting your own disappointment trip over into self-pity; trying to rise above jealousy.

Now tell me how you measure that.

I feel a bit guilty about writing this after today's team meeting with our new team builder, because he and it were much, much better than previous ones. Less nonsense, more cricket. But I still believe that the best way to foster the right team chemistry is to have the right personnel (i.e. marginalize those who undermine others) and the right leadership. The leaders merely tweak the team culture at the margins; the body of the work is already in place. I believe, for what it's worth, that we're not far off that at Kent.

20 March

Today's schedule: 7 a.m., circuit training in the gym; 10 a.m., basketball; 11 a.m., climbing; 3 p.m., swimming; 4 p.m., two-hour team meeting; 6 p.m., collapse in exhaustion on to my bed; 7 p.m., dinner; 9 p.m., hit the night spots of Maidstone. I don't think so. Nor did half a dozen others. Instead of putting on our dancing shoes, we stayed in the dining hall, sitting on plastic chairs beside canteen trestle tables, playing board games and taking the mickey. Primary-school strip lights flickered unsympathetically overhead.

The go-outers popped in to say, 'We're off, any of you changed your mind?' We hadn't. But I did get a good look at my reflection in Martin Saggers's improbably shiny polo shirt. He had, unknown to me, already been mercilessly teased by everyone else for picking out the Eric-Bristow-meets-*Saturday-Night-Fever* garment. And I had meant to say something completely different when I got his attention across the room. But as he turned in my direction, baby blue shirt glistening under the harsh lights, somehow I couldn't escape the image of a darts player strolling up to the oche. Before thinking, I mimed a darts throw. The team's laughter was rather too enthusiastic.

The 'old men' who resisted the charms of Thursday night in Jumpin' Jacks nightclub were Patel, Banes, Walker, Sigley, Brayshaw and Smith. They are not always so restrained. All of us were ringleaders on the equivalent night exactly one year ago in South Africa, when I ended up trying to swim from Port Elizabeth to Bombay. Sadly, I did not start in the ocean, but on the concrete floor of the car park.

But tonight, it is 'Cranium' board game and banter. A varied half dozen: Min Patel, born in Bombay, educated in England, quick, witty, clever, a gambler and fittingly hard to read; Matthew Banes, who was at school with me, and whose quiet public persona evaporates into infectious laughter in the right company or after a few drinks; Matt Walker, schoolboy sports prodigy, captain of Young England in both hockey and cricket, and a popular team mate; Martyn Sigley, a pro cricketer and a pro physio, for Central Districts in New Zealand and Kent respectively, who treads a healthy line between management and being one of the lads; and 62-year-old Ian Brayshaw, all-rounder for many years for Western Australia, and now Kent's coach.

I play the first couple of rounds of 'Cranium'. The problem with board games is, everyone expects me to be much better than I am. I'm OK on factual questions, useless at charades and often out of the loop on mass popular culture. Matt Walker carries us to a respectable second (out of two teams).

When the game changes, I drop out. I have promised to read my dad's new book in manuscript form before he gives it to his publisher. So I sit next to the games table, turning the photocopied pages, wondering how much of the author is in the fiction. I drift from wanting to find out what happens next to wondering how much of it is real. I am hooked.

As the white wine bottles open and empty, the disputes about rules and regulations get louder and more frequent at the games table. There is just the right amount of spice in the contest. They are not laughing, and yet they are laughing, and it is all the more fun for the suspension of adult seriousness. They are – we are – big kids, even the 62-year-old.

But I am also nicely aware of the unselfconscious warmth and arguments of the board game a few feet away. There are no ego battles tonight, no hidden agendas, no wishing-he-wasn't-with-us feeling. Nor is it a clique who had planned a night apart from the group. It just worked out that way. Occasionally, I look up from the book without being noticed, or get called upon to adjudicate a disputed answer. It could easily pass for a tipsy family on holiday somewhere. I am happier than I have been for weeks.

That is what team life is like at its best. No formality, no sense of event or pressure, but a lot understood without being spelled out, and a lot shared. I could have gone to bed hours earlier than I did, but I stayed. No big deal, nothing special – just the resonance of laughter without malice or social ambition, washed down with cheap Australian white in an ugly, curtainless cabin.

But it matters, it matters a great deal, more to me than to most, and I doubt anyone knows that. Nor does anyone want to hear it. We sportsmen like sentimentality to remain implicit. But it is there all right, the secret comforter that keeps us going.

23 March

After an over-long and often disappointing tournament, today is the Cricket World Cup Final. The right two teams are playing, Australia and India. Australia are definitely the best bowling side in the world and possibly the best batting side – India being the only alternative.

So what do all neutral cricket fans want? India to win the toss and play to their strength (batting), get 300 and set up a thrilling finish. I woke up just after the start of play and switched on to see Gilchrist and Hayden batting. Oh dear, end of game. Worse was to follow. India *won* the toss. I am dumbfounded.

Didn't Pakistan make the equally silly opposite error four years ago? Their strength was bowling, and they chose to bat first on a damp wicket at Lord's. And didn't Nasser Hussain, by his own admission, make the same error in the first Test match of the recent Ashes series in Brisbane? Vaughan and Trescothick, at that stage, were arguably our biggest asset, but we chose to bowl first.

I know India bowled badly; I know Ponting batted brilliantly; I know Tendulkar was out first over; I know it is easy with hindsight. But even at the time, a huge number of us were screaming, 'Play to your strengths.' India didn't, and it cost them.

Two Kent players were playing, Andrew Symonds and Rahul Dravid. Symmo didn't bat and bowled a couple of overs at the end;

Dravid got 47 and kept wicket. Rahul batted number three for Kent in 2000 (I batted four); 2003 will be Symmo's fourth season batting at four for Kent (I now bat three). So I have batted a lot with both of them. Appearances don't lie: they are indeed polar opposites.

Rahul is a composed, considered, patient batter, always studiously searching to better his technique and learn more about the game. His game is based around excellent technique and the ability to concentrate for long periods. Off the field, he is further proof that the last remaining gentlemen are usually Indian: fair, courteous, private, humble.

Before Symmo reaches for his shooting rifle, I am not about to say he is unfair, bad mannered, noisy and arrogant. But he is a vintage Australian, and he likes to play up to that image. His mobile phone rings to the tune of 'Waltzing Matilda'. He vigorously supports Australia at every sport, and if Australia aren't playing, he supports the team who are up against England. He wrestles and stabs pigs, shoots low-flying birds and fast-running mammals, fishes wherever he can and likes to eat as much meat as fits on the barbecue. Dave Fulton began a recent article about him with the lines, 'My first thought when I met Symmo was: I wouldn't want to fight him.' Mine too.

When he gets out, Symmo often says, 'Should have hit it harder.' If you say well played when he gets less than 150, he says, 'Only half a score.' He tries to out-macho opponents: staring at them, standing next to them, looking down at them. But he is happy to have a drink with them after the game. If they can play, that is, and don't talk about themselves. He is a galvanizing influence whose philosophy on sport mirrors the basketball player Charles Barkley: 'I'm just here to kill 'em and let God sort them out later.'

It will not surprise anyone who has been to Australia that he also has very good manners and more respect for people than it might seem. When he bumped into my mother at the cold, windswept Southend cricket ground, he greeted her warmly as 'Mrs Smith' and ran inside to get her a spare sweater. He came to the launch party for my book last summer – not the kind of night he dreams about – and when I was fraught and busy, he helped me move chairs, fold out tables, pass round drinks. Helping people comes as naturally to him as shouting at them.

The big question about Rahul is: does he think too much? Should he express himself more? The big question about Symmo is: should he think more and be more disciplined in the expression of his vast talent?

I don't know. Rahul certainly has more gears than he likes to use. Symmo is exasperating one day and irresistible the next. They are at the extremes of sporting experience, and in their journeys we see our own internal arguments writ large. When to analyse, when to just do it, when to think, when to fight. We bounce from doing it wrong in one way to doing it wrong in another. The hope is that we eventually end up near the right answers for us.

Symmo's answer? 'Quit the bullshit, Ed, and just bloody well compete!' He'll be able to tell me in person in a few weeks. As long as he doesn't expect me to listen just because he's won the World Cup.

24 March

Cricket at last. The St Lawrence ground, after months of winter preparation, has come alive. The nets are up, the square is being rolled, the stumps are in place. No cricketer can fail to respond to the smell of the early season, the signposts that spring is on the way. We don't use linseed oil on cricket bats any more, but I still associate it with this time of year. Damp grass cuttings, brisk mornings sometimes yielding to warm afternoons, the steam from the shower room, the deep sleep of tired limbs.

One legacy from Steve Waugh's month at Kent last summer is a reciprocal arrangement between Kent and New South Wales. As part of an exchange of ideas and coaches, we have been joined by Trevor Bayliss, ex–New South Wales batsman and coach. He will be with us for the first six weeks of this season, focusing particularly on improving our fielding.

Borrowing from baseball coaches and the Australian Test fielding coach, Trevor has devised a series of fielding practices designed to improve the specifics of fielding technique – throwing technique, catching technique, gathering the ball technique. If that sounds basic, it is. But it is amazing how the technical element of fielding is usually ignored. I have enjoyed working with Trevor and think I have made big improvements as a fielder.

He had this to say about coaching: 'In Australia now, we look at the techniques of the best fielders and say, "Why can't we teach everyone to do that instead of the textbook way?" It might not always work, but usually it does.'

Worth comparing with an English coach who once complained about my (at that time) high batting back-lift. 'So what about the high back-lifts of Ponting, Lara and Dravid?' I asked when challenged.

'Ah, but you can't copy geniuses.'

A word about Kent. How good are we? We are definitely a 'big' club; we have never been relegated in either the championship or the one-day league; people have heard of us; we are often near the top of the table. But 'this side' has never actually won the championship. The famous sides of the 1970s did. We have challenged for the highest honours without going all the way. We won the one-day league in 1995 and 2001. But most people think we could have won more trophies than we have. The challenge for us this year, as it has been every year since I have been around, is to go from being a good side to a championship side.

Last week I asked Robert Key, one of Kent's movie buffs, to lend me some DVDs. Quite out of character, he remembered, and five films were sitting by my seat in the dressing room this morning. Then, just before lunch, Rob announced he was off to buy some magazines from the corner shop. 'Grab a paper for me too,' I said.

I was even more surprised, fifteen minutes later, when *The Times* landed on my soup bowl. 'Christ, Rob, steady on, not one favour in seven years and then two in one day.' Murmurs of amusement were followed by proper laughter at his reply, 'Don't think it means I like you.'

Rob learned – or intuited – very early that a cheerfully cynical temperament is very well suited to dressing-room life. Cockiness, an absence of sentimentality, taking the world at face value, avoiding hazy theorizing, a wise-cracking wit: it goes a long way.

It helps if you can play, too, which he can.

My favourite Robert Key story is from another outward-bound team-bonding trip, this time in the Welsh mountains four years ago. One exercise was canoeing. He was paired with Matt Walker. It was an exhausting day, and Matt was feeling the strain in the front of the canoe. He upped his work rate. Still the boat slowed. He pulled harder still. It didn't make sense. Matt could hear Rob pulling harder than ever in the back of the boat, and he was giving his all at the front. So he turned to ask Rob's advice.

What he saw was Rob lying back, admiring the view, feigning effort by sighing loudly, 'Uh . . . uh . . . uh' in time to Matt's rowing stroke.

Rob would have flashed that I-know-I'm-busted smile that doubtless got him out of countless detentions at school. No denying it, sir, I admit, I was just doing what I could get away with. I'll turn over a new leaf tomorrow . . .

One other thing. Someone said today that Buckmore Park – our base for team bonding – has gone bust. Ours will be the last flip charts ever to grace their whiteboards.

26 March

Today is the lunch ceremony for the W. H. Smith/Sports Club book of the year. My last book, *Playing Hard Ball*, has been nominated as best newcomer. But we are only three days into pre-season practice, a time when captains and coaches like to keep everyone together. So yesterday, when I told Dave Fulton about the lunch, I suggested that I didn't go. 'No, you've got to go,' he replied.

'Have your net early and then go up to London at midday. It's not every day you get nominated for a book award.'

Then this morning, before practice, Dave made a quick announcement to the squad about my nomination. I was very touched by the dressing-room applause and 'Good lucks'. How much we like people to be proud of us. I drove off to London feeling ten feet tall (and fairly sure I wouldn't win).

The lunch was a big bash at the Café Royal in Regent Street, well supported by players, publishers and press men. I bumped into Mike Atherton, whose autobiography I reviewed last summer. It was a positive review, but the words chosen by the sub-editors to go alongside the photo of Atherton were, 'Mike Atherton: could come across as cold and aloof.' His words, in fact, but they looked like mine. Hardly poisonous stuff, but I mentioned it to him nonetheless. 'That's what I wrote anyway!' he replied cheerily.

I sat next to Alan Samson, my friend and my publisher from Time Warner, who gambled by publishing *Playing Hard Ball*, and made a bid for this one – only to watch me desert to Penguin. Instead of accusing me of disloyalty to him and Time Warner, Alan simply said, 'Congratulations on your deal with Penguin, your new editor is one of the best.'

Walking down the stairs on the way out after lunch, I bumped into Bob Willis, ex-England captain and now Sky Sports commentator. He asked me what I thought of the county system and the state of English cricket.

I made my usual arguments: I am a reformer. I would prefer fewer counties not eighteen, with better pitches and practice facilities. We can all agree on that. But despite being in favour of reform, I do not think county cricket is always 'to blame'. Do people really think the standard of English professional cricket is worse than that of South Africa, New Zealand, India, Pakistan?

I am also one hundred per cent in favour of the Academy. But it is worth remembering that nearly all the Australian side are in their early thirties, and – contrary to rumour – most of them did not 'make it' in their early twenties. Ricky Ponting and Steve Waugh did. But Damien Martyn, Justin Langer, Matt Hayden,

Mark Waugh and Andy Bichel became international regulars in their mid- to late-twenties or early thirties.

I could have gone on indefinitely, but let Bob Willis walk off into the London sunshine to get tickets to the Royal Opera House. I enjoyed our chat. It was good of him to ask.

I didn't win, by the way.

April 2003

11 April

It was snowing when I woke up this morning – big flakes. So the prospect of fielding all day in a practice match did not thrill me with anticipation. Nor did reflecting on my run-out yesterday. I had scored 9 when Michael Carberry and I ended up looking at each other in the middle of the wicket before I turned and ran towards certain death at the bowler's end.

The snow stopped before the start of play, but the easterly continued to blow, as it often does near the east coast. The Gloucestershire batters got in and got going, Phil Weston making 140 and Matt Windows 150. They hit the very cold ball very hard.

At tea, just when I was thinking it couldn't get much worse, the coach Ian Brayshaw closed the dressing-room door. 'I've got some bad news. The captain [Dave Fulton] has been hit pretty badly in the eye. He's in hospital now. We're keeping this between ourselves until I make an official press release later today.'

Fults chose not to play in this game because he is in good enough form not to have to. Instead, he practised facing bouncers against the bowling machine in the Astroturf nets. Only two days ago, we had both done something similar in the indoor school – he had thrown balls at my head for me to duck or hook, and then I had returned the favour. I wore a helmet; he didn't. He is like that: he enjoys the buzz of bravery.

In fact, today he had turned the machine up to top speed at 90 m.p.h. One came out when he was slightly unprepared. It squeezed through the gap between the helmet and the metal grille and hit him flush on the eyeball. The odds of a ball squeezing through the grille are slight; the odds of it missing all the protective bone around your eye are slighter still. It couldn't have been unluckier. It was an ugly and distressing scene apparently.

'Look after your eyes; they are the most precious thing you've got.' My dad has said that to me countless times, a preoccupation doubtless prompted by the fact that he has written a novel about the painter Sir Alfred Munnings, who lost an eye in an accident. Eye injuries certainly make me feel more squeamish than any other injuries.

We always leap to ask the questions that cannot be answered, seeking reassurances that could only be hollow. How long will he be off? Surely there's no chance of him losing sight in one eye? It couldn't be the end of his career? But there are no answers and, in truth, even the bleakest scenario is not impossible.

Fults has been one of the best batsmen in the country over the last two years; he has taken well to captaincy; at thirty-one he is in his prime. His injury is a hammer-blow to all of us.

Who will captain in his absence? There are six senior players. In order of age: Mark Ealham, Min Patel, Martin Saggers, Matt Walker, Ed Smith and Rob Key. Min has a serious injury of his own and will not play for six or seven weeks; most people think it is very hard to captain as an opening bowler like Martin Saggers; Rob Key will probably be busy playing for England. That leaves Ealham, Walker and me.

Ealy is a 33-year-old Kent stalwart who has been a regular first-team pick for over ten years. He is Kent's beneficiary this year, with all the distractions and pressures involved. That is one consideration. Nor am I sure Ealy would want to become captain. He might once have done, but I am not sure it remains an enduring ambition. But he has a commonsensical, natural intelligence, 61 one-day internationals for England and a winning lightness of touch. He is the likely choice.

I think Matt Walker would be happy to be captain, though he wouldn't petition for it, especially as he is a close friend of Dave's. Matt is a naturally compelling sportsman, always the first to get his knees dirty in the field and give hugs in team huddles. When we are winning and he is playing well, he is our standard-bearer:

carefree, talented, instinctive. But he was out of the side for quite a lot of last year. At his best, Matt is probably the best batsman to watch out of all of us, but his troughs of bad form – a fact of life for all batters – go on much longer than they might. What has never been in doubt is his popularity and sense of fun.

I would be a brave choice as a caretaker captain. Some players may think I am too analytical, too difficult to read, too harsh a judge – though less so than they used to. Some committee men may fear I am too young. Nor might they want to reveal their hand that I might be a long-term successor. The fans might wonder why older, more experienced candidates had been overlooked. The management (the coaching staff) may worry that the very qualities that make me a candidate – independent thought, knowledge of cricket, and an interest in what makes people tick – might mean I would be difficult to control once I was in the job. They might be looking for a consensual voice.

My view? If Ealy is keen to take over, he will. But if he would rather not captain, I would happily do the job. I will say as much if I am asked. I would rather be seen to be ambitious than watch someone be encumbered with a job he didn't want. There are higher gods than humility and team-blokeishness (both of which demand I say nothing).

My prediction is I will not become captain.

I have given more space to the captaincy issue than I might, given how much it is all outweighed by a sense of tragedy. Fults deserved to play for England last year, deserved to be a successful captain, deserved the support and loyalty of his team mates. He still has the latter; but he has lost – temporarily, we desperately hope – vision in his right eye. It will be a hard journey for all of us from here.

13 *April*

Dave Fulton is staying at the William Harvey Hospital in Ashford, four miles from my house. I went to see him twice today.

I did not have high hopes after speaking to him yesterday, soon after he had come out of two and a half hours of surgery. He sounded groggy, depressed and desperately short of sleep. He had spent the night of the accident in a general ward, surrounded by the terminally ill, and it was starting to rub off.

Today he was transferred to a private room with a shower, TV and a window. He even managed a proper meal and a full night's sleep, admittedly with the help of some heavy-duty painkillers.

When I arrive, Dave is in the shower, being helped by his girlfriend Claudine, who has been with him ever since the accident.

'Soap!' he says shortly.

'Soap, please, darling.'

'All right then, soap please.'

I am glad they are feeling bubbly enough to bicker a bit.

'Shall I come back later?' I say through the partition door. 'I feel like an extra in a porn movie.' I am determined to keep things as light-hearted as I can, and I am glad to get a laugh from them both when they come into the bedroom.

Even here, in a comfortable and secluded ward, my mood sank as soon as I walked through the swing doors of the hospital. I tried looking straight ahead as I attempted to find Dave's room. But I still caught glimpses of old and ill-looking people with mostly empty expressions. I remembered the theory of an octogenarian friend of mine: 'No, I'm not going to hospital – people get ill in hospitals.'

'You should have seen the ward last night, Eddie,' Dave says straight away. 'I've never heard such coughing and crying. The guy next to me had throat cancer and spoke through one of those voice boxes. Made me feel positively blessed.'

'Good for the sense of perspective,' I say, and immediately regret the metaphor.

'Which is otherwise not at its best, given the fact I can't see through one eye.'

Why do we do it? Why can't we avoid saying exactly the wrong phrase when dealing with tragedy? Soon after a friend of mine had lost a brother in a car accident, I remember having dinner with him. Cars, death, bereavement, crashes: they kept involuntarily coming into the conversation. Sensitive phrases, which I had planned to avoid, were like magnets that I couldn't avoid being dragged towards. And now, in forty-five minutes with Dave, I manage two 'perspectives' and one 'blinding' (I meant it as a synonym for terrific).

He wants to know how people played in the rest of the warm-up game; how is the mood of the camp; what's news; who should we play in the first game? I get the feeling he desperately needs to feel in the loop, temporarily suspended from action but soon to return, still running the show. That, I suspect, is keeping him going. 'Maybe I'll be back in three or four weeks, who knows.' Maybe.

Dave is full of optimistic phrases, and I endorse them. He will be back very soon; we will have a great year; just a little set-back that might bring us together. But beneath the surface, inevitably even for someone as optimistic and well adjusted as Dave, there is panic and despair. Will I ever play again? Must I say goodbye to unfulfilled ambitions: playing for England, winning the championship? Is the dream over for me, not just this year, but every year?

Claudine, his girlfriend, has been brilliant, but she too is looking drained. It is harder still, perhaps, on the carers rather than the cared-for. I wonder, if it was me propped up at 45 degrees in a bed, unable to walk around or stand up for long in case it scars the eye – would I send people away after a while for fear of them getting depressed? Perhaps I would cling to them regardless.

I give him a copy of *Esquire* magazine, *The Economist* and a copy of *The Great Gatsby*. 'Something to please the eye [there I go again!], something to help you to sleep, and the best novel of the last century.'

'I don't think I'll be given too many other novels from the boys. Get your head down and get some runs.'

'I will. You keep yours up.'

'I will.'

14 *April*

The management called a meeting of the senior players (Ealham, Walker, Key, Saggers and me) at nine this morning. I know I will not be made captain because I would have heard by now. It probably means Ealy has been offered the job and has accepted.

While we wait to learn of the appointment, the five of us joke light-heartedly. That is what sportsmen do. We try to find humour when seriousness threatens to darken the mood. When coach Ian Brayshaw arrives, we quickly discover I was right about the appointment – Ealy apparently accepted 'with alacrity' – which means he is obviously keen to do the job. He is very experienced and people enjoy his company, so he starts with two major plus-points.

The rest is familiar, though perhaps necessary, platitudes about 'all of you are lieutenants' and 'leadership from the senior players'. We have three days until the start of the first-class season and a hugely difficult challenge ahead.

There is a practice game today involving several old Kent players, a tradition started last year by Richard Davis, Kent's ex-left arm spinner. He wanted to keep recently retired players close to the club, and use the day to raise money for cancer research. Richard, though currently well and active, has come close to dying from a persistent brain tumour. [Sadly, Richard died on 29 December 2003.]

The old players are mixed in with the current staff to make two even teams. It turns out I bat against almost the full Kent attack – Saggers, Trott, Khan, Tredwell. I am glad to get some time at the wicket and I hit the ball nicely. I am 'retired' at 80 not out. Not a big game, of course, but decent practice. I have felt in good form all pre-season without getting many runs in the warm-up games, so it was nice to confirm things in a game before the season proper starts on Friday.

We have an informal dinner for players, administrators, ex-players and all their families. Richard Davis makes a short speech about cancer, Ealy a brief comment on his captaincy. Driving home across the downs, it feels a long time since the meeting this morning. I set my alarm for five thirty. It is the A.G.M. of the Professional Cricketers Association in Birmingham at eleven tomorrow, and I am getting the train. It will probably be the longest day of the season.

17 April

Pre-season is now over. No more practice games. The first-class season starts tomorrow. I am back at a place that was once my home – more than just home, in fact. Seven and a half years ago, straight from school and just turned eighteen, I arrived for my first term at Cambridge on one of those perfect early-autumn days that graduates spend their lives associating with going up to university.

Ten weeks later, Rob Ashforth – three-year rugby Blue and soon to be my room mate – drove me to the cricket ground at Fenner's. 'Here it is,' he said, getting out of the car and pointing at the square. 'You'll be great.'

I was touched and embarrassed in roughly equal measure. The day before, Rob had starred in front of 50,000 at Twickenham in the rugby varsity match, throwing a long miss pass in injury time that won the game. He was already a hero on a much bigger stage; I hadn't even made it on the smaller one yet.

When my time came, I was proud of the great tradition of Cambridge sport – from Majid Khan and Peter May to Rob Andrew and Mike Atherton. I felt part of a blood-line of Cambridge sportsmen. I also argued passionately that Cambridge cricket should keep its first-class status. I was wrong, though having benefited so much from Cambridge cricket it feels disloyal to say so even now.

Whether they should have counted or not as first class, I got lots of runs at Cambridge: a hundred on debut, followed by a fifty or a hundred in each of my next five first-class games. I don't think any other English first-class cricketer has done that, though I am not sure, nor am I particularly concerned either way. The next year, I started with an 80, then 190 against the Champions, Leicestershire.

I am, however, keen to put the record straight about who was bowling. We all know that many county teams don't always put out full-strength teams against the universities, but that doesn't mean they don't care or can't bowl. My debut hundred was scored off Steve Watkin, Darren Thomas and Robert Croft; game two was against Devon Malcolm and Dominic Cork; Angus Fraser, Richard Johnson and Phil Tufnell at Middlesex followed.

I concede that it is possible those games were played at a slightly lower intensity than championship matches and on good wickets. But I am also certain that the opposition were trying to get me out and it was hard work. I have been waiting for five years to say that. I can say it now, because I get as many runs for Kent in the championship as I once did for Cambridge in non-championship first-class games.

Tomorrow, I have a more straightforward ambition than setting any record straight. Runs; play well; start the season running.

But this afternoon, I have tea with George Watson, a literary historian and English don at St John's. I am trying to edit and find a publisher for his collected essays. He talks in the way that only academics can, and he looks surprised when I say anything that might be pertinent. I like professorial disregard for the social game of pretending we are all intellectual equals. They tell you things and expect you to listen.

It is a sunny 80 degrees, so after tea I sit alone for a while on the riverbank where the lawns of Trinity College meet the River Cam. The daffodils are turning, but the tulips and bluebells are in full bloom beside the neat stripes of the fairway-like lawn. In front of me is the austere classical symmetry of the Wren Library, to the right is King's chapel, to the left the mock-gothic splendour of St John's New Court. It was always my favourite spot.

Two eighteen-year-old girls, obviously undergraduates, are discussing their top ten best-looking men in the university; three lads idly throw around a rugby ball; people punt by, drinking white wine and arguing affectionately; someone is thrown in the river, amid laughter, recriminations and theatrically planned revenge. It is their world now, as assuredly as it was once mine. My smile is probably starting to look unconvincingly fixed.

Back at the University Arms Hotel, one of the many potentially attractive provincial hotels butchered by barbaric interiors, the Kent lads are in the bar, unaware that Arcadia is a few hundred yards away. Golf is on the TV, so we talk about good swings and dodgy handicaps; conversation starts and stops fitfully; piped music plays predictably; bar food is picked at and shared. We tussle over wanting to be the one to buy drinks as enthusiastically as some of my friends at university used to avoid their round. We could be in any hotel in any town. Strangely, perhaps, I feel more at home than I did by my favourite riverbank.

I go to bed saying the following to myself, 'Don't think it will be easy tomorrow; imagine it will be difficult; then at least you will practise getting into the right mental state.'

So, tomorrow; it all starts tomorrow.

18 April

My determination to take today very seriously wasn't helped by an opening stand of 258 between Rob Key and Michael Carberry. At the start of play, I watched – in fact, waited – like I would in a championship match: quiet, watchful of the bowling, weighing up the challenges. Fenner's is one place where I am remembered, so I didn't want to entertain an endless series of conversations about the old days and the years in between. The plan was frosty courtesy and championship-style intensity.

After a while I thought to myself, what the hell am I doing? You have played hundreds of innings, probably thousands, like this one or harder. There's no point pretending that you're nervous because you're not. At some point today, you will be called upon to bat. When that happens, switch on and play well. Until then, it doesn't really matter a great deal whether you occasionally chat or not.

Over the past few years, I have learned to rev at lower intensity before I bat. Waiting can be hard work, particularly if, like me, you used to open. The best mindset, I think, is a kind of alert but neutral state.

I did eventually bat, when Michael Carberry was out after making a compact 137 on his Kent debut. Rob Key, himself near a hundred, looked almost indifferent as to whether he stayed in or got out. By the time Kent declared, I had made a measured, controlled 61 not out. I can't think of a single memorable shot. It was a dead wicket, an old ball, and a drab day in a place full of happy memories.

The whole Kent team had dinner in Browns, opposite the rooms where I lived in my first year at Peterhouse. I felt slightly weary being back. Seven years ago exactly – the evening of the first day of the 1996 first-class season, my first day of first-class cricket – I was 13 not out overnight against Glamorgan. I bumped into two older players from the Blues team, graduates who had already played county cricket. 'How are you, Ed, not too nervous?'

'Nervous? I'm on fire! I think I'll get a hundred tomorrow.'

They laughed affectionately, saying, 'Good lad,' but probably thinking I was an amusingly deluded debutant.

I got a hundred the next day. I was the youngest person on debut ever to do so for Cambridge. It was here, in Browns, that I celebrated.

It's unlikely I will get another chance to make a hundred in this game. If I did, it wouldn't make me happy for long.

Kent 408/3 declared, Cambridge University 56/0

20 *April*

We bowled badly today and the University batted well. Allowing a university to declare on 395 for 8 is an undignified failure.

Credit to Cambridge: it is their job to heap indignity upon counties. When Arfan Akram reached his maiden hundred, in only his second game, he leapt as joyfully as Michael Slater in his pomp. The David-against-Goliath feeling of succeeding as a student playing against pros adds an extra joyous dimension. I remember it well.

The captain Mark Ealham decided that Michael Carberry, Rob Key and I had had enough batting practice in the first innings, and elevated the middle order to open our second innings. Greg Blewett played some trademark pull shots that had helped bring him to the attention of the cricketing world back in 1995–6; Ealy moved steadily through the gears *en route* to 64; Matt Walker made a smooth 92. It was a placid and unremarkable day.

Fenner's has a small but eccentric core of loyal members, among them some unusually interesting characters – university lecturers, retired surgeons, Second World War veteran pilots, unidentified eccentrics. I got to know them in my three years here. But now, five years on, some old faces are missing. These are not the types who move on; they have died.

But I did talk to one familiar old man, a surgeon and medical academic. He always watched me carefully while I was an under-graduate, and he made intelligent remarks about cricket and history. Today, he sat next to me in the pavilion while I watched the Kent batsmen. I had no interest in repeating the banalities of my ambitions for the season, so I drew him out about medicine. He talked in detail, but not boringly, about the moral dimensions of subjects I know little about: abortion, euthanasia, donating organs. 'I used to be in favour of abortion,' he said, 'then I performed one – I am now like a soldier who was at the front line and turned pacifist.'

For an hour I listened to a humane, sympathetic man who has looked hard at life and felt its pain and injustices deeply – and who wanted to talk about it. Whether I agree with him is irrelevant. It was probably the only conversation like that I will have in a cricket pavilion all season.

I drove out of Cambridge on a beautiful spring evening, feeling flat. It was a bit of a non-game, with little real battle to sustain me. It was also strange being back there.

But as I passed Grantchester on the way out of town, where I walked with my first girlfriend seven years ago and my last girlfriend several weeks ago, it felt that something had ended. I am not only no longer a student, I am not even anything like a student. It is one dream I have woken up from.

On the pitch, harder challenges begin on Wednesday with Leicester's visit to Canterbury. I have scored heavily against Leicester over the past few seasons. They have returned the compliment by verbally abusing me more than any other team has done. It will be very different from Fenner's.

Kent 408/3 declared & 256/3 declared, Cambridge University 395/8 declared. Match drawn

23 April

Today is the first day of the championship, and I am suddenly out of sync. No kidding. Nor am I imagining it. One week into pre-season, nearly a month ago now, I had a meeting with the coach. He said simply this: 'You are hitting the ball so well you must be dying for the season to start. Just try to hang on to it.'

Then, during the last week, I have gradually lost that sharpness and rhythm. Three days at Cambridge without decent nets or good opposition bowlers didn't help. More likely, it was just a random shift in the capricious pendulum known as form. So here we go, day one of the real thing, and I am thinking about why my feet aren't moving well, instead of simply watching the ball.

With each year of extra experience as a player, practice diminishes in importance and the ability to get up for match play becomes more important. No one, least of all you, is much interested in how well you can hit the ball in practice. You have hit the ball well for six thousand first-class runs. It's performance that counts. Hence the first proper game of the year feels less like the culmination of a pre-season process and more of a real beginning. It's on again: me versus the bowler.

So I wasn't overly worried – in the way I would once have been – by my slight loss of rhythm. I have scored plenty of runs without being in top gear. Perhaps more than when I am batting in my pomp. I made a virtue of it in my private pre-match thoughts: 'Good, you'll fight today and take nothing for granted. Get out there and scrap.'

We lost Rob Key after just over an hour, so I joined Michael Carberry, making his championship debut for Kent, with more than an hour to bat before lunch. The wicket was not a typical Canterbury batter-friendly surface, but a difficult April green-top. It was hard work and I was thankful to get through three overs without major alarm.

Then, backing up at the non-striker's end, I watched the bowler try to stop a straight drive from Carberry. Charlie Dagnall just got his fingertip to it, enough to deflect the ball on to the stumps at my end. I had seen what might happen and was desperately trying to get my bat back into the crease. I did. But just after the ball hit the stumps. Run out for 3, backing up, the unluckiest dismissal in cricket. What a start!

I didn't say much in the dressing room. 'Was that out?' Yes – just – most people thought. That was what I thought too. I was determined not to mope or be self-pitying. It is a once-in-a-career dismissal that warrants no analysis, a straightforward slice of bad luck that it is best to get out of the way early. One of those things. But still . . .

Kent 245, Leicestershire 101 / 3

24 *April*

In my last book I described the curious phenomenon of players performing exceptionally against their old teams. The example I used was Paul Nixon, playing for Kent against his old club, Leicester, hitting 14 off the last over of a championship match in August 2001 to win the game. It had given me the biggest high of my career – earlier in the day Andrew Symonds and I had shared a 200 partnership that set up Kent's highest last-innings run-chase since 1934.

Today, Paul Nixon returned the favour, this time playing (again) for Leicester against us. He was released at the end of last summer to make way for our talented wicketkeeper-batter Geraint Jones, and went back to his old county. We had two good players, and only one spot. The more experienced man got the chop.

The crowd gave him a very warm reception as he walked in, then watched for four hours while he took the game away from us. It was a fighter's innings, the kind of attritional cricket Paul thrives on. It was also, of course, an up-yours to the people who had initiated the sacking.

One idiot in the crowd shouted, 'Go home, Judas!' not realizing, or not caring, about who parted company with whom.

We did well to restrict Leicester to a lead of only 25. Rob Key and Michael Carberry again started well, and I went in with the ball starting to get old and the wicket looking a bit flatter. I have got back some of that rhythm, and hit two nice boundaries in my first few balls. Then, sensing a ball from Phil DeFreitas was there to be hit through the on side, I went for my favourite leg-side clip. It was too straight and I missed it: lbw for 8. Two failures out of two.

Greg Blewett and Michael Carberry soon followed, and at 70 for 4 we were in serious trouble. Mark Ealham and Geraint Jones (perhaps with a point to prove of his own) got us through to stumps at 6.30.

I am giving a barbecue for all the players and their wives and girlfriends tomorrow. Out twice and extremely frustrated, I remember at eight o'clock that I have yet to construct my brand new barbecue. It takes two hours – 'Not a second more than twenty minutes,' the shop assistant had promised – of screws, allen keys, trolley legs, wooden slats, sweat, frustration and some amusement. I was actually quite glad of the distraction.

Leicestershire 270, Kent 245 & 147/4

26 April

This might have been an exciting game, but some rain breaks and more good batting by Paul Nixon made it an inconclusive draw. The battle between the wicketkeepers, in fact, was the game's best feature. Yesterday, Geraint Jones replied to Paul's 113 with a sparkling hundred of his own. Geraint faced 152 balls for his 104, hitting 2 sixes and 10 fours. Though it is not his first-class debut, it is his first game as the regular first-team keeper. He looked about as un-overawed as he could be.

Three years ago, when I was playing in a second-team game, I remember seeing this 'wicketkeeper' bat for the first time. Standing at the crease, Geraint looked exactly like a batsman, wicketkeeper or not. He batted brilliantly that day – as he did yesterday – with attacking self-belief, quick feet, assertive shot-selection, uncomplicated technique and a preparedness to attack spin from ball one. I said at the time, 'If he can keep well, he'll play for England.' I haven't changed my mind.

A few Leicester players, Paul Nixon among them, came to my house-warming party last night. It was supposed to be a barbecue, but it rained hard and unceasingly, forcing forty of us into my sitting room while the team chef stood under a golfing umbrella doing the cooking in the garden. 'I'm thrilled for Geraint,' Paul said to a couple of us, late into the evening. 'He got the nod over me and I wish him every success. No hard feelings at all. He played brilliantly.' Paul is like that.

Just to add one final ironic touch, while we tried to bowl out Leicester today and force an unlikely win, Paul Nixon dug in again, adding an obdurate 53 to his first-innings ton. He's like that, too.

Leicestershire 270 & 255/6, Kent 245 & 411. Match drawn

27 April

I don't expect to be writing this very often: today went exactly according to plan. We batted first in our first National League one-dayer, exploited the fielding restrictions in the first fifteen overs, played sensibly in the middle, and then slogged well at the end. Mark Ealham, in his first one-day game as captain and pinch hitter, made a big-hitting 41; Greg Blewett held things together with 46; Matt Walker paced his 82 not out perfectly, leaving Kent 254 off their 45 overs. I was the only real blip, making a scratchy 10 off 22 balls.

In the field, we bowled well and never looked threatened. Ben Trott, bowling with the kind of control and bounce that makes us all wonder why he isn't a more consistent match-winner, took two early wickets; James Tredwell bowled with level-headed intelligence; Peter Trego picked up the tail and finished off a good personal debut.

It really was like that, a nerve-calming victory that has relaxed the expressions of everyone around the club. We desperately need some wins to distract us from the tragedies and upheaval of the last few weeks. Without a winning momentum, the self-pity of bad-luck stories and ready-made excuses will look dangerously tempting. So thank God we got off to a running start today.

Equally importantly, Mark Ealham had a great game, because every new captain craves the authority that comes with good personal form. He also made an interesting point to me after the game. 'I know you got a good ball today,' he said, 'but it looked to me like you were a bit anxious. Don't fret after a few dot balls in one-day cricket. You will always score quickly enough when you get going. Take your time. You'll make it up later.' I've been wanting someone to say that to me for a while, not only because it's comforting, but because it's true.

Paul Nixon, the jack-in-the-box Leicester keeper, read it more simply: 'It was an absolute jaffa, mate. Don't give it a second's thought.'

So three county innings and three failures: a good ball, a bad shot, and a freakish slice of bad luck. One year – next year? – I would love to start the season with 180 not out and take off some of the pressure. But it is 27 April, too early, surely, to be saying 'maybe next year' to myself?

Kent 254/4, Leicestershire 200. Kent won by 54 runs

May 2003

2 May

Writing this diary is turning out to be more difficult than I had thought. More difficult to find the time to write, more difficult to go over painful recent memories, more difficult to clear a space for my computer in the tiny room I have been sharing with James Tredwell, more difficult not to watch TV, go out, call someone or sleep instead.

It doesn't help that we keep losing and I can't get more than 30-odd. We lost to Sussex inside three days, I got 23 and 33, and there's something not right about the way we are playing.

Me first. For this game, I at least got back that good rhythm of pre-season. I played fluently enough for 23 in the first innings, before getting a good ball that I nicked. Greg Blewett and Matt Walker also played nicely for 41 and 40. But 23s and 41s and 40s don't win games, nor even very often do they save them. Nearly always someone has to get a hundred.

In the second innings I thought it would be me. I was in for two hours – a long time compared to the short visits I have been spending at the crease this year. For the first time this season, I felt the thrill of competition, the needle of a good game of cricket in the balance. We needed 293 to win, and wickets were tumbling at the other end. 'Just this wicket and we're through,' Murray Goodwin, Sussex's Zimbabwean overseas professional, kept saying. 'Get Ed and the rest will go easily.'

Today, I started once again to use external cues as mental prompts. When I am batting well, my positive mental side – my 'good voice' I call it – uses whatever stimuli it can find in the outside world as added incentives. It might sound silly or trite, but I use the most eccentric things to re-focus. Today, just as I was getting into the contest, I saw a white feather – a symbol of cowardice – next to the batting crease. 'If you get out softly now, you might as well give yourself that white feather as a mark of your own cowardice! Get stuck in, be here at the end, just be here.'

So to get out, caught at cover off a seamer, back-driving at a decent ball – *caught cover* – left me close to despair. To do the hard work, get back into good rhythm and good thought patterns, then *caught cover*! It stopped, I think, 'got stuck in the pitch'. But it always does, doesn't it, when you get caught cover? It stopped. Frankly, no one cares. You were caught cover and Kent lost by 133 runs. You were the man in and you got out.

But nevertheless I felt I had it back today, that certainty and self-belief and total absorption. It's the getting lost in it, not having an extraneous thought or problem in the world, not thinking about the pettiness of humdrum, everyday life – that's what I love about batting.

There is a loner's streak in many good batsmen that cuts across styles of play. You would pick Mike Atherton – persistent, astute, stubborn – as an angler before a professional sportsman. It is easier to imagine Ted Dexter – fearless, bold, undaunted by what-ifs – as a solo pilot or racing car driver than as a soccer player. If not cricket, it wouldn't have been team sport at all. Different men and different batsmen, but they share, I suspect, a certain delight in isolation.

Not all batsmen are like that. Some find the loneliness of batting one of its chores rather than its pleasures. But many of us find solace in the solitude. In my case, I love being in charge of my thoughts and my game, controlling the tempo and the destiny of the game, winning battles in the privacy of my own world – all the time not having anywhere to hide. No matter how sociable I may otherwise appear, that private world is central to my life as a cricketer. Today was the first time I have got close to finding it this season.

So what about Kent? We are struggling in several areas. First, we can't finish off tails. Sussex were 166 for 6 in poor batting conditions on the first day, then they recovered to 279 all out, with Mushtaq Ahmed getting 37 and number eleven Jason Lewry slogging 22. That shouldn't happen. It's not often that 279 is a match-winning total, but in this game it clearly was – the other three innings were under 200.

Secondly, we are all getting out when we are in. None of us is in properly bad form. Greg Blewett is adjusting to these slow, green, English wickets, Michael Carberry looks in deft touch, Rob Key and I are simply short of time in the middle, Matt Walker is playing fine. None of us is struggling technically. If that sounds good, it isn't. A technical flaw can be ironed out in a few nets. Ironically, playing decently and not scoring heavily, especially throughout a team, might be more problematic – a reluctance, perhaps, to stand up or stand out.

The only solution is that someone needs to make a big score and end the cycle of cameos.

Thirdly, we don't have as much competitive presence as we should. There is nothing wrong with the team spirit. There is plenty of laughter, fun, affection. It's just that when we take to the field, we aren't translating that into making life unpleasant for the opposition. You can be the happiest camp in the world for a few games, but if you don't start winning, you never stay happy. That's the first rule for creating lasting team spirit: win.

No one is necessarily to blame. But we need to fire up in the field, be more ruthless with the ball, and get stuck in with the bat. That's three clichés in one sentence – all of them true.

As for me, I am getting there. I said so when I spoke to my mother on the phone tonight. 'That's nice, Ed,' Mum said wearily, in a way that suggested, 'What poor deluded souls these sportsmen are, always thinking great things are around the corner.' Later, an ex-girlfriend called, and asked – as a brief aside – how I was playing.

'I think I might be on the brink of playing better than I ever have,' I explained.

'Good to hear nothing's changed, you always were at about that stage,' she replied.

No, no, no, you don't understand, I'm back, I AM BACK!

Sussex 279 & 198, Kent 185 & 159. Sussex won by 133 runs

5 *May*

The last time I crossed the Severn Bridge I was travelling to give the address at my grandmother's funeral, two years ago. My grandfather was Welsh, and we spent many family holidays walking in the Brecon Beacons or by the sea on the Gower Peninsula. Hardly Martha's Vineyard, but the beach cricket is better on Rhossili Beach.

No one would guess that I am even one-quarter Celt, but I feel a surprisingly deep affinity with the Principality. Talkative, emotional and friendly, Welsh people are good at making you feel at home.

I have never played at Sophia Gardens in Cardiff, and it feels strange sitting up in the dressing room, waiting to bat. In the old days, when there was only one division and one-dayers were on the Sunday after a four-day championship match, you never had to turn up out of the blue on the other side of the country for a one-off 45-over game. You settled in for the week. The danger now is that one-off games like this one can be over before you have got used to where you are. If you don't impose yourself, it's like it never happened.

So before the game started I told myself to imagine myself out there batting, feeling at home, here to stay. Just as well: we won the toss, batted, and I was in at 20 for 1.

They bowled well up front and I took a long time to get into double figures – perhaps 25 balls. In previous years, when I felt under pressure for my place in the one-day team, I might have fretted. What would my team mates be saying: 'Why is Ed using up so many precious overs?' But today, my thoughts were: you've done the hard work, don't give it away now; it will be harder for the man coming in; you always score quickly enough when you are in; today is your day.

It could have been. At 101 for 1 off 20 overs, with both Rob Key and me going well, I played across a straight ball and was lbw to left-arm spinner Dean Cosker. Well batted, they said in the dressing room, you've given us a good platform. But I know that good platforms often don't materialize. It didn't today. Following my dismissal, Rob Key and Greg Blewett holed out, the middle fell away, and we collapsed to 192 for 9.

Glamorgan approached the total positively, attacking up front with pinch hitters (in particular Robert Croft) in the first fifteen overs. When you don't pinch hit, and the opposition does it successfully, you always feel: what were we doing, pushing and poking out there? I don't deny pinch hitting works well for some teams. But I am still not convinced that it suits us.

Whatever. Glamorgan cruised to victory with seven wickets and four overs in hand.

Lessons: first, if you get in, go big; second, take responsibility, don't leave it to someone else; third, today shows me the way I am going to play one-day cricket: calmly, with the confidence that I will make up for a slow start with free scoring once I am in.

Just go on next time and make a proper score. And yes, I am partly to blame for today's loss.

The team is wobbling a bit. Draw, win, loss, loss. I am travelling with the captain, Mark Ealham, and we inevitably talk a bit about team selection, tactics and politics. He is clearly worried about Kent, perhaps more so than I am. He has always liked being informal and approachable, but as captain there is inevitable isolation. Whatever anyone says, you cannot be just the same as before, one of the boys and nothing more. There is also extra pressure concerning your own performance. Captaincy is a tough job. I listen to many of Ealy's opinions about Kent, but I also try to keep things light: there should be a time limit on any post-mortem, particularly only two weeks into the season.

A muted dinner in Cardiff tonight. We travel to Cornwall tomorrow – my favourite county in England, apart from Kent – for the C&G game on Wednesday. I plan to arrive early in St Austell, then make the extra hour drive to visit the Tate Gallery in St Ives.

Kent 192, Glamorgan 195/3. Glamorgan won by 7 wickets

6 May

There isn't time to get to St Ives, so instead I decide to go for a walk along the beach near our hotel in St Austell. I get the impression the others aren't enjoying the sleepy seaside atmosphere of the Cornish coast as much as I am, and I leave them playing pool in the dingy bar of the hotel.

It isn't hot, but warm enough down on Carlyon Bay to lie on the rocks, sunbathing, and I doze off, listening to the Atlantic. After eight hours of driving in two days, two hours of stolen solitude in the sun feels blissful.

How funny that three of our first away games should be in Cambridge, Wales and now Cornwall, all of them full of non-cricketing memories for me. The last time I came here, in December last winter, I was trying to persuade an American that England can do beaches and seascapes as well as lawns and country houses. In fact Cornwall's magical quality – its lush but windswept headlands, its early Christian settlements and mythical atmosphere – is as distinctly English as Bath's Georgian orderliness or Oxford's Gothic spires. It is scarcely surprising that so many English myths, from King Arthur to Tristan and Isolde, are set here. Of all the places I know, it is the easiest to imagine a dragon emerging out of the sea or a castle conjured from the mist.

With the decline of slate and tin mining, tourism is Cornwall's main – almost only – industry. But I am still surprised that even more people don't visit. Most cricketers, for example, are more likely to have been on holiday to Barbados than to Cornwall. I concede that the weather is never guaranteed, but in terms of pure landscape I don't know any coastline – whether it be Australia, Massachusetts or Provence – more beautiful or inspiring. I feel better already for being here.

But I promise this diary won't go on like this. There will be no special memories in Derby, no ex-girlfriends in Chesterfield, no family holidays in Northampton. Over the course of the season, there will be plenty of soulless cinemas and colourless towns. But for the time being, cricket is taking me to some interesting places.

The evening ended, incidentally, with me playing pool in the bar as well, doubtless with more enthusiasm for not having done so all afternoon.

7 May

Almost every year a professional first-class county side loses one of these games against an amateur minor county. It had better not be us. With our captain injured, and having lost our last two games, now is not the time to crash out of the C&G Trophy to a team of enthusiastic club players.

Truro is a stunning ground, carved into a hillside, flanked by the River Fal on one side and Truro Cathedral on the other. But its prettiness should not obscure what a horrible venue this is for us. If you are playing tennis against someone much better than you, what is the best way you can improve your chances? Play with squash rackets or put boulders on the court. Anything which introduces an element of pure lottery will assist the person who trails in skill.

That is why minor counties sometimes produce the slowest, most difficult wickets they can prepare when they play against first-class sides: a faster pitch with true bounce means the better side will win, and win quickly. Today was a classic minor county pitch, described by one of my team mates as 'a bit like rolled snot'. Hence the game becomes, in another cricketing metaphor, a potential 'slippery banana skin'.

We won the toss, decided to bowl, and watched our fast bowlers struggle to get the ball to bounce above ankle high. Cornwall crawled to 62 for 8, then recovered to 140 all out, just enough on this wicket to make it a potentially nerve-racking chase.

Most pro batsmen despise playing on wickets like this one, particularly against slow-ish 'trundler' bowlers. It is very hard to play fluently, harder still to play elegantly. It drags you down to club level. But over the last few years I have changed my view a bit. Yes, it is hard and often grim work. But it is also a different kind of technical challenge, one which English players from older generations were much better at than us. They grew up on uncovered wickets and played later and more watchfully. I am not advocating, as some people do, a return to those days. But I do believe that the ability to change gears – to swing the bat later and straighter – is a useful skill. If you can adapt your game at will, you must be playing well. It is also good practice in case we have to play a real county side on a low, difficult wicket. We also have a game to win, and I am a bit anxious.

James Tredwell is out in the first over, and I bat slowly and solidly with Rob Key. Rob plays more shots but departs for 27. Greg Blewett, our South Australian overseas pro, really struggles. He has not yet hit form this year, and this is probably his nightmare wicket. At the other end, I am quietly enjoying the struggle. Just when I am starting to congratulate myself on how well I have adapted to the wicket – 'Gosh, I'm maturing as a player' – I spoon one to mid-on and depart for 25. The ball did undeniably 'stop' as it bounced, even more than usual for this wicket. But that is what pros always say. Yes, it did stop, but I might also have been careless.

More importantly, it starts another collapse. 69 for 2 becomes 83 for 5, and I am blaming myself in the dressing room while Geraint Jones and Matt Walker painstakingly recover our innings. By the end, it looked easy at 141 for 5. Most people will forget how close we were to disaster. I won't. I started it.

BUT. I am playing with some authority. Even if I do keep getting out for twenties and thirties, I have got back that good rhythm of pre-season. So I am both pleased to have won and feeling privately optimistic as we start the longest drive of the year. Six hours in the driver's seat lie ahead.

It could not be a more beautiful spring evening, and as we drive over Bodmin Moor the yellow gorse is lit up in the last of the May sunshine. Then, in Devon now, we pass over the harsher, bleaker but still wonderful Dartmoor. Mark Ealham, my fellow passenger, is on the phone to Rob Key, who is complaining about the long drive. Rob and I are cheerfully antagonistic in our opposite natures.

I shout out to Mark, 'Tell him to stop moaning and think how lucky he is to be expanding his experience of the English landscape.'

'The what? Looks terrible to me,' he replies, via Mark. 'You see solitude, Ed, but all I see is boredom.'

Two hours later, now in Thomas Hardy country, dusk is settling on Salisbury Plain, which lends itself perfectly to the still half-light. I am tempted to say, 'Just like *Tess of the D'Urbervilles*,' but decide against.

Several of us stop for food at a service station. Ahead of us in the queue are eight friends – perhaps in their last year of university, or their first year at work in London – clearly returning from a few days on holiday. They are lightly tanned, clear-skinned, bright-eyed, with public-school voices. They've probably been surfing in Polzeath, or yachting in Salcombe, perhaps dipping a bit too enthusiastically into daddy's case of cabernet sauvignon last night. One or two of them would not look out of place in a Ralph Lauren advert.

'Posh tossers,' one of my colleagues says to me with a smile.

Cornwall 140, Kent 141/5. Kent won by 5 wickets

10 May

I'm not lying, honestly, I have been playing better. So what happened today at Chelmsford against Essex? A miserable 2, almost every ball of which was unconvincing. You can't keep losing form – or whatever it is that makes you play well – overnight. I am genuinely confused why I played badly today.

We also lost, less heavily than we might have done. At 33 for 5, batting first on one of the best wickets in England, it didn't look like being a game at all but a rout. We recovered to 176, then bowled and fielded well to take the game into the last over. We had our old hustle and self-belief in the field today. We certainly played with more spirit than at any stage earlier this year.

I spent more time this pre-season working at my fielding than I ever have before. Today it paid off. I took a tricky catch in the deep quite easily, and then made a direct-hit run-out from mid-on to get rid of Darren Robinson. Waiting for the decision of the third umpire, we chatted animatedly in a huddle of Kent players. 'Do you think you got him, Ed?' Mark Ealham was certain. 'Definitely – I was square of the wicket. He was a foot short.' It was a crucial moment – though Essex were still favourites, a wicket would give us a fighting chance. I almost broke James Tredwell's ear-drum when it was given out.

I normally take little notice of whether games are televised or not, but I was glad to field well on TV today. Most people agree I can bat – they may disagree about exactly how well – but I need to convince people I can field well, especially if I am going to play for England. Hopefully today will help kick start my fielding on to another level.

But another loss for Kent. I need runs, not just for myself, but to get the whole top order going. I am usually good at getting back into form quickly. Kent need me to do that now more than they ever have before.

Kent 176, Essex 179/7. Essex won by 3 wickets

13 May

Even though we had a close and tiring game on Saturday, yesterday (Monday) I practised on my own with the coach, Ian Brayshaw. I don't like to let my game lie when it is plainly out of sync. And today (Tuesday), even though we practised as a team, I stayed on afterwards with my batting coach, Chris Stone.

Dave Fulton asked me to watch the video of my innings on

Saturday with him. It was a video nasty: 13 balls, two thick edges, two lbw appeals, a mis-hit drive, a handful of decent shots. Bob Willis was not much impressed on the commentary. Fair enough. Nor was I. Dave thinks my balance is too far on my back foot, causing me to be late on the shots. He is right. I am pleased with the analysis. It is easy to put right, and the rest of my game looks OK. But it is never easy watching yourself bat poorly. Bob Willis sounded appalled on the commentary. Fults looked anxious on my behalf.

This evening an ex-girlfriend invited me to the opening of an exhibition of her new paintings. It was at my old school in Tonbridge, where she was an artist-in-residence. (No, not when I was a pupil there.) Just outside the exhibition, I stopped and looked at the famous Head cricket ground – where Colin, Chris and Graham Cowdrey, Richard Ellison and several other Kent players including me learned to play. I had it all mapped out in those days: the Head, then the St Lawrence ground at Canterbury, then England . . .

Inside, cricket still follows me around. Paul Parker, ex-captain of Sussex and now a schoolteacher, asks how I am going.

'Me or Kent?'

'Both.'

'Both badly.'

'I'm surprised.'

A cellist in her late thirties comes up and tells me her son Alex has a poster of me on his bedroom wall. 'You're his hero – he follows your scores every day.' There can't be that many Alexes out there, but even a few is enough to make you feel slightly special.

I get talking to a few people about why Kent haven't got going yet, why we aren't scoring runs, why I'm not scoring runs. I try to be honest, amused, balanced – panicking, me? – full of confidence that things will come right eventually. They buy it. I can see them thinking, 'He'll be fine, obviously got a good head on him.'

'Of course, knowing the lines is one thing,' I add. 'Doing it is another thing. I'll be nervous as hell at eleven o'clock tomorrow.'

And seriously worried about another failure and another collapse.

I bought an abstract painting for my new house.

'Do I get a special rate as your ex-boyfriend?'

'Sure – half as much again.'

I listened to Bob Dylan in the car on the way home. Rob Key, who must be hoping that he hangs on to his England place when the team is announced shortly, is staying the night at my house. We both could do with a score tomorrow.

14 May

One of Steve Waugh's ideas is never to take negative thoughts into a game. Whatever doubts you might have, sort them out as best you can before play starts. If you can't sort them out, deny them to yourself.

That's what I decided to do against Middlesex today. I am sick of team meetings, sick of talking about form, sick of endlessly going round in circles about team spirit and helping each other and cliché-ridden banalities. The only way out is to perform. So what if I'm not playing perfectly? I am good enough even when I am not playing perfectly to get runs. I decided to look forward to getting in, look forward to hitting the ball, and to avoid siege-mentality fear of failure. If I nick one, so be it. I am going to impose myself on the day.

At my first ball, from Aussie fast bowler Joe Dawes, I played a cut shot. I missed it, and said to myself, 'Forget it – just hit the next one.' I did and got going. Suddenly, far from being worried about a decent start, I was looking around for gaps in the field, trying to put pressure on bowlers to bowl where I wanted them to, feeling dominant rather than dominated. It was nice to be back on song and to sense a little apprehension in the opposition.

I got 103 off 144 balls, a decent scoring rate, with 19 fours. I played well but unexceptionally. More importantly, I established our first good batting day of the championship season. By putting on a big stand with Greg Blewett (60) we re-established some authority as a batting side. It was also good to watch, and we are paid to entertain.

Should I have gone on? Well, that's what people always say. In truth, I didn't relax on 103 and lose concentration. I got a very good ball which bounced unexpectedly. Disappointing, yes. Culpable? Not particularly.

We have to keep going like this: backing our talent as a batting side. We are too good to get cagey. It is not a sign of character to retreat into defence as soon as things get difficult. This was the first hundred of the year for a top six batter. If it helps to kick start our season, it might be the most significant hundred I have ever made.

Kent 291/4

17 May

We had a good chance of winning this game, but rain ruined it. Kent made 472, then bowled Middlesex out for 221. Following on, Middlesex were still 251 behind. From that point, given a normal full four days, you would back yourself to win most times. But for two days it drizzled and depressed us and damaged the game irreparably. So we will have to wait for a win.

The Oval and Surrey await tomorrow. I have never made big runs at the Oval or against Surrey.

What do cricketers do when there is a longish break for rain? Some do the crossword, some read magazines, some practise indoors, some sleep, some play cards, some log on to the internet connection in our dressing room. I do all of those things sometimes. Sometimes a nice chat develops over coffee in the players' dining room and the old stories are dusted off, exaggerated and embellished. Sometimes, perhaps not as often as I think we should, we talk cricket.

But today, I did something different. I wrote a letter to a younger friend of mine who has just become a professional cricketer. In some respects, he is like me. So writing from somewhere in the middle of my career, to him at the beginning of his, is a bit like writing to my younger self. What advice really would have helped? This is what I wrote:

1. Look for the good. Despite the frustrations and pitfalls, being in a sports team is infinitely more fun than almost any other job. And sportsmen are rarely worse than other tribes and often better. Enjoy the ride – the banter, the escapism, the practical jokes, the inanity, above all the warmth and affection. You've got the rest of your life to be serious and solitary. And the best way to build team spirit is not by talking about building team spirit but by forming real friendships. Don't be semi-detached.

2. That said, you're also on your own. Some people will help you, a few support you, one or two might even promote you. But ultimately you are on your own. You and the ball, you and the bowler. That's what it boils down to. The rest is incidental. Apart from the fun and the winning. And the best way to win and have fun is for you to win as many of those one-off battles with the bowler as you can. That is the best way, perhaps the only way, to make a real contribution. One ball at a time. Before blaming a 'lack of team spirit', or unhelpful senior pros, or bad pitches, or poor umpiring, first think about how you can maximize your chances of winning more contests with the bowler tomorrow than you managed today. It's your job and a big chunk of your life, so you may as well give it primacy of place. Get used to looking in for the answers and looking out for laughs – not the other way around.

3. Technique. Think hard before changing it too much or too soon. Of course you are ambitious and will be impatient to get better. But every 'improvement' carries with it the risk of damaging another part of your game. Never sacrifice a major

strength to solve a minor weakness. Stubbornness or cynicism – no. Courteous scepticism – yes.

4. Politics. It will be everywhere – in the dressing room, the car park, at the cards table, in the night club, round the table with the players' wives. We live in a political world, as the Bob Dylan song goes. Some people will be in it for themselves, prepared – with varying degrees of subtlety – to run down rivals and promote themselves. That will concern you, annoy you, depress you. Don't let it. Through politics people might be able to bullshit their way into the team for a game or two. But it doesn't work in the long term. Play a long-term strategy. Keep your counsel. Your opinions will eventually be worth all the more when they are known not to be self-interested. In the meantime, enjoy having freedom that comes with not being expected to have an opinion and just play.

5. Don't jump to say the right thing. Have a strong work ethic, be privately self-critical, inwardly tough, quietly ambitious. But don't shout about it. Piousness is both irritating and threatening. It also leaves you no room for self-improvement when times get tough. Like Prince Hal in *Henry IV Part 1*, it helps to be able to turn over a new leaf. Fail when you still have a bit to learn, and people will try to help you; fail when you appear to have all the answers, and people will think there is no hope for you.

6. Don't apologize. For your accent, your education, your good fortune. It fools no one and demeans yourself. Acknowledge your luck, but don't despise it. Almost always teams eventually learn to love people who are cheerfully themselves. It might take time. But they will never like you if you are pretending to be someone else.

A bit teacherly maybe. But both my parents are teachers, one uncle and an aunt also. Both my grandfathers were headmasters. So I plead genetic inheritance.

I have been lucky to have had several great teachers, a couple of them cricket coaches. I enjoyed absorbing and learning from what they had to give. The thrill of discovery can be as good as it gets. But so too is the converse: being able to help someone else. I don't have the patience of the professional teachers in my family. But recently I have started to understand why they have spent their life working crazily hard and earning a pittance.

There is performing – acting, playing sport, writing – with its joys and despair. But even the most focused performer can't perform all the time. There is art – a great novel, a thrilling concert – which can give you a present-yet-absent euphoria, a break from introspection or wordly worries. But most of us can't escape into that world all the time.

So what else is there? How else do you lift your day? Teaching, in its myriad forms, is one way. I can't remember when I first realized how thrilling it is to inspire that smile of recognition – got it! the off drive! – on someone else's face. A smile you know so well, coming back at you. Suddenly, the 'dead' half of practice – when you are throwing the ball for someone else to hit – came alive.

I must be getting old . . .

I wonder if my friend will smile like that when he reads what I wrote. I wonder if I would have.

Kent 472, Middlesex 221 & 249/4. Match drawn

18 May

The most exciting innings I have ever played and the best game I have ever been part of. Today we scored the highest ever second-innings total (316) in the history of the Sunday League and lost by six runs. I got 99, my best in limited-overs cricket.

The Surrey batting line-up reads a bit like the England batting order – probably because they've all played international cricket.

Ali Brown, the most feared one-day player in England; Ian Ward, who scored more runs than anyone else last year, English or otherwise; Mark Ramprakash, who, alongside Graeme Hick, has been the most prolific county player for the last decade; Graham Thorpe, generally regarded as the best English Test batsman of the last ten years; Rikki Clarke, who played for England last year as a twenty-year-old; Adam Hollioake, former England one-day captain, who can make even the Oval seem like a children's pitch; Azhar Mahmood, the Pakistani all-rounder.

So we won the toss and elected to bowl first!

Brown smashed 44 off 24 balls, including a couple of huge sixes; Ramprakash made an unbeaten hundred; Thorpe and Ward added 30-odd each; Mahmood scored a sensational 70 off just 41 balls. They finished with 322 for 7 off their 45 overs. It was the biggest battering I have ever seen.

To make things even worse, in the last over of the Surrey innings I injured my right hand trying to catch Mahmood on the deep mid-off boundary. Back in the dressing room between innings, I picked up my bat and played a few shots. It hurt like hell. After a series of expletives, I told captain Mark Ealham that I doubted I could bat in my usual number three spot. 'I don't think it's broken, but I'm really struggling.'

Our physio suggested he throw me a few balls on the outfield before the start of our innings as a kind of fitness test. I hit them pretty badly, but I felt my right hand wasn't getting any worse, so I said, 'Good enough,' when I got back upstairs and rushed to put on my pads as Rob Key and Mark Ealham walked out to the wicket. As it turned out, we decided I would bat next if Rob Key went first, and Peter Trego – more of a big hitter – would go in if Mark Ealham was out.

I went in at 62 for 2, with both Ealham and Trego gone. Rob Key followed almost straight away, leaving us 71 for 3. Greg Blewett, though short of form, was likely to be a key player for us. You need class to chase 322, and he has it. I felt that he and I had to get a stand together if we were to have any chance at all. So, despite the enormous run rate, I was prepared for both of us to take a little while to get set. We would make it up with fast scoring when we were settled in.

The first part of the plan worked well – we were both in and playing nicely – when Saqlain Mushtaq bowled Greg with a straight-on ball that looked like an off-break. It was the kind of magic moment that great sides produce when they most need it. With Kent 137 for 4, our overseas star out, Matt Walker on nought, and still needing nearly 200 off 22 overs, we must have been at least 12–1 against.

I have made big scores in one-day cricket, but always measured ones. I have never completely let off the handbrake. My team mates often complain that I hit big sixes in the nets but not in the middle. Too much self-control, they say, or, less generously, a fear of failure that is not suited to the one-day game. I answered some of that today when I decided to go for it when Walks came out. I hit the next ball for four with a big heave to midwicket – 'That's not you at all, Ed,' the Surrey wicketkeeper John Batty, who has known me since university days, immediately said. I hit the next one for four through extra cover. 'That is,' he added.

It is a big mistake to think that players who are able to share a joke in the heat of a game are somehow less committed to ruining the other guy's day. I remember seeing two major league baseball players sharing a joke during the World Series and thought, 'If these guys can rise above the pressure and still enjoy it, why can't we?' No one would have me marked down as a devil-may-care joker, and I'm normally quiet and self-contained at the crease, but I am also happy to enjoy the ironies and asides that give sport much of its colour.

Today there were several, mostly involving Adam Hollioake. Much is made of Adam's hard-man image and bullish self-confidence. But less is said about his intelligence and ability to understand the huge role that luck and chance play in one-day cricket. Adam is clever enough to understand that a lot of captaincy isn't about cleverness – but being a sensible gambler and retaining the aura of self-certainty when your gambles go wrong. Above all, one-day cricket favours people who bowl or hit the ball with purpose and self-belief, and he has plenty of both.

When I was trying to work out how many we needed to have to be ahead on Duckworth-Lewis (i.e. what our score had to be for us to win the game, should it rain), Adam laughed and said, 'This is where your degree comes in handy.'

'Not mine, it's in history, which is no use for anything.'

Later, when Kent needed 55 off eight overs, Adam tried a bit of gamesmanship and kidology. 'The run rate has crept up to nine again,' he shouted to his team mates while standing next to me.

'If your maths is that bad, Adam, you should have read history.'

He laughed, like he often does to alleviate pressure.

Earlier, his first ball to me had been a truly dreadful long hop, which I mistimed truly dreadfully for one.

'Terrible cricket all round, Adam.'

'Yes, but something for you to write about in one of your columns.'

Later, he tried a knuckle-ball, a baseball-inspired slower ball that dips at the end of its flight, dropping towards your toes. I picked it and hit it for one. 'That's a knuckle-ball, right?'

He paused for a second. 'That one was, yes.'

A few balls later, I hit his next knuckle-ball for six, but decided against saying, 'So was that one.'

Meanwhile, we were quietly winning the game and Surrey were not so quietly losing it. The good thing about playing against any team of all-stars is that they sometimes lose hunger when things go against them. They have had so many big days before: if today goes wrong, well, life goes on. The danger is that with so much talent stacked against you, a moment of brilliance could take the game away from you at any moment.

With Kent needing about 36 off five, Matt Walker on 70 and me on 95, we were probably 6–4 on. We had scored at nearly 10 an over for twenty overs. Neither of us had gone through a quiet spell or put too much pressure on the other. We had both batted fluently throughout. We had been winning the game for some time. Whenever a boundary was needed, one of us came up. We were running the best side in England ragged. It was as much fun as it gets on a cricket field. It was not a big crowd at the Oval, but it was full of Kent fans roaring me on, even chanting my name – which, no matter how well you are playing, never happens in four-day cricket.

I was also close to the limit physically and was continually draining the sweat from my helmet so it didn't run into my eyes. In the 80s, feeling tired for a moment, I told myself that fitness training in the winter was designed specifically for days like this. This was when it counted.

On 95 I decided to run down the wicket to Azhar Mahmood and hit to the short leg-side boundary. I hit it well enough and got four. 99 and we had never been better placed. I said to myself, 'You are winning this over, and this match, be sensible, be ready for a good ball.' It came all right. A faster, inswinging yorker that flattened my stumps. Bowled for 99; game level.

I got a standing ovation from both sets of fans, the first time that has happened to me. 99 off 86 balls, with 9 fours and 2 sixes. Short of being something I will never be – a brutally big hitter – I couldn't have played much better. But I could scarcely believe my bad luck. I had done nothing wrong, just been beaten by a good ball. I felt suddenly frozen out of the most exciting game of my life. I sat with my head in a towel on the dressing-room balcony, scarcely able to watch the balance swing towards Surrey. We couldn't lay bat on ball. The dot balls mounted. New batsman Geraint Jones holed out to third man.

Incoming batsman Michael Carberry faced the toughest challenge: going straight into a clutch situation at the 'death' as a proper batsman more used to playing long innings. It wasn't his day or ours. Adam Hollioake bounced back to bowl a great last over. 11 required off three balls (still breathing) became 10 off two (only just) became 10 off one (let the post-mortems begin).

I couldn't speak. I walked down the steps to shake the hands of the Surrey players, hoping no one would see I was crying waterless tears. The Surrey players, I hope, were too happy to notice. They were also uniformly gracious.

I was present at the team meeting afterwards but couldn't tell you exactly what was said. I must have said thanks to lots of people who said, 'Well played,' though I can't remember who. I do remember sitting in the dressing room with Greg Blewett and Matt Walker, Kent's numbers four, five and six, long after everyone else had gone home. The ground was deserted and the London skies were turning from dusk to dark. We were half reminiscing about moments in the game, half getting changed, sometimes laughing, sometimes sighing in disbelief. 'To come so close . . .' Moments like that are what bring team mates together.

If someone had offered me a crate of beer, a bowl of pasta and a pillow, I would happily have spent the night in the Surrey away changing room.

Instead I eventually got my act together and joined Dave Fulton and his girlfriend for dinner. Tomorrow, he sees a Harley Street specialist about his right eye. He wants to play in the second team this week. To prove the point, as we walked along the Marylebone Road after dinner, Dave covered his good eye and said, 'Now I'm going to tell you when I can read that road sign thirty yards away.' He managed it fairly quickly.

'The only difference,' I added, 'is that the road sign isn't a small red ball coming towards you at ninety miles an hour with a little bit of inswing!'

'Fair point.'

I stayed at my sister's house in London. She had been at the Oval with her husband, baby daughter and a few friends. Amazingly, when I walked off for 99 today, having taken just a few forlorn steps from the middle, I gazed absently into the middle distance and noticed my brother-in-law changing seats in the crowd. I am extremely superstitious, so I jokily blamed my dismissal on him moving seats.

'Sorry, but your sister is so superstitious she wouldn't move when you were in, so I was looking after the baby.'

'Tatiana says sorry, too. She started crying when you were on 99.'

'Just the way I like it. Everyone is blaming themselves except me.'

Upstairs, holding my water glass in my injured right hand, I dropped it on the bathroom floor. Bloody hand. With glass shards all over the bathroom floor, I ended the evening picking them up on my hands and knees while trying to avoid cutting myself.

In bed, I allowed myself to trawl through the day's events. After I was out, I remember walking off the field quickly, without any great show of emotion or public display of disappointment. Some might have misconstrued that as me being happy with my lot. That isn't true. This game, I think, has left me with three separate feelings. First, I think it was a breakthrough innings for me personally, and that is satisfying. I am also very proud to have been central to a great game of cricket: the highest scoring one-day league match in history. The third feeling is desperate disappointment that my side were on the wrong end of a great spectacle. Those three feelings coexist equally strongly. They are not mutually exclusive.

What a full, thrilling, disappointing day.

Surrey 322/7, Kent 316/7. Surrey won by 6 runs

19 May

I am parked in a 'residents only' street, so I have to move my car before 8.30. I am due to meet a friend in Bond Street for brunch at eleven, leaving me with two hours to kill in central London. I buy some papers and sit in Starbucks, while the working world revs up for the new day and the new week.

Like most players, I do sometimes read the press, I do like praise, and, yes, we all enjoy headlines. Today's *Telegraph* is 'Smith leads charge as Kent go close'. There are some nice reports about my partnership with Matt Walker. It was, they all agreed, a great game. Consoling? Only a bit.

I am very much the odd one out here. Everyone else is trying to switch into work mode after the weekend – shoes shined, ties done up, hair styled – squeezing in an espresso before a long day at the office. I am recovering from five days' non-stop cricket, a hundred and a 99, and looking forward to my version of a weekend: Monday and Tuesday off. A cricketer's week is upside down. I look like I have rolled out of bed straight on to the Starbucks sofa. I can scarcely get my eyes open, or change the expression on my face. Walking to meet my friend, I move at about half the pace of the rest of the street.

It's good to have brunch with a non-cricketing friend. 'Yes, yes, well done on the runs,' she says, 'but what are you reading at the moment?'

Reading? I've lost the knack. Can't even talk, apart from about yesterday. I am in a swanky London restaurant with a beautiful girl, and all I can think about is Azhar Mahmood. Something is not quite right here.

The drive home – Hyde Park Corner, Victoria, Vauxhall Bridge – takes me straight past the Oval. 'Welcome to the Oval, home of Surrey County Cricket Club.'

What if. 'On a day of high drama and emotion at the Oval yesterday, Kent pulled off a miraculous run chase, the highest in the history of the Sunday League. Having just hit a four to reach 99, Ed Smith decided the time had come to settle the issue. His next shot, a six over midwicket, not only brought up his hundred, but also effectively ended Surrey's resistance and ensured Kent went into the record books . . .'

Back home, with just me and three loads of laundry, there is only one thing for it: Birgit Nilsson singing the Immolation Scene at the end of Wagner's *Twilight of the Gods*, turned up to full volume. Even the gods go up in smoke. Cricket? Never heard of it.

24 May

I was looking forward to this game, and vile weather ruined it. Kent versus Warwickshire at Edgbaston, two good teams at a famous ground – and it yielded almost no good cricket, because we scarcely played for more than two hours at a stretch without light but persistent drizzle forcing us off the field. I got a steady 43, which was a perfect example of an average day at the office: some good shots, some moderate ones, not much to report.

Result, draw; amount of competitive fire, minimal; level of frustration, very high. It was the kind of week that makes me despair.

The best came just before the end. By the time Mark Wagh walked out to the wicket at the end of the fourth day, the game had ceased to drift and had stopped dead still. That doesn't change the fact that his sweetly struck drives on the up clearly stood out. He is, in my opinion, one of the best strikers of a cricket ball in England.

Mark and I have had parallel careers: we were exact contemporaries at university, he at Oxford, I at Cambridge, where runs and hundreds came quickly for both of us; we both had early success with our counties, then quiet spells when people questioned whether we were openers or middle-order players; we have both come back at number three and scored heavily; you could say we are competitors for an England shirt; we both have interests outside cricket. He is a more extravagant shot player than me; I think I fail less often.

People have sometimes said of Mark that he is aloof and self-contained. I'm not sure that is fair or true. What people might mean is that he is not a run-of-the-mill county pro, full of acceptable opinions and studied modesty. He is different, difficult to read and unimpressed by mediocrity. And the problem with all that?

I am writing this in an Italian restaurant in Worcester, where we play a Sunday League game tomorrow. I make a point of getting out of the hotel whenever possible: one of the best things about being a professional cricketer is the opportunity to experience the rest of the country. You learn, if you look, that things change quickly from county to county. You notice smiles come more easily in some grounds and cities than in others. You learn that some counties harbour more hatred of government, or London, or flashiness. You hear different attitudes to money, to drink, to sport.

The philosopher Jacques Barzun believed that 'To understand America, you first have to understand baseball'. I wouldn't go as far as that about cricket and England, but there could be few better introductions to the texture of English life than a year playing or following county cricket.

Warwickshire 311 & 124/2, Kent 376. Match drawn

25 May

We were whipped today and are in danger of going into free fall. We have lost three out of four games in the National League (the one-day league). It is now not quite impossible to win it – but nearly impossible. We are plumb bottom of the first division of this competition and just off bottom in the county championship.

We bowled dreadfully, allowing Worcester to get 271 on a wicket where 200 would have been above par. Before I indulge the classic batters' excuse of blaming the bowlers, I should add that we didn't bat much better either. My 28 was top score in a total of 132.

It was probably the best start I have ever had to a one-day innings, better than last week at the Oval. I hit three consecutive fours off Kabir Ali – who is in line for an England call-up next week. It looked like being one of those days when everything hits the middle of the bat and timing comes easily. Then David Leatherdale bowled a short ball that scarcely bounced above ankle high. The scoreboard should have read, Ed Smith, bowled, groundsman. I hate being bowled – the most comprehensive mode of dismissal – but today was out-and-out bad luck. And, no, I won't make a habit of saying that.

When Greg Blewett, who also started well, was run out, the slide to inevitable defeat began. It's not just that we lost; worse still, we played with no fire or passion, drifting along towards defeat. Dave Fulton, recovering well from his eye injury but still watching from the sidelines, looked distraught. He has now started travelling with the team, hoping to inject some extra leadership and a greater sense of purpose.

In a circular team meeting after the game, there was much talk of a lack of 'noise' when we are fielding, as though a few more hand claps will put everything right. It isn't hand clapping we need but more character and a greater sense of personal responsibility and pride.

There are three main competitions: the championship (one off bottom), this one-day league (bottom) and the C&G knock-out cup. The fourth round of that is on Wednesday. There will be no second chances.

Worcestershire 271/4, Kent 132. Worcestershire won by 139 runs

26 May

How does a Wagnerian get over missing out on tickets for *Tristan and Isolde*, the first ever production of Wagner at Glyndebourne, a performance described by *The Times* critic as 'One of the greatest nights of opera of my life'? Easy: tickets for Bruce Springsteen at Crystal Palace sports arena.

Writing a diary about this cricket season carries with it the implicit conceit that my life is worth reading about. I might as well broaden the script by writing about how I keep sane the rest of the time – the consolations, if you like, for a career which demands improbable amounts of time in cars, hotels, crowded dressing rooms, and (in my case) on my own. Music is high on my list of consolations, and Bruce Springsteen my most reliable musical remedy. He has got me home on countless long drives after bitter defeats, picked me up when I was sick of the inside of my car, made me want to try when I felt defeated and played out. Tonight was the first time I have seen him live.

With the exception of my sister, who looked like she had just returned from a Fifth Avenue shopping jaunt with Carrie Bradshaw in *Sex and the City* (I suggested she change into a denim shirt, or else they might not let her in), it was not a glamorous crowd. Gone are the days of Courtney Cox being plucked from a swaying mass of American beauties. Most wore old jeans, clumpy shoes, shapeless T-shirts; many had grey hair. They were there for the music, and for The Boss. Our group – two friends my age, my sister and both my parents – was not unusually multi-generational. Unlike Prince, David Bowie and Madonna, who reinvent themselves with the seasons, Bruce has only ever had one image: himself, probably the reason why he has not only endured but never embarrassed his fans.

I leave most rock concerts feeling either bored or short-changed – they either quit too early or go on without sustaining the emotional energy. Bruce sings for three hours without a pause, no support band required, no gimmicky light effects or side shows – just him and the E Street Band, and the same sound and energy they have had for thirty years. He must be one of the very few singers who often sound better live – as his live albums prove – than in the studio.

What makes Springsteen unique is the combination of profound moral seriousness and an unmistakable sense of fun. The world he evokes is often a blue-collar one – the working week, the daily grind, looking for meaning among mundane routines. That is not, as critics suggest, phonily Everyman. It is the real thing. If I can relate to a song about working construction in small-town America, the chances are that the explanation lies in the song's authenticity, not its sentimentality.

Profundity and cliché, as Wordsworth said, are closer than we imagine. Many of Springsteen's songs are simple but finely worded, clichés in somebody else's hands, startlingly clear in his. His social commentary, though bleakly realistic, is never pious or smugly liberal; his patriotic optimism, despite Ronald Reagan's infamous misreading of 'Born in the USA', is ever present but not blindly supremacist. In other words, with Springsteen you get both sides of the American dream, often in the same song. The verses are the blues, the chorus is the gospel.

He is the most likeable of The Big Three (to a large number of rock fans, Bob Dylan, Van Morrison and Bruce Springsteen belong in a category of their own). But unlike Dylan, there are no lyrical pyrotechnics, no obfuscation or occasional pretentiousness. Unlike Van Morrison, there is no hazy rural idyll. It is the real thing all the way, a personal journey recorded in music, from Jersey City to LA and back again. He has really been there, not just the highways and the hometowns, but the fully lived human condition. It is not always easy, he sings; we know, but it is easier because of these songs.

Springsteen moves more slowly these days, more Gus Fraser than Jonty Rhodes (Dylan, meanwhile, is starting to resemble Trevor Bailey coming on for a second spell late in the day), but the joy is undiminished. It is two-way traffic, too, from the stage to the crowd, and the crowd to the stage. He doesn't talk about making you a part of the evening; you can feel it for yourself.

I am not trying to link tonight artificially to the sporting theme of this book, but one word that recurred in my head throughout the concert was leadership. Springsteen has the ability unashamedly to take the lead – no mock modesty, no it-ain't-me-that's-running-the-show, no modish anti-heroics. He does not deny the egotistical thrill of what he is doing; in fact, it is clearly a big reason for him carrying on doing it. But that doesn't diminish the affection he has for his fans, or the debt to his band.

Anyone can duck leadership; and those who crave it mostly abuse it. Springsteen does neither. He is clearly a good man; he just might be a great one too. Now that is my kind of hero.

If he gave our team talks I would definitely listen.

28 May

When you are at the bottom of both the championship and the one-day league, cup matches take on extra significance. They are a lifeline to more glamorous challenges and happier days. A cup run can be the perfect catalyst to ignite a season.

So we played Gloucestershire at Canterbury today with the extra burden of knowing that the C&G Trophy is now our best chance of winning some silverware this year. We lost, and must now refocus on extricating ourselves from the mess we're in.

It was a big day for Dave Fulton. Six weeks after being hit terribly on the right eyeball, after hospitalization and eye operations, after thinking he might never play again, then thinking he could be back much earlier than it actually turned out, after the most draining physical and psychological saga – he played for the first time today. He wants to get out there and captain, to take control and get us back on track. I have no idea if he's ready, but I admire his bravery.

His return lasted three balls, the last of which reared and took his glove. I doubt better eyesight would have made much difference. Greg Blewett, batting well and on 50, was out three balls earlier to exactly the same delivery. We never recovered momentum from that double-wicket over, and our total of 194 looked 30 short.

Earlier, I had made 14. Again, I promised much more, starting with a flick for four then a pull and good rhythm all round. Mike Smith, in the middle of a probing spell, angled one across that I nicked. If you are playing well and get out to an out-and-out defensive shot, it was probably a good piece of bowling. I am sick of writing that. No one is interested – and nor should they be – in my technique or 'form' or good rhythm. Kent just need runs from me.

We threatened briefly with the ball. Mark Ealham and James Tredwell, who have been our most reliable one-day bowlers this season, both exerted pressure in the middle of their innings. But Jonty Rhodes showed how to win awkward, low-scoring games.

Like Michael Bevan, he took his time, played the percentages and – above all – was there at the end. It was experienced, nerveless batting.

We have now not won a game since Cornwall. Our captain is back but struggling with his eye and his hamstring. Our batters are still not coming up often enough. The bowlers are below their best. We need to start winning – even if we're not going to win a trophy this year.

Kent 194, Gloucestershire 195/5. Gloucestershire won by 5 wickets

June 2003

2 June

I am running out of phrases like 'free fall'. We lost again today, a four-day championship match against Lancashire, who we beat twice last year. The truth is not that we played badly, as has often been the case this year, but that they were all-round better than us. In fact, it is the best we have played this year in the championship, and the best game of cricket I have played for months.

Lancashire 347, Kent 267, Lancashire, 334, Kent 339 – Lancashire won by 75 runs. The difference between the sides was a spectacular 154 from Andrew Flintoff. He came in with Lancashire at 43 for 4 and played as well as Ian Botham in his pomp. There is no one else to compare him to when he bats like that: correct, balanced, brutal, old-fashioned, uncomplicated, a natural batsman with unnatural power. As only Graeme Hick can do among contemporaries, Flintoff made it look like men against boys. If he can bat like that for England – and there is no reason why he can't – crowds around the world are in for a real treat.

I played almost flawlessly for 26 in the first innings, before dragging a wide ball on to my stumps – just like against Warwickshire. I have a bad dose of what I call 'first-mistake syndrome', a lethal affliction that causes batsmen to get out with their first mistake. Sometimes, it seems you can make twenty errors and still survive. When you have first-mistake syndrome, it is one mistake and all over. It is the primary cause of madness in cricket. In my last five innings, I have made less than a dozen real errors: twelve errors, five dismissals. Considering that Terry Alderman, the great Australian swing bowler, believed that on average it takes ten plays-and-misses to get one edge, this means my luck is seriously down.

So when I was playing well again in the second innings and was dropped by Gary Keedy, I thought, 'Here we go, that's the bit of luck you have deserved, make it count.' I carried on nicely to 56 before, unbelievably, I presented exactly the same caught-and-bowled chance to Keedy. He caught that one. I walked back to the pavilion at the end of the third day, with Kent 121 for 4 chasing 414, not quite dead but nearly. If I had survived the last five minutes of play that night, we would have had a slight but significant chance of a famous win on the fourth day. Two years ago, when Andrew Symonds and I both got hundreds, we chased over 400 on the last day to beat Leicester. This could have been even better.

This was a competitive game with plenty of attacking bowling and batting. Like Surrey, Lancashire are not only a good side but also a fun side to play against. They are confident enough to be able to relax and enjoy the game while still competing hard, and their respect is worth winning. My 56 also included some good banter with their close fielders, particularly Andrew Flintoff.

'Freddie' was in the same England Under-19 squad as me in 1996. Even then, he was already known as a hugely powerful hitter. I remember being introduced to him in the dressing room at Old Trafford – me with foppish Hugh Grant hair and just back from my first year at Cambridge, him sixteen stone and planning a night out in Manchester. He looked at me as if to say, 'Jesus, where on earth did this bloke come from?'

Dozens of England games later (and the odd night out too), Freddie isn't much changed from that likeably laddish Lancastrian eighteen-year-old. Everyone knows he is talented and generous spirited; he is also witty and fun-loving, and today he was in full voice.

ANDREW FLINTOFF: Come on, let's get Ed out and let him go beagling on the downs!
ES: Beagling? That's a good word, Andrew. Are you sure you know what it means?
AF: All right, let's get Ed out and let him go punting on the Cam!

And on it went. 'Come on, let's get Ed out and let him get to the ball tonight at the Polo Club! Come on, lads, let's get Ed out and give him time to iron his new Ralph Lauren shirt before the dinner party! Come on, let's get Prince William out!'

When Peter 'Digger' Martin came on to bowl, Mal Loye, fielding at cover, shouted out to him, 'Here's your chance to get out Number One on the Posh Hit List!'

Later, when Gary Keedy came on to bowl his left-arm spin, Warren Hegg asked if it was true that I had been to Bombay in the winter to practise playing spin bowling. 'Let's see it then, Ed,' added Flintoff. 'Let's see this new wristy Indian batsmanship.'

I hit the next ball off the back foot through the leg side. I thought I'd hit it well, so said to the close fielders, 'There it is, lads,' as I set off for the first run. In fact, I hadn't quite timed it, and the ball pulled up short of the boundary. I trotted back for two to find an amused Lancastrian slip cordon.

'Jesus, Ed, we can all clunk it for a mistimed 2. You could have saved the money on the air-fare to Bombay and learnt that in a weekend in Bury!'

I think that is the kind of banter that makes the game more amusing. It neither makes the batsman feel matey and at home (which is unprofessional) nor is it abusive.

And no, none of that had anything whatsoever to do with me getting out. I am old enough now to be able to enjoy a little by-play and still switch on when the ball is coming towards me. It would be a boring game if we always played in the strait-jacket of humourless conformity.

But it will be a long season if Kent can't find a win from somewhere. We have one day off, then another four-day game at Tunbridge Wells, then a one-dayer on Sunday. That is nine days of cricket in ten. County grind? What county grind?

Lancashire 347 & 334, Kent 267 & 339. Lancashire won by 75 runs

5 June

It is Tunbridge Wells week, played at the stunning Nevill Ground, near where I grew up. Last year we beat Sussex convincingly in the same fixture.

We will need to play a lot better than we did today and yesterday, if we are to repeat that this year. On an awkward batting surface, we had Sussex 174 for 6 but again failed to finish off the tail. They finished with 311. I don't mind Mushtaq Ahmed having a say in this game with the ball, but he is making a horrible habit of scoring important runs too. He got 43 today and shifted the momentum towards Sussex. Robin Martin-Jenkins, continuing his good form with the bat, top scored with 67.

Kent finished on 188 for 5. I am out, lbw Kirtley, for 13. We talk in the game about 'looking guilty' when you are hit on your front shin. I sometimes ask umpires what batsmen look like when there is a big appeal but they feel innocent. Perhaps then I might master it. Today, I looked – and was – very guilty. The ball decked in and would have hit halfway up middle stump if my pad hadn't intervened.

Our keeper-batsman Geraint Jones, prepared to use his feet and hit Mushtaq over the top, sparkled towards the end of play. He has been our best player this year. Andrew Symonds, in his first game back at Kent after winning the World Cup with Australia, also looked in great form with 54. When he plays well, he looks a world beater.

In case you don't understand how overseas pros seem to come and go each week – don't worry, you are not alone. As I understand it, each county is allowed up to five overseas players, though only two can play together at any one time. Until today, Greg Blewett has been our only overseas pro; he and Andrew Symonds will play together for just this week and the forthcoming Twenty20 Cup; then Blewett leaves and the Pakistani quick bowler Mohammad Sami arrives and will partner Symonds.

Yes, it is a circus, and an expensive circus. Though it is true

overseas players bring in increased gate receipts, they also – particularly when there are five of them – cost a huge amount in air-fares,
accommodation, sponsored cars and perks. I have no complaints
about Kent's overseas players. Nor do I mind the law changes
which have allowed two overseas players. But a constantly shuffling
pack of five, from which two are selected?

Sussex 311, Kent 188/5

6 June

If I don't write much about today's play, don't think it doesn't
hurt, or preoccupy me, or it isn't ruining my mood. We are behind
in this game, against our local rivals, Sussex, who we normally beat,
on a ground that is usually kind to us. We are not ourselves, and it
is depressing.

There was, however, one non-cricketing highlight today, and
writing about that will probably lift my mood more than picking
over the bones of a frustrating cricketing day.

Apart from glory with bat or ball, what does a professional
cricketer dream will happen on the Thursday afternoon of a typical
championship match? Let me tell you. He hopes to return to his
fielding position on the boundary, glance into the crowd – perhaps
a small crowd, with each face clearly visible, mainly the faces of
retired men reading the *Telegraph* or drinking warm beer over the
crossword – and see not another balding comb-over and club tie,
but a beautiful girl looking at him.

That is what happened to me today at the Nevill Ground, one
of the prettiest backdrops in cricket. There she was, just in front of
the famous purple rhododendrons, a few feet away from where I
was fielding at third man. I am trying to think of a description that
avoids 'English rose', but I can't. Extremely pretty, slim, willowy,
brown hair, green eyes, demure smile, floral skirt, casually eating
cherries out of a brown paper bag. Seriously.

It didn't take my team mates long to notice. 'Keep concentrating, Ed!' Greg Blewett shouted from first slip, loud enough for the whole ground to hear. 'Stay ready down there, Ed,' said Andrew Symonds in his broadest Queensland accent. 'The game's over this way!'

The worry, of course, is that a girl like that is not really there for the cricket at all, but has merely been dragged reluctantly through the gates by an aggressive, tattoo-covered, body-building boyfriend who is about to return from the bar with two pints of Stella.

The hope is that – aside from what is already obvious – she is intelligent, witty, cricket-loving, amusing, interested and interesting. Well, as luck would have it, that was exactly the character sketch that emerged after talking to her briefly on my way out of the ground. Nor could I discern any tattoo-covered boyfriend.

Now here's something for the sports psychologists to ponder: I wonder if I would play better if she watched Kent every day?

Sussex 311 & 188/5, Kent 275

7 June

Leaving aside the bowling, which he can do and I can't, I have been comprehensively out-batted this game by Robin Martin-Jenkins. When Robin and I sat around in Bombay arguing about who would win the new season's games between Sussex and Kent, I didn't have in mind humiliating defeat on our home ground, with Mushtaq taking nine wickets, and Robin getting 67 and 84 to my 13 and 40. Today, when we chatted after the game, I remembered how different it had been last year, when I had made 81 in an exciting Kent win.

We let Sussex get too many today, but I threw every positive thought I had into believing we could make 323 batting fourth. In fact, I was more deeply 'in the zone' for my 40 today than I have been for weeks. I felt complete indifference to extraneous distractions, a reluctance to waste energy or words, a determination bordering on possession. I am starting, I think, to bat angry. I have no idea if it will turn out to be a good thing in the long run. Today I hit 7 of my 61 balls for four, several of them back-foot square cuts – my new favourite shot. At lunch, Greg Blewett, who had fallen early in his final championship game for us before going back to Australia, came downstairs to the dressing room to speak to me. 'Hitting them sweet, Ed,' he said.

But not for long enough – yet again. With Mushtaq bowling relentlessly well from one end, our only chance was to put pressure on the bowling at the other end. Perhaps I was forcing the issue too much against Jason Lewry when I was caught behind. Counter-attack, I reasoned, was our only chance. It started another collapse. We were eventually all out in the mid-afternoon for 131 off 47 overs. Only Michael Carberry and I got in, and we could only manage 40 each.

We have now lost four games in a row and six games out of eight. We haven't won a game since Cornwall. I can't remember playing in a sequence like this. A friend who is a great Kent fan was at the ground. He called me as I drove home. 'What is going on out there?' I had no answers.

Sussex 311 & 286, Kent 275 & 131. Sussex won by 191 runs

8 June

Last night we had a meeting at the ground to 'clear the air'. We sat in the dressing room and talked about what was going wrong. Given that Kent are in deep trouble, everyone seemed remarkably keen to be nice to one another. I am not against team meetings. But there is no point in them if people aren't honest. We all like praise and we should look to praise our team mates whenever possible. But you don't dig yourself out of trouble by avoiding harsh realities.

After the meeting, I got a phone call from our New Zealand physiotherapist, Martyn Sigley. With typically Kiwi-style candour and can-do attitude, he said, 'Rather than going too deep into reasons and explanations, just grab a few players and do some extra practice, keep it simple, work hard, and – above all – get loads of runs. That's the best way to help.'

This morning, our preparation still felt rushed. There were lots of helpers and coaches around, leading and cajoling, but I felt light on net practice and straightforward catching. I did some more just before the league game against Yorkshire started in order to take a good feeling into the game with me.

It didn't last long. It was a cold, grey windy day at Tunbridge Wells and a difficult wicket. I was quickly in and out at number three, caught behind off a perfect away-swinger from Ryan Sidebottom. Two balls earlier, he had bowled Rob Key with a big in-ducker. I had to play the ball, and I just nicked it. I really have nothing to say beyond that.

I checked with the umpire, Ian Gould. 'Don't bullshit me, was it a good ball or not?'

'I'd tell you if it was a bad shot, but that was a jaffa, mate.'

It was such a terrible wicket that even Greg Blewett, who is normally a fluent and free-scoring player, crawled to a crucial 46. We eventually made 208, which should have been – and was – enough. Ben Trott bowled beautifully with the new ball, then Andrew Symonds bowled and fielded with huge presence.

We needed this win, for the table, for the fans, for us. But it doesn't feel like the kind of conclusive victory that will set us up for the rest of the season.

Kent 208/7, Yorkshire 186/9. Kent won by 22 runs

15 June

Today was supposed to be a day of celebration as we unveiled our new ground at Beckenham. Kent is a densely populated county, but many live in the London suburbs in the north-west: Canterbury is a distant concept, both in miles and in atmosphere. The Kentish Londoners, who have plenty of other competing distractions, belong to a more metropolitan set that likes sport to be round the corner. Beckenham, an old ground recently redeveloped, is meant to attract a whole new set of Kent spectators. If a packed house today is anything to go by, it will.

The combination of a white wicket and blue sky demanded that we bat first. Inexplicably – to my mind – we collapsed to 10 for 3. I was one of them, having scooped an easy leg-side shot to square leg on nought. Andrew Symonds said simply, 'I've never seen you miss one of those before.' Back in the pavilion, I tried to convince people that it wasn't a bad wicket at all – just a freaky start.

An hour later, while Andrew Symonds stroked it around easily, we looked to be back on course. On 56, he hit a regulation on-drive to long-on and ambled slowly towards the bowler's end. Mark Alleyne, sensing Symmo might be being too casual, charged in, threw down the bowler's stumps and was awarded the run-out. It was the most bizarre dismissal I have ever seen.

Symmo has now replaced Mark Ealham as caretaker captain while we wait for Dave Fulton to return. This was announced to the team yesterday, with not much more information than those bare facts. I am not being evasive. I just don't know much about the process. The good news is that Ealy and Symmo are great friends, so there will be no problem between them about the leadership issue.

Despite some brilliant late hitting from Geraint Jones – who must be the best keeper-batter in the country on current form – 222 would be enough only if we bowled brilliantly. We didn't. Gloucestershire cruised home four wickets down with twenty-two balls to spare. It ended up being a contemptuous rout.

A new ground was opened today, and we lost. A new competition – the jazzy, trendy, innovative Twenty20 – opens at the same place tomorrow and we need to win. Preparations for today weren't helped when two of our team got lost in the London maze and missed part of our warm-ups. 'If need be,' Dave Fulton said at a meeting afterwards, 'we'll get here three hours before play tomorrow – whatever it takes to win.'

Dave wants to play again straight away, to take control and lead from the front. His hamstring is not yet healed, and his eye is improving but is still a long way from being right. But I admire his guts – so long as he is fit enough to survive out there. We'll find out tomorrow.

16 June

I have been a regular in Kent's championship side since 1997, and I haven't missed a game since 2000. Until this season, I have been in and out of the one-day side, for a variety of reasons, one of which was that people thought me unwilling to improvise. This year, I was guaranteed selection, and after my 99 at Surrey, captain Dave Fulton said in the dressing room, 'Ed came of age as a one-day player today.' Since then, I have hit the ball harder and more cleanly than I have ever done, never more so than in the practice game we played two days ago. That was an internal Kent warm-up for the new Twenty20 competition. People were surprised, I think, that someone who is concerned about correct technique, as I am, can also slog the ball out of the ground when he needs to. The two skills don't seem mutually exclusive to me.

The Twenty20 Trophy has been introduced this season to attract younger crowds and win over new cricketing converts. It doesn't 'count' towards official cricketing statistics – they are therefore to some extent exhibition games – but the prize money and the silverware count, and the big crowds will mean plenty of nerves and a desire to excel. Every county plays five games each in the zonal phase, with the matches starting in the mid- or late afternoon. The plan is to entice the after-work crowd, and serve up an entertaining brand of attacking cricket for them to enjoy over a drink or two in the high summer sunshine.

Our batting order will doubtless be fluid; but most people, including me, have assumed I would bat somewhere between three and five. It never occurred to me that I wouldn't play, not because I am conceited or particularly desperate to play 20-over slog cricket, but because, with the exception of Andrew Symonds, I am hitting the ball as cleanly as anyone in the team. Leaving aside technique and temperament, I thought I would get in on hitting alone.

So when Dave Fulton asked to speak to me before the game, I assumed he wanted my opinion on tactics. Instead, 'I'm coming back into the side today, and you are missing out.'

'You're kidding, right?'

'No. We're playing all the all-rounders to go all-out at the top of the order, and there's no point you batting at nine.'

'Where are you batting, Dave?'

'Eight . . . You can pull all the faces you like, but you're not playing.'

I was amazed. My gut instinct is that something doesn't add up here.

I have hit the ball well and hard all year. Aside from solid form in four-day cricket, I scored 99 off 80-odd balls a few weeks ago against the best team in the country. I played very well in practice the other day. I am totally unconvinced that playing all the all-rounders at the top of the order is better than playing a blend of batters and hitters throughout the order.

I have not yet performed as well in my career as I should have. My 6,000-odd runs in first-class cricket have been scored at an average of about 38. I can do better than that. But it remains a fact that almost no one else of my age has. I am fairly confident that I must be close to having the best record of any English batter of my age, especially in the first division. More to the point, I am scoring runs in championship and one-day cricket quicker than anyone, apart from Symmo. How fast do I have to score before people change their opinion of me?

I deserve better than being thrown the drinks bottles ninety minutes before the start of a 20-over match. Over the years I have become better at seeing things from the management's perspective, but this feels seriously wrong.

Once the game starts, I try to forget any personal disputes and do the best I can to help the players who are on the field. Fortunately, what happened on the pitch tonight was so extravagantly brilliant that it lifted everyone's mood, even mine.

In reply to Hampshire's respectable 145 off their 20 overs, Andrew Symonds smashed – there is no other word – 96 not out off just 37 balls. He hit 14 fours and 3 sixes. We won in the twelfth over – with *eight* remaining. It was the most extraordinary display of hitting I have ever seen. As Greg Blewett put it afterwards, 'That was truly scary.'

We desperately needed a win. To play with such style was a huge bonus. It was, however, a solo effort. It could scarcely have been otherwise. Symmo didn't leave much for anyone else to do.

My guess though – and I don't usually lose my judgement in times of disappointment – is that it will be harder to repeat in the other four games.

21 June

When Andrew Symonds isn't terrorizing bowlers with savage off-drives, he can normally be found shooting or fishing. A day which passes without him putting on his predator's hat is a day wasted. I live next to the River Stour, renowned for its trout, so today I asked him to give me a fly fishing lesson.

To get a one-day permit, I had to visit the secretary of the Stour Fishing Association. I was welcomed into his hall, where I stood underneath a stag's head while the bewhiskered, elderly secretary wrote out the permit. He initially looked a little unimpressed by my loud Hawaiian shirt and sunglasses. 'Are you Australian?' he asked, scarcely opening his jaw to speak.

I am about the least likely person in east Kent to have a stuffed stag's head in my house, but I couldn't resist admiring the secretary's genteel courtesy and the timelessly rural atmosphere of his Old Rectory. All very Kentish – albeit not my Kent at all – but we would be the poorer if it were lost forever. 'No more than two brace of fish are to be killed in any one day,' he explained, as I glanced at his fishing waders and hunting books.

'That's four, right?'

'Yes, four. I do hope you have a good day.'

Symmo, on the other hand, really is an Aussie. When the England management asked him to play for us in the mid-1990s (he had dual nationality), he said no: 'I'm a fair dinkum Aussie.'

As a cricketer, Symmo's hallmark is brutality. He stands still at the crease, upright and uncomplicated, a stationary mass of fast twitch muscle ready to explode at the ball. He quite often misses the first ball, often groaning as he does so. 'Oooaah!' he says. 'Jeez, that one bounced a bit,' even if it didn't. I sometimes do impressions in the dressing room of him taking his first ball. 'Very funny, Ed. But it takes me at least one ball to wake up.'

If you're the fielding side, you'd better hope he stays asleep. Five days ago, he got 96 not out off 37 balls, including one hit – now lost somewhere in Crystal Palace – off Shaun Udal that was one of the biggest sixes I have ever seen. The umpires had given me a box of spare balls for that very reason, so I ran out with a replacement. 'Hang on a minute, Ed,' Shaun shouted as I turned back to the dressing room, 'better give us two replacements just in case.'

The patience and cunning of fly fishing is not an obvious pastime for someone who is probably the most brutal hitter of a cricket ball in the world. 'It's being a predator I love,' he explained, casting out the line with a deft flick of the wrist. 'Bingo! Right in the zone on top of that trout! Jeez, he's not even nibbled at it! Cunning bastard. I'd have gobbled that one up, but then again I wouldn't have lived very long if I'd been a fish.'

I had a go, too. 'Imagine it's one of those flicks for four you do off your pads,' was Symmo's advice. 'It's all in the timing.' And looking out across the river at the rolling downs at seven o'clock on the longest and balmiest day of the year, I could imagine it, definitely – giving up vast chunks of spare time trying to outwit fish. A cerebral world of solitude and competition and adrenalin: a rare trio of emotions.

The plan was to cook some fish for a few team mates on my barbecue afterwards. But aside from a couple of grayling, we only caught one trout, and it was too small to kill, so it went back into the Stour to fight another day.

'Reckon you hurt him much, Symmo?' I asked as he took out the fly from its gullet.

'Nah, scarcely scratched the little fella.'

So it was an old-fashioned steak 'n' sausages for an unusual mix of my friends and colleagues, one half friends from London, the other half professional cricketers from Adelaide and Copenhagen and Brisbane. 'Right,' Symmo exclaimed just before dark, 'I'm going back to the creek to get that trout.'

23 June

Today was everything the Twenty20 was supposed to be: noisy, exciting, fun, young, and sold out. On a hot afternoon, Kent needed to win to have a realistic chance of going through to the semi-finals. We also, more subtly but no less importantly, need to give our fans something to cheer.

In any Twenty20 game against Surrey, your first concern is their hitting. What happens if Ali Brown and friends get going? It's a terrifying prospect. So it was ironic that Mark Ramprakash, more noted for technique than power, held the Surrey innings together with a perfect blend of proper batting and inventive strokes. He set things up for Azhar Mahmood to smash 57 off 31 balls, including 5 huge sixes. On current form, Azhar is one of the best all-rounders in the world. Today he radically changed the momentum: having controlled Surrey for the first twelve overs, we got ready to bat feeling deflated, having endured Azhar's explosion. We had let it slip and knew it.

Andrew Symonds, about to open the batting, sat with his helmet on, staring blankly into the middle distance, looking thunderous.

'Are you OK?' I asked.

'Yeah,' he said, as if he meant, 'Does it look like I'm OK?'

This could go one of two ways, I thought: he could get a hundred off 30 balls, or get out in the first over. He did indeed try to hit every ball for six. After hitting 2 fours and 1 six (17 off 5 balls), he hit the sixth straight up. It was good while it lasted, but he is too good a player to waste like that.

I was due to bat at number six, after Peter Trego, James Tredwell, Mark Ealham and Matt Walker. With three wickets down, and me next in, Sky Sports interviewed me in the dug-out by the boundary. The ECB is determined to 'take Twenty20 to the people', and the players have been asked to co-operate with whatever the media requests.

'Well, you're all padded up and ready to go, Ed. Will you be batting normally out there or slogging?'

'Hopefully an intelligent mixture of both.' I might be obliged to give interviews, but not to bat one-dimensionally.

I went in at 44 for 4, with Kent needing 125 runs at about 10 an over and all our recognized match-winners out. You win those games once in ten. But I also remembered that it was almost exactly the same equation the other day at the Oval – when Matt Walker and I got so close. The difference then, of course, was that Matt and I both had decent scores already on the board. But if I could get to that level of fluency straight away, we had as good a chance today.

I have been furious about being left out of the Twenty20 for three games, and tonight I walked out to the middle trying to prove a point. But trying to do that with grim determination, as I might in a four-day game, would be counter-productive – it might confirm the misplaced criticism that risk does not suit my game. Instead, I resolved to get into the spirit and tempo of the game and, above all, to express myself.

Perhaps because I have played well against Surrey this year, I felt comfortable and started well. One shot very rarely recaptures form, but it can define and set up an innings. That's what happened tonight when I came down the wicket to Azhar Mahmood and hit a one-bounce 4 over wide mid-on. I said to myself, 'If you're going, go one hundred per cent, no what-ifs, but don't overhit – just trust yourself to time it.' I got it sweetly, and the next 40 runs was some of the best fun I've ever had on a cricket field. I hit 2 sixes, 4 fours and got to 50 in 30 balls. We kept up with the rate of 10 an over.

With Matt and me still in, we always had a chance. But when you need more than 10 an over, you take risks almost every ball – either in shot selection or when running between the wickets. Going for a tight 2 with 40 needed off four, I was run out from third man. Not bad luck, a simple misjudgement.

Twice now against Surrey I have been at the top of my competitive range, fully engaged, living it to the full. Again, I was distraught to leave it in other people's hands. I had, though, proved a point.

We didn't keep up the momentum, and fell short by 18 runs. The mood afterwards was reflective. There is a mathematical – though remote – chance that we can still qualify. Realistically, today, on our home turf in front of a full house against the old enemy, was it. We are now unlikely to win anything this year; the rest is playing for second prize.

So am I a Twenty20 player? It is true I relish the sustained examination of four-day cricket. But in these two shorter games against Surrey, I have felt a different kind of absorption: the thrill of hitting sixes, the excitement of a game see-sawing in seconds, scampering when you're exhausted, double guessing the bowler, backing yourself, finding out what you're capable of. I've loved every minute.

I was also delighted that today was at the St Lawrence ground. I've never batted like that in a home game and, truth to tell, I was thrilled to entertain. Later in the evening, someone said that both Nasser Hussain and Mark Butcher, two of England's most intelligent cricketers, had said very complimentary things about my innings on Sky TV.

After the game, all the Kent players and a few Surrey guys stayed for a drink and some food. 'That's it, Ed,' Adam Hollioake said to me with a smile about the two sixes I had hit off him, 'I'm sick of bowling to you with a short boundary! Next game at the Oval, I'm telling the groundsman to have proper boundaries on both sides. If necessary, I'll mark them out myself . . .'

24 June

Before warm-ups this afternoon, a few of us chatted about the best way to bat in Twenty20, particularly against the new ball when big hitting is at a premium.

My theory is that we have got carried away with 'clearing the front leg'. The idea is to move the front foot towards the leg side before the ball is even bowled – hence removing any obstacles that might stop you 'accessing the channel' in which the ball will arrive.

The whole trend grew out of a specific development in the evolution of one-day cricket: death bowling. As more bowlers started to bowl yorkers and low full tosses to stop batsmen from getting under the ball and hitting sixes, batsmen found themselves getting cramped for room. They got hit low on the pad or on the boot. If the ball reversed into them, they found it even harder to get their 'hands through the ball'. By 'clearing the front leg', batters were able to hit (some) death balls for fours and sixes with semi-cross-batted shots straight down the ground. Azhar does it brilliantly for Surrey and Pakistan.

So far, so good. In the run-up to Twenty20 this year, we heard a lot about 'clearing the front leg' – it started to sound more and more like the answer to everything. But what happens if the bowler doesn't bowl yorkers and bowls length or back of a length instead? Often, the ball goes straight up in the air. It is a huge risk to swing the bat at forty-five degrees with the ball bouncing at different heights – and the combination of a new white ball and anything less than a perfect wicket means uncertain bounce is guaranteed. Against Surrey, I think we offered seven skied catches, of which five were caught.

If I'm sounding like a wise guy after one decent innings, I'm not. But I do think there is still a big role for conventional cricket shots, more attacking adaptations of the shots we play every day of the week. It needn't be binary: either normal batting, or super-high risk. Often the best one-day players are the ones who can bat for longest within the middle range of risk taking.

None of which makes any difference if you get run out for 10, like I was today. Michael Carberry knocked the ball beautifully into the off-side gap; I set off, he looked down, I turned round halfway, scampered back (too late) and was run out at the bowler's end. My run-out was in the middle of a Kent collapse which led to our small total of 114.

We had Sussex 2 for 1 and then 6 for 2, but a stand of 82 between Bas Zuiderant and Chris Adams decided the game. One moment stood out. With the scoring rate increasingly irrelevant, we attacked in search of wickets. So, for Mohammad Sami (Greg Blewett has now passed on the baton to Sami as Kent's second overseas player), Dave Fulton set a Test-match style slip cordon. Sami is one of the two or three fastest bowlers in the world – no one, surely, imagined Twenty20 would be about Mohammad Sami bowling at 95 m.p.h. and Chris Adams batting for his life.

When Sami bowled a no-ball, Sussex were given a free hit. Adams guessed it would be a yorker and hit it unbelievably hard for four straight down the ground. An express ball met with extreme power and bat-speed, two elemental forces of nature: it had all the ingredients that make a baseball home run one of the great spectacles in sport.

Kent, though, are knocked out and all but knocked down. If July isn't hugely better than May and June, next year we will be playing all our cricket in the second divisions. Everyone looking inwards – what can I do to turn this around? – is the only place to start.

28 June

Before this game against Essex, now two days old, Dave Fulton came up to me with a list of the two teams. 'Let's match up the teams, man against man,' he said. 'I have to bat better than Darren Robinson, Keysey has to outplay Paul Grayson, you have to get more runs than Nasser Hussain . . .' And so on.

That was a nice prospect: outplaying the England captain. What a great way to focus the mind. I have felt in fantastic form in the nets since that thrilling Twenty20 game against Surrey. I went into this game feeling quietly confident that my season is now about to take off properly. The phrase 'double hundred' came into my mind more than once. The mini-ascents of May were finished. I felt ready to get my season into fifth gear. What better circumstances could I ask for? Essex are a struggling team; my opposite man is the England captain; I am playing well but am hungry for runs after plenty of disappointments this season; Chelmsford is a flat wicket; the weather is set fair.

I got o, lbw first ball. It swung in – a bit. A goodish ball to get first up. Just one of those things. The runs will come. You've already heard it all before. But *first ball*? At *Chelmsford*? Yesterday was difficult to shrug off as bad luck. It was a hammer blow.

Nasser, meanwhile, my 'opposite man', ended today on 192 not out. I spent last night and all of today watching him bat from five feet away at short leg. He opened up, in fact, instead of batting three, and faced a couple of seriously fast overs from Mohammad Sami last night just before the close of play. It was as quick as anything around these days. 'It's just starting to swing away a bit, Nas,' said Darren Robinson from the non-striker's end as the light turned gloomy and Sami walked back to his longest run-up.

'Thanks,' Nasser said with a pointedly ironic tone to no one in particular, 'but the *swing* is not my primary concern at the moment.' The next 90 m.p.h. short ball flew off the shoulder of the bat through fourth slip.

He survived last night on 4 not out and cashed in today. He

played the off-spin of James Tredwell extremely well, and the rest comfortably. He just batted, and went on and on and on – with the same tempo from one hour to the next, the same application, the same determination, the same demeanour. It was relentless, professional batting, not scratchy, but highly pragmatic.

I fielded at short leg for most of it and I both willed his dismissal and watched him carefully. After the enormous pressures of captaining England in recent months, I expected him to look played-out and restless in this game. In fact, he looked calmer at the crease than I have seen him recently. He is always a fierce concentrator and animated at the crease – he talks to himself, curses his mistakes, demands more from within, blazes with disgust at perceived weakness in his own willpower.

He did all that, as I expected. But he was also more measured and relaxed than he sometimes appears on TV. That may be because he is under less pressure in a county game, or it may simply be because he has been through so much recently that he has come out on the other side a little more philosophical. He will never under-rev or take this game lightly. But perhaps, at thirty-five, he is determined to express himself in this phase of his career.

Fielding so close to the bat today was a reminder how much playing top-flight sport takes out of you. In most professions, a thirty-five-year-old is scarcely in his prime. He can still jauntily enjoy the prospect of getting better and moving up the professional ladder, brushing aside older, slower spirits. Nasser, on the other hand, looked every day of his thirty-five years. He has lived cricket as hard and fully as anyone, and he will not care that it shows.

Hussain 192 not out; Smith first ball 0.

At dinner with my parents tonight, I said that watching Nasser's innings might kick start my season. 'When you watch someone bat all day like that, it reminds you how much you want to do it yourself.'

Mum wore that look people have when they've been around optimistic sportsmen for too long.

Kent 381, Essex 423/5

29 June

Today was much better. Twice as good, in fact. I faced two balls for 0. This one certainly wasn't a good ball. It was a leg-side length ball from Graham Napier that I somehow managed to scoop to square-leg. Aftab Habib, who looked to be deep in conversation with the square-leg umpire, at first wandered in a few steps. I thought, 'I can't believe my luck, it's going to land over his head as he comes forward.' Then Aftab took a step back, reached over his head and held the catch.

A pair is the final indignity, the first time I have experienced it in my 104 first-class games. I have faced three balls on this flat Chelmsford wicket, survived one and been out twice. I have never even worried about getting a pair before. Then, bang, I've bagged one. A pair. What the hell is going on this year? There is no rational explanation. A pair. It is unbelievably grim.

I hit dozens of throw-downs afterwards in practice. Eventually, Ian Brayshaw said, 'This is a waste of time, there's nothing wrong technically, Ed. I've got nothing to add. I know how you feel.'

Does he? Does anyone? I feel impotent – I can see nothing to put right, but I have got a pair. I have never been someone who waits for things to fix themselves, but I am at a loss. Throughout this pre-season and the season proper, I have felt on the brink of great things. Now I am under pressure to survive. A text message from a friend said, '165 at the Oval next week.' I would pay huge money for that.

The overwhelming likelihood is that Kent will draw this game tomorrow and I will have little to do with the rest of the game. Don't expect a diary entry. In fact, you may not be hearing from me for some time. It is that bad.

Kent 381 & 278/5, Essex 514

July 2003

1 July

I have been practising with Chris Stone since I was thirteen. Then, he was the cricket professional at my school; now, twelve years on, he is Director of Kent Youth cricket. As you get more experienced as a player, you should become better at curing your own technical problems – so I go for weeks, sometimes months, without practising with Chris. When I do, he might simply say, 'This looks different,' or 'When you're playing well, you look more like this.' He is an extra pair of eyes, a skilful observer, as much as a 'coach'.

I nearly didn't practise today on the theory that sometimes getting away from the game is the best preparation of all. At the last minute, in the middle of the morning before travelling to London to play against Surrey tomorrow, I changed my mind and rang Chris. 'Twenty minutes, that's all I need, Chris.'

'Sure, come to the ground, we'll use the indoor school nets for as long as you need.'

At the ground I saw a few of the second-team guys. It is a dreadful condition being in the second team: the failure of others in the first team may well provide you with opportunities. They knew I had got a pair last week. They also knew I was here practising, trying to find some self-confidence. While we talked, they looked at me as if they were thinking, 'Is Ed tottering here? Might his place be up for grabs soon?' That's OK, simply human nature.

We went through the usual routines, checking my bat swing was straight, my preliminary movements were in rhythm, my balance was right. 'I can't see anything wrong, Ed. What's been the problem in the middle?'

'I haven't been out there long enough to tell – there might not be one.'

'Your technique looks normal. Maybe you just need to practise hitting the ball cleanly without worrying about technique. Just hit it.'

So I hit some pulls, a shot I don't normally play unless I am feeling confident.

'That's better. Just hit it.'

So I did. I hit it hard and often and without inhibition for twenty minutes at the end of practice. It felt different, better, more natural, less cluttered by unnecessary thoughts.

'That's enough, Ed. You start on nought tomorrow.'

'Thanks for reminding me, Chris.'

'After two noughts, then two hundreds. You're that kind of guy, aren't you? A pair of noughts then a pair of hundreds. I won't ring you to say well done after the first hundred. A pair of noughts then a pair of hundreds.'

While I tried to thank Chris afterwards, he cut me off, saying, 'I've got work to do upstairs, sorry to rush. I won't call you after the first hundred.'

I drove Rob Ferley (a left-arm spinner who has just finished at Durham University) to London tonight. He is in the Kent squad for tomorrow's game at the Oval and might make his championship debut. I tried to convey no nerves or stress about my own form. No matter what I am going through, Rob will be much more nervous. The support should flow in that direction.

I went for a quick walk near our hotel off Hyde Park. After so much Wye, I am badly in need of a dose of big-city life: just the smell, the street tempo, the colour and texture of London life gives me an instant lift.

Before I fall asleep, my phone bleeps with a text message, from Matt Banes, the second-team player most likely to win my place should my season implode. 'Get a big hundred tomorrow.'

2 July

Today was good cricket. Mohammád Sami bowled somewhere between 90 and 100 m.p.h. and Mark Butcher played brilliantly. He got an undefeated 117 out of Surrey's 245 for 3.

When Mark Butcher got recalled to the England side in 2001 after a battle to keep his place even in the Surrey side, I remember a now retired Kent player saying to me, '*Butcher?* He'll get blown away by Australia.' Like most pros, I hesitate before praising other players in print, but I did say then, 'One thing he won't be is "blown away" – he's too good a player of fast bowling for that.'

He has scored a lot of runs for Surrey and England since then, often batting with flair and fluency as well as a simple, uncomplicated technique. Like Alec Stewart, he is a natural back-and-across batter – probably because he grew up on Oval wickets that were faster and bouncier than they are now. But unlike most natural back-footers, he is also a terrific driver when he is playing well, particularly straight and through the off side. Being such a free driver and so naturally adept at playing off the back foot also means bowlers find it hard to bowl a length to him.

I have often wondered why he hasn't won more games for Surrey in one-day cricket. He is such a good timer of the ball and such a quick-scoring batsman that one-day cricket should come just as naturally to him as the four-day game. Anyway, that isn't my or Kent's problem. We have to find a way to get him out tomorrow.

Before the start of this season, Kent coach Ian Brayshaw asked me to keep my eyes open for social events during the season that were different from the dinner/drink/movie norm. So today I bought a few tickets for a new West End play called *Hitchcock Blonde*.

    ES: Anyone interested in coming to the theatre tonight?
    [Murmurs of disapproval]

ES: Rosamund Pike, the new Bond girl, totally naked, first-row
  balcony seats . . .

I should have bought more.

Surrey 245/3

3 July

Some people don't believe in form. Just one good shot away from
getting it all back, they say. I do believe in it. I know what it feels
like to stand at the crease full of confidence, with stacks of runs
under my belt. I also know – a feeling I can retrieve from memory
with greater clarity and sharpness (fear is so much more memorable
than comfort) – the quiet turmoil of bad form. Please God, give
me a start, just a start, and I will be all right.

That was what I was thinking today, crouched over my bat on
nought, waiting for my first ball from Saqlain Mushtaq, one of the
best bowlers in the world. After two noughts at Chelmsford, I was
unusually nervous. Another failure and the questions would start.
'I know Ed is a good player, and he played well last year . . . but how
much longer can we go on with him? I mean, is he really that good
anyway?' You are never far away from those questions, which
you spell out in your private thoughts, when form has deserted you.
'How dare they question me! I'll show them,' shouts your defiance.

I hit my first ball in the middle of the bat, a forward defensive
for none. At least I didn't get out first ball again. Remember, I only
survived one ball in two innings at Chelmsford. I felt much happier
a few balls later when Saqlain bowled me a straightish, shorter ball
on my hip. I played a back-foot flick to leg off my pads – four runs
and finally free from the fear of my third nought in a row. Thank
God for that. Now get in and don't give it away. 'You're smiling
again, Ed, which is great to see,' said the umpire Ian Gould, who
was also umpiring at Chelmsford.

I have spent much of the last week talking to Ian, me fielding at square leg, him umpiring at square leg. I enjoy talking to umpires. They are well placed to form independent opinions on the game, and especially how it has changed. There is sometimes an element of nostalgia and conservative romanticism in their views: it was much better in our day and all that. But mostly they simply say what they see, and it is worth listening.

I asked Ian about the dressing room in the two counties he played for, Middlesex and Sussex, particularly the influence of Mike Brearley at Middlesex. 'He was a very calm man, a very private man. We were completely different – he was a Cambridge philosopher, I wanted a drink and a bet on the horses – but he let you get on with your life and expected you to allow him to get on with his.'

I batted well this evening and finished at 33 not out. Ian Salisbury, the Surrey leg-spinner, told me to look after my bat. 'It's an absolute beauty – and we've seen more than enough of it this year already.'

'Essex didn't, last week!' I said.

It is true, I have played well against Surrey this year – 99 in the one-day league, 56 in the Twenty20, and a good start today. I was privately pleased to see we were playing Surrey after my pair, not just because I did well at the Oval in May, but because they are a class side. They are a better side than many international teams. Ironically, I expected that fact to make me less nervous than if they had been a poor side. I would be too worried about the technical challenge of facing Saqlain and Co. to indulge many psychological fears. That was exactly as it turned out. Straight in against Saqlain, and the immediate challenge of picking his various balls and surviving them, quickly dominated my thoughts. A flat track and bad bowlers would have left much more scope for private worries.

I left the ground feeling confident of a big score tomorrow. How 33 undefeated runs can change your mood. Form? Never believed in it anyway.

It's great to be back in London. I miss the buzz of big cities, especially after a week in a miserable hotel in Brentwood. I am determined to enjoy London this week, just as I am to play well against Surrey – in fact the two might well be connected. I play best when I am engaged and stimulated. That doesn't mean staying up all night drinking. But it might mean seven hours' sleep not nine, if the other two can be spent doing something that will lift my morale – whether that is a conversation with a team mate or watching a play.

Tonight I met up with an old friend for dinner in a noisy, hectic, crowded bistro in Notting Hill. Last time we met up in London, incidentally, I got 99 the next day.

I was ready for sleep after dinner, but I had promised Andrew Symonds I would have a drink with him and a friend on the other side of town. In truth, I am only going because we are the not-out batsmen and will walk out to bat together tomorrow at 11 a.m. Sometimes you take the warmth of the previous evening out to the middle with you and play with a closer sense of partnership. Kent need something from us tomorrow.

Surrey 401, Kent 101/2

4 July

Got it! That hundred. About bloody time, but it felt good nonetheless. I played really well today for 135, reaching my hundred off only 138 balls before lunch. It was how I like to play: positive but with little risk, controlled (mostly) but aggressive. It was one of the best of my thirteen first-class hundreds.

It was doubly nice to get it against Surrey, not only because they are such a good side, but because they have several opinion-makers in their team. If you are ambitious, as I am, you want to impress the current England players. As wicketkeeper, Alec Stewart had a good view of my innings, even saying 'Great shot' to me a couple of times. And Mark Butcher, Surrey captain and one of the best cricketing analysts in the England team, had plenty of reason to think hard about my strengths and weaknesses. Scoring runs is what counts, and winning the game is even more important than that, but I cannot deny that I also want to be rated by people who count.

A few times in my career – notably when I got 175 against Durham in 2000 – I have moved into top gear and really attacked the bowling full on. Normally, I operate best just below top gear, still exerting some self-control over my natural desire to hit the ball. For the most part I hung on to that today – except for a brief spell after lunch when I hit two drives and two pulls, 16 runs, off Jimmy Ormond's first over following the break.

'Drugs test?' laughed Matt Walker, who was batting with me. Jimmy, meanwhile, went nuts at my onslaught, unleashing just about every swear word I have ever heard. It is flattering to make a bowler so angry, particularly Jimmy, who rarely says a word. He has also won plenty of battles with me before, so it was nice to get one back.

From a technical perspective, I was pleased with my cut shots and back-foot back-drives through extra cover. That meant the bowlers came to me, giving me plenty of balls on the stumps to hit off my pads. By improving your weaknesses – as I did in India this winter – you get more opportunities to express your strengths.

I also played the spinners Saqlain and Ian Salisbury much more fluently and positively than I would have done before my two trips to India. Thank you, Min Patel and Rahul Dravid, for telling me to go. Good advice.

But above all, today was an internal battle. I see batting as a battle between two competing voices, one weak, the other strong. Your weak voice tells you one of your team mates will get runs if you don't; your weak voice says you are tired and that a day in the pavilion recuperating wouldn't be such a bad idea; your weak voice tells you that next pre-season you will put right the things that are going wrong now; your weak voice says there will be another day; your weak voice says that you have always found this bowler hard and that doesn't mean you're a bad player, just unlucky today; your weak voice says you are looking out of your depth and if you get out it would save embarrassment – you can make it right another day; your weak voice gives you an endless stream of escape clauses.

Your strong voice says someone has to get the runs and it might as well be you; your strong voice says you bat best when you're tired and that you hate the impotent feeling of watching others bat when you are out; your strong voice says that most technical problems are best solved by batting for five hours in the middle not by talking about them in the nets; your strong voice wonders why not today, rather than tomorrow, given that all tomorrows one day become today; your strong voice says there is no better time to win this battle with the bowler; your strong voice doesn't care whether you look pretty at the crease, and knows that no one remembers a scratchy start if you get a hundred; your strong voice keeps coming back to now, this day, this match, this bowler, this ball. It says this ball is the only way to achieve what you want.

The best players do not always time the ball better than the norm; they do not always have excellent techniques; they are not always exquisitely gifted. What they all have in common, I suspect, is the capacity to make that strong voice drown out the weak voice with more consistency than lesser players. The big mistake lies in thinking great players don't have that weak voice. They do. They even go under to it some days. But less often.

'People reckon I'm this mentally tough guy who never has any doubts,' Steve Waugh told me after he got nought at Taunton last year. 'That's absolute bullshit. I've got more than enough fears and doubts. I've just been better than most at silencing them.'

I silenced my bad voice for most of today's innings. But it was pretty loud at the start – as it always is after two noughts.

Early in the day, I saw a girl in a white coat walk in front of the pavilion. It looked like that girl from the Nevill Ground in Tunbridge Wells but I couldn't be sure.

After the day's play, I agreed to go on Phil Tufnell's radio show on Radio 5 Live. All good knock-about banter about today's play and my book on baseball, but I was tired and ready to stop performing for the day. Tomorrow will be another challenge. We declared behind in order to set up a game. In the taxi from the BBC to the hotel, I called my dad. He was pleased but withheld much praise. 'Go again tomorrow. Make it count.'

Surrey 401 & 249/3, Kent 352/5 declared

5 July

I didn't make it count, and we lost easily. In fact, I didn't get off the mark, caught Butcher, bowled Ormond for 0. So Jimmy didn't have to wait long for his revenge, and I didn't get to savour the feeling of having scored a ton. My sequence is now 0, 0, 135, 0.

This 0 was the most frustrating. I had scored a hundred the day before and the side needed runs from me. Surrey went up a gear today and we – I – didn't respond in kind. We wilted. I like games with a keen competitive edge and it hurts doubly that I was out playing an expansive drive outside off stump.

It was a quiet and reflective drive home. I am sick of getting 0 after hundreds. That is the third time I have done it: 175 then 0 in 2000, 154 then 0 in 2002, 135 then 0 today. I'm not doing it next time.

I scarcely had time to put my laundry in the machine before falling asleep. We play yet again tomorrow, this time in the Sunday League against Glamorgan at Maidstone.

Surrey 401 & 251/3 declared, Kent 352/5 declared & 114. Surrey won by 186 runs

6 July

I have always loved playing at Maidstone. Canterbury is probably my favourite county ground, but Maidstone, as a natural amphitheatre, has a special closeness between spectators and players. Getting my first one-day hundred in front of a packed Maidstone crowd ranks as one of the best days of my career. It was hot, sunny, and great fun. Given a blank sheet of paper before the game on which to plot an ideal one-day innings, I would have drawn a graph very similar to how it turned out.

We changed tactics today: we moved Mark Ealham from pinch-hitting opener to the middle order, and I moved up to open with Rob Key. Initially, Rob was the one to start briskly, hitting two early boundaries with his usual untroubled authority. At the other end, I played out half a dozen dot balls while I got the pace and bounce of the wicket. Then, without taking any risks, the boundaries started to come, beginning with an on drive, then a front-foot square drive. I had 40 after eight overs without having hit a ball in the air.

With Kent 60 for 0 and still several overs of fielding restrictions remaining, it was the perfect time to exploit our good platform. I decided to take on the fast-medium Alex Wharf while the field was still up. In his first over, Wharf had settled comfortably into a line and length, angling the ball in to around middle-and-off. I reckoned that by using my feet and getting down the wicket, I could get outside the line (eliminating the chance of getting lbw) and play 'pick-up' shots through the leg side. That was one area I hit well during the televised Twenty20 game against Surrey. I remember thinking before my first lofted shot today: 'No fear, no worries, just watch the ball and don't overhit – if you get even one-third of it, you'll clear the infield.' I got all of it. In all, I took 20 off Wharf's second over, hitting 3 fours and 1 six.

We were now well ahead in the game. This effectively took away the need to take many risks in the middle of the innings and, when Rob Key went for 40, Andrew Symonds and I were able to knock the ball for ones and twos in the middle section of the innings. The difficult thing in one-day cricket is getting far enough ahead to allow the late-innings risk-taking to be free from fear. Without pressure, most batters can play amazing shots. Once you know you are likely to win, it is easy to play without any fear and completely dominate. It's like playing in the nets. That is the part of your innings everyone remembers, the spectacle. But the nitty-gritty are the ones and twos that put you in the position from where you can express yourself.

I hit only one boundary from 50 to 100, but I never got bogged down. That pleased me as much as the cleanly struck boundaries. I aimed mainly down the ground to long-on and long-off for singles and twos. 'Christ, Ed,' Robert Croft exclaimed when I had 80, 'there seems to be an electric fence in front of your bat.' Andrew Symonds, who has won one-day games single-handed for Australia, talked encouragingly throughout. A seemingly bland push for one down the ground prompted him to say, 'Shot, Ed!' We were earning the right to have some fun later.

The tempo is much higher in one-day cricket, and a long one-day innings is almost always more tiring than a long innings in a four-dayer. And although it was hardly like Bombay, today was hot enough to make it hard work. 'If you're struggling, take your time between balls,' Symmo said, 'but keep running the first run hard or I'll kill you.' He looked like he might kill someone anyway when a reverse sweep went wrong and he was caught for 45.

The fun, when it came, was when I hit three sixes off three consecutive balls. Andrew Symonds had just got out, and Matt Walker had yet to face. I hit the fifth ball of Robert Croft's last over straight down the ground for six to the right of the sight-screen. It wasn't a big six, but it took a while to find the ball in the tent. Matt came down the wicket to chat.

'I'm going again this ball,' I said.

'OK, whatever you think – but keep playing the percentages.' It's exactly what I would have said to him if our roles had been reversed.

'I'm going again anyway.' I hit the next one better, over the marquees behind mid-on. Matt got a single off the first ball of Adrian Dale's new over. I hit the second delivery for six over square leg. I've never hit a sequence of three sixes out of three before.

The plan in one-day cricket is: one person bats through the innings for a hundred; you attack in the first fifteen overs, taking calculated risks that come off; you consolidate in the middle, without losing wickets but without losing momentum; you accelerate strongly at the end; you win easily. All of that happened today. Best of all, Kent recorded their first win for weeks, and our confidence will be hugely boosted.

Three hundreds in
Maidstone week

A boundary at Blackpool

'You might have 203 but I'm 5ft 8!': Matt Walker congratulates me on tiptoes at Blackpool

Kent's game against South Africa, in which I was captain

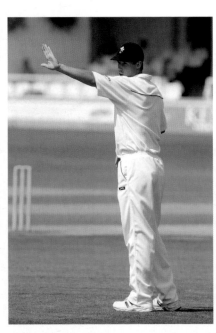

Being capped for Kent with Rob Key by the Duke of Kent, Canterbury 2001

And by Michael Vaughan for England, this time with James Kirtley,
Trent Bridge, August 2003

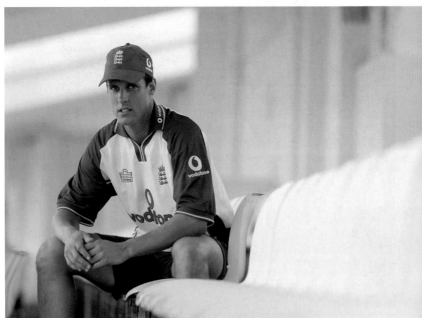

Before my first Test at Trent Bridge

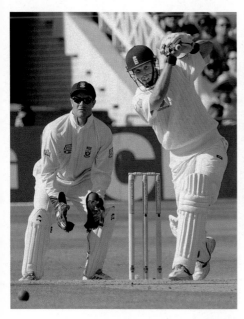

Instant success and instant failure – 64 and 0 at Trent Bridge

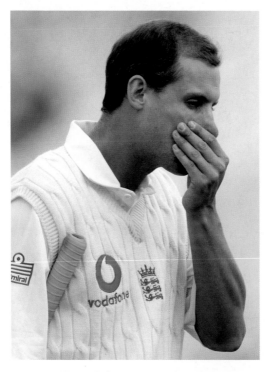

Four at the Oval – my favourite photo from the Tests

Catching and
celebrating (I'm in the helmet in the middle)

Four key players for Kent: (*above left*) Andrew Symonds, (*above right*) Matt Walker, (*below left*) Martin Saggers and (*below right*) Dave Fulton

I should be happy, and I am. But I am also a little angry. I could have been doing this in one-day games for years, but for the 'one-day specialist' theory which has dominated Kent selection for five years. I am all for one-day specialists, given one proviso: that they are better at one-day cricket than the four-day specialists. Often they aren't.

Even sillier is the idea that you have to play one-day cricket in one of two clearly prescribed ways. I was told hundreds of times, 'Either you've got to be a big-hitting risk-taker, OR you've got to nurdle it around for ones and twos.' Where does that leave Mark Waugh? He does neither (or both), preferring just to bat well. And what about if you start an innings in one manner and end it in another? That used to be considered part of the art of batting.

I call this phenomenon – either you're one thing or you're the other – the ghetto-ization of sport. It is conceptually easy, which appeals to people: 'I am Big Hitter, you are Mr Ones and Twos.' It takes away the need to think on your feet, to read the situation as it unfurls. It doesn't always help us to understand, or play, the game any better.

It is something the Americans are very bad at – that is to say they do it all the time. They have power hitters, contact hitters, low-ball hitters. Having a category for everyone appeals to their sense of scientific rigour. But though tabulating performance can clarify the essence of a sport, over-categorizing performers can distract from the only question that really matters: is he a player who will help us regularly win games? That is a harder question than 'Is he a nurdler or a slogger?' because the answer requires judgement, and where judgement is difficult, categories are easy.

Glamorgan, incidentally, were last year's one-day champions. So that's two hundreds in three days against the respective champions of four-day and one-day cricket. A radio interviewer asked me after the Surrey game how on earth we thought we would win against the one-day champions, given our poor form. 'I don't even think in those terms,' I said a bit sharply. 'I don't care who we're playing. If we turn up and play as well as we are able to play, we can beat anyone. That is what I will be trying to do tomorrow.'

After today's game, near the end of the half-hour drive from Maidstone to my home in Wye, at the roundabout off the M20, I rolled absent-mindedly into the back bumper of the car ahead. I can't have been going more than five m.p.h., but that was enough to give his bumper a tiny dent.

'You're a Kent player, aren't you?' the other driver said. 'How did it go today?'

'We won and I got a hundred.'

Enough to escape for free?

No chance.

'Give me your number then, and I'll tell you how much it costs.'

Perhaps in moments of personal triumph, after settling old scores or debunking the myths our critics have shrouded around us, we shouldn't be allowed to drive. Success, after all, can have just the same intoxicating effect as alcohol.

Meanwhile, Kent finally has something to celebrate. Those lectures I gave myself after Cardiff and Cornwall – when I had good starts in one-day games then failed to go on and make match-winning innings – paid dividends today. My concentration was the best it has ever been in one-day cricket, partly because we needed a win to-day more than in any Kent game I have ever played. Above all, we need momentum, and a feeling of confidence in the whole club. The only way to get that is not through talk but through performance.

Kent 291/4, Glamorgan 239. Kent won by 52 runs

7 July

Sometimes, when cricket is quiet or I need a complementary challenge, I am glad to wake up and remember that I have a newspaper article to submit that day.

With my muscles stiff and achy, and my mind sleepy and happy, today was not one of those days. But I have promised my editor at the *Sunday Telegraph* that I will e-mail my review of a new novel by midday today. I haven't started the piece yet. In fact, I haven't finished reading the book.

It is a warm, sunny morning, and I don't bother with breakfast or getting dressed, but lie on my sofa with the doors open, feeling the air getting hotter and the early-morning sun burning off the dew on the lawn. It is one of those summer days when I am very glad to live in the country rather than a city.

Fortunately, John Burnside's *Living Nowhere* is one of the most interesting books I have reviewed, a Lawrentian examination of memory and families and friendship. In case it sounds too rushed to finish the book and write the review in one morning, I should add that I have spent plenty of hours thinking about it. It should write itself.

But, like many journalists, I look at the empty page, the blank white Word page on my iBook, with a sinking feeling. Where to start? Why am I doing this, this morning of all mornings? I could be reading reports in the newspapers on Kent's win yesterday and having a leisurely breakfast. It takes twenty minutes before I write a word. Like a cricket innings, the first sentence is usually the hardest but, once off the mark, the article flows quickly.

An hour or so later, I re-read it with quiet satisfaction, glad that I didn't cry off from doing it. Writing short reviews is a challenge of style and form as much as of judgement or critical faculty. Sometimes the harder you try to be clever, the worse and more congested the review becomes. It is like a miniature sketch, and some themes and ideas need to be suggested rather than spelled out in full. My best ones are probably written the most simply.

I will have a better, more relaxing day because I used my mind for a couple of hours this morning. Now I can put it back into neutral for a while without feeling bored or restless.

Now for the morning papers and plenty of praise. *The Times* first, I think. Headline: 'Smith Slays Dragons with Show of Class'. The main photo is an on-drive of mine. Favourite description: 'wonderful' . . .

This could be a nice day.

9 July

As always there was a lot of talk about the wicket before the start of today's four-day game against Nottinghamshire. 'It's very soft,' said one senior player. 'A few days ago it was wet through.'

It was. But it's been hot and sunny for three days and I think the wicket will play very well, not unlike Sunday's pitch when I got a hundred. I enjoy playing on different types of pitches and the challenge of adjusting my game accordingly. But when things are going well, knowing the surface will be predictable adds an extra degree of self-confidence. I hope we win the toss and bat.

We did and Dave Fulton was out quickly, leaving me taking guard at the Mote ground not long after 11 o'clock on another high summer's day. I played an off-drive first ball and missed it. 'He's had his fill,' said the New Zealand all-rounder Chris Cairns from mid-on. 'He looks like a guy who got a hundred on Sunday and doesn't have much hunger for today.'

If true, that would be unforgivable. I have had a difficult season which is just coming right. Today the odds are stacked in my favour: good form, fine weather, a placid pitch, a struggling opposition. I will play other games, doubtless just around the corner, in poor form and on terrible wickets. 'Don't be satisfied,' I said to myself just after Cairns's comment, 'be ruthless and cash in.'

But you often still need a touch of luck. My first scoring shot was a front-foot clip off Andrew Harris. I hit it well but at catchable height through square leg. Guy Welton dived but couldn't quite reach. It was the closest I came to getting out all day.

In terms of timing and placement, I don't think I have ever played better than this morning. At first Notts bowled outside off stump to me. But since that net against the bowling machine in India, I have been cover-driving much better this year. More importantly (because I rate back-foot shots as more destructive against better bowlers) I have also been hitting my cut and back-foot drive very well this last week. The result of playing those two shots effectively is to squeeze the length and line that bowlers can get away with. When you are playing well off both feet, if the length isn't just right, you always have an attacking option.

After a handful of boundaries, Notts switched to bowling straighter, freeing up my leg-side shots off my hip. Placement is difficult to explain – some days you do it well, others not – and today I kept hitting the ball crisply between fielders. When I had about 30, Chris Cairns said with a curious tone of voice, 'OK, so we know you can play. Why aren't you in the England team?'

For a while it looked like I would score a hundred before lunch – something I have never done. The last over of the session was bowled by off-spinner Kevin Pietersen. I had 94. The first three balls were dots. 'Come on, Ed, fortune favours the brave,' Pietersen said. 'You know you want that hundred – imagine sitting through lunch in the nervous 90s.'

I had decided to go for my hundred anyway, and I went down the wicket to the fourth ball, aiming to hit a straight six over the top. I got too close to the pitch of the ball, couldn't get the elevation, and hit it hard but on the ground straight to Pietersen.

OK, I thought, it wasn't meant to happen before lunch. Just stay put and take your time. I clipped the next ball off my hip for four, blocked the sixth and walked off on 98 not out.

Today's morning session was among the most bizarre I have ever played in, or even seen. When Geraint Jones and I went in for lunch, the score was 170-odd for 5. A team normally scores around 100 runs per session, perhaps less in the first session. When wickets fall, as they did today, the rate of scoring is usually slower while the batters 'rebuild'. For 170 runs to be scored *and* for five wickets to go down is scarcely believable. Everyone looked a bit stunned. It was, quite literally, all happening.

I had a light lunch, drank lots of water, glanced at the paper and intermittently chatted in the dressing room. 'Come on then, Ed, what's the secret?' James Tredwell asked with an amused, quizzical expression, 'How do you hit every ball on your hip for four – you didn't miss one, literally every one went for four.'

I got the hundred in the first over after lunch, with a back-foot drive for four off Chris Cairns through extra cover. I was again genuinely touched by the reception I got from the Kent crowd. They, too, have waited a long time for us to play well this season.

I was eventually out to a lazy, sloppy sliced cut, caught in the gully. I had made 149 off 143 balls with 22 fours, probably the most attractive innings of my life. Until today I have always considered a 40 against Middlesex at Fenner's in 1997 as the most perfect I have ever played. That was in the middle of my first glut of run-scoring as a nineteen-year-old. I wouldn't quite say that day six years ago has haunted me, but it is true that I have always wanted to improve on it. It wasn't nice to reflect that as an out-and-out striker of a cricket ball, I hadn't improved in six years. I am glad to have changed that now.

Interestingly, that Cambridge innings is more typical of what you usually get when you are playing at your absolute best: 40. The perfect days almost never last. You tend to hit every ball in the middle for half an hour and then get out to your first mistake. That was the pattern for that 40 at Fenner's: I almost sensed it would end as a pretty cameo. So I was doubly delighted to make a big hundred today. It was a cameo that went on to become a real innings. That is the best fun of all.

I hope to play again like today, and on a bigger stage. But I also accept that I may not, and I will one day look back on a sunny, high summer's day at the Mote ground as the closest I ever came to being completely in charge at the crease.

Meanwhile, I shouldn't forget that I still only batted for a session and a half. If I can bat at that level for a day and a half, I really will be on the brink of something.

Having got out, I asked the dressing-room attendant if he had seen my dad. He is definitely here, came the reply, up on the grassy bank. I was thrilled that he was here – I leave a ticket for him every day, so I often don't know if he's at the ground or not. Today is one innings I wanted him to see, a memory to keep, a snapshot for the nostalgic photo album in his mind.

When Kent bowled at Notts, the wicket looked rather more

difficult. That, as is often the case, is because we bowled better: Mohammad Sami is quick, very quick.

I cooked dinner for a friend at my house tonight. Afterwards, as the sun faded but the light lingered, we walked by the River Stour, which runs through the meadows a few hundred yards from my house. With a drink in one hand, a hundred to celebrate, and the affable tiredness that good friends permit, I reflected that the good times really were here and now.

I hit my pillow, knowing that my first conscious thoughts tomorrow will be quietly happy – 'What is my mood? Ah yes, good: yesterday I got a hundred.' A moment later, still not really awake, that will be replaced by, 'And today? – now I remember . . . another chance to bat well.'

You see, no matter what I preach about balance and perspective and finding solace in landscape, music, humour or friendship, my innermost mood, the secret state of my soul, owes much – too much, perhaps – to how I am playing. And right now I am playing well.

Kent 362, Nottinghamshire 137/5

10 July

I arrived at the ground at the usual time this morning: 9 a.m., two hours before play starts. It seemed far too early today. I am lethargic from yesterday's innings and will probably cruise through warm-ups, trying to preserve energy for the game. Ideally, I wanted only twenty or thirty catches and throws, then fifteen throw-downs in a net. I reckoned my success today would depend much more on hunger and application than on preparation.

There was only one technical thing I wanted to practise: the leave. One problem with being in great form is that your eyes light up too easily and too early in your innings. You know you are capable of playing a full range of attacking shots, and you can't wait to play them. The danger, then, as I did in the second innings at the Oval, is that in your first few balls you play a shot you would hit for 4 nineteen times out of twenty if you had 80 not out. But you don't have 80 – not yet – and your current odds are more like four out of five. That's too big a risk, given that a good, solid start will almost inevitably bring big runs. When you are in a purple patch, the challenge is to play with the discipline you have when you are struggling and yet retain the confidence of good form.

Last night, I thought about how I would approach this morning's practice. I am swinging the bat well, so why bother to swing the bat in practice? The most likely thing that might have stopped me making a hundred today is a rash shot early on in my innings. A few, good early leaves, I felt sure, would set me up nicely. So in order to practise that muscle-memory, I asked Dave Fulton to throw me a dozen balls just outside off stump: I left all but two of them and said, 'That's all, thanks, mate.'

'What, no drives? Unheard of!'

He was right. In previous years I have been guilty of hitting balls for the pure pleasure of timing them well. Today – after yesterday's fun – I just wanted to get runs, ugly runs if necessary.

My muscles did remember this morning's training, and I left ten of my first fifteen balls from the Notts left-armer, Greg Smith. From then on, after a much more sedate and less sparkling start than yesterday, I felt I had a good chance.

I got 113, a much more workmanlike innings than yesterday. I rate it much worse than yesterday aesthetically, much higher in terms of character. Character didn't come into yesterday much. I played like a kid in a candy store: with delight. Today, it was harder work. But, much as I like to entertain, character matters much more to me. Falling short as a personality, playing without any steel, hits me very hard. I would have felt just that if I had nicked an extravagant cover drive on nought today.

When I walked off to another lovely reception both from the spectators and from my team mates, I took off my pads and thigh pads slightly numbly. Two hundreds in two days, and four hundreds in eight days. I glanced in the mirror and saw a look in my eyes I have never seen before. 'What have I done?'

While Rob Key and Andrew Symonds moved towards hundreds of their own, someone told me my family were watching. Four different generations were all sitting by the furthest boundary, in line with a flick through wide mid-on. My niece, just over a year old, tottered up and down the grassy slope; my sister, in red polka-dots, watched a mixture of baby and batting; my parents, more familiar faces at Kent games, probably looked equally nervous about two things: that I might get out, and that they, if I stayed in, might be perceived as looking even remotely smug. Most important, my grandmother, now in her nineties, watched every ball. I think it was from her husband, a wonderfully stubborn Yorkshireman who died three years ago, that I inherited my strongest sporting genes. This book is dedicated to him.

The greatest thrill about being a sportsman is being able to make people happy. To give the people you love, in particular, a day to celebrate and share is the grandest repayment imaginable for the physical exhaustion and psychological torture of the days that end in failure.

Kent 362 & 418/3 declared, Nottinghamshire 156 & 29/2

11 July

We wrapped up a great win today. How we needed it. After the tenth Notts wicket fell, Dave Fulton suggested we clap the Kent supporters. They have stuck with us over these last two difficult months. Now, I hope, we are back.

It was harder to get the Notts second-innings wickets. Jason Gallian played typically correctly for a very determined 106 off 293 balls. Kevin Pietersen and Chris Cairns, two of the cleanest strikers in our competition, smashed fifties. Pietersen, in fact, looked like he was just getting going when he charged Andrew Symonds's off spin and hit over the top, to my left at mid-off. I dived and took a two-handed catch at full stretch. It meant as much to me as the hundreds. Even Symmo, who is not given to exuberant praise, admitted it was the best catch he'd seen me take. I am determined to keep fielding better. It was perhaps the best single moment of my season, a significant catch in the middle of a crucial win.

It is not often that you score two hundreds and come second in the most-valuable player stakes. But this match belongs to Mohammad Sami. He took 8 for 64 and 7 for 50, bowling fast, straight and often brilliantly. He has a perfect side-on action, great natural athleticism and star quality. He slept through much of my two innings, which I didn't mind at all. He looked to be resting with intent.

He proved in this game that genuinely fast bowling changes games even on placid wickets. He can swing the ball, too, though I am inclined to agree with Nasser on that point – it would not be my primary concern. If Sami can stay fit for long periods, it would be a surprise if he does not become a dominant player on the world stage. I know he can really bowl because Andrew Symonds is being nice to him.

I have become a big believer in the Australian philosophy of celebrating wins, the principle being that team spirit is forged in shared experience of good and bad times, especially the good. So the whole team sat in the dressing room this afternoon, remembering what we did well and laughing about the odd slip-up. It was the happiest scene of the year so far. If Sami – quite rightly – got the biggest cheers, I was secretly content to have helped make today happen.

The worrying news is that most of the team have family commitments tonight, leaving only Symmo and me to celebrate in Canterbury. Short of throwing drinks over my shoulder, I am not sure how I will keep up with him. 'Stop talking, Ed. Start drinking,' he said this afternoon. It was three o'clock.

For anyone interested in fate and coincidence, that girl from

Tunbridge Wells week has now seen me bat three times. I have scored three hundreds.

> Kent 362 & 418/3 declared, Nottinghamshire 156 & 337. Kent won by 287 runs

15 July

Sky Sports televises one county championship game a year. This is it: Lancashire versus Kent at Blackpool. 'What on earth do they want to televise this one for?' Mark Ealham wondered. I was rather happier to see the Sky lorries and commentary box scaffolds.

Before the game, the players and commentators inspected the pitch. 'The cracks are so big the plates are moving!' one of my team mates worried. I think it will be low and flat and that the cracks won't make much difference either way. It is a very hot day and I desperately hope we bat first.

It is easy to get distracted when you are playing well. People talk to you. Today's television commentators, normally just courteously minimal with me, made a point of saying well played with that 'well-done, son' expression ex-players are so good at. I noticed David Lloyd, once England coach, now Sky commentator, watching me carefully during my net before the game.

What the hell, I thought, now he's looking, I'll see if I can hit this one for six. It is pretty out of character for me to change the way I practise in order to seek to impress bystanders. I hit it into the sight screen on the full, then, immediately fearing hubris, blocked the next one.

Into the real thing, Rob Key nicks out off Peter Martin for one, so I am quickly in against the new ball. After one or two plays and misses, I get the pace and bounce of the wicket. It is low, skiddy and not moving much in the air or off the seam. What that means to me as a batsman is the following: look to play the ball, not leave it; play straight-batted shots, not pulls and cuts; draw imaginary lines on the wicket and swing the bat up and down the line of the ball – what we call 'lining it up'. So much for technique. More importantly: with little help for the fast bowlers, and in the absence of a quality Lancashire spinner, I told myself that if I could concentrate, there was a very good chance of another big score.

I had 88 at lunch (10 less than last week at Maidstone), and Charles Colville from Sky interviewed me as I walked off the field.

'Three hundreds last week, 88 not out at lunch today, it's a pretty easy game for you at the moment, Ed.'

'It's never an easy game.'

'You must be hoping for 12 more after lunch and another hundred.'

'Hopefully a few more than 12 more. The only way to win four-day games on wickets like this is to get a long way ahead and stay there.'

You have to walk through the home dressing room at Blackpool to get to the away one. A few minutes into the break, trying to find the dressing-room attendant, I popped my head round the door into Lancastrian territory. He wasn't around, so I apologetically asked the scattered Lancashire players where I could find a can of Coke. 'You can fook off, that's what you can do,' said Peter Martin.

I batted fluently after lunch. I found that the skiddy wicket enabled me to drive a lot of balls on the up – even if they didn't go for four, most of them went hard-ish to mid-off and mid-on. I think that crisply hit defensive shots and measured check drives wear down bowlers' morale as much as scoring shots. They are statements of assurance and confidence.

Just after tea I was out for 203 off 257 balls. I hit 35 fours and 1 six. When I got to 194, I passed my highest score in first-class cricket, which until that time had been 190 for Cambridge in 1997 when I was top of the national batting averages in May. Much more importantly, at 194 I also became the first player this season to pass 1,000 first-class runs for the season. That is certainly the best achievement of my career so far. A few minutes later, I got my first double hundred. I didn't even throw the innings away – the ball which bowled me from Carl Hooper kept very low and squeezed under my bat.

Perhaps the reaction of the crowd meant more than the milestones. The Lancashire fans have no reason to support me, but most of them stood and clapped more warmly than I had expected. I am paid to get runs, not to bat prettily, but which of us, deep down, doesn't also like the idea of being an entertaining and pleasing player to watch?

I also like the old-fashioned, no-bullshit atmosphere of northern cricket clubs. People sometimes suggest I am happiest in idyllic Home Counties grounds like Arundel and Tunbridge Wells. In fact, I have performed much better at grounds like Blackpool, where middle-aged men drink warm beer at lunch and put hankies on their heads to keep off the sun, but who often know the difference between a good shot and a lucky one. My grandfather, even though he was from the other side of the Pennines, would have fitted in perfectly at Blackpool.

Many pros hate festival weeks like Maidstone and Blackpool. They resent the lack of practice facilities and bemoan the discomfort of the dressing rooms. But I would rather sacrifice a little comfort for more atmosphere and a bigger crowd. So long as the wicket is up to first-class standard – and this one certainly is – I think we should continue to play a few games away from county headquarters like Old Trafford and Canterbury. We have to keep selling county cricket as well as we can.

Kent finished the day on 384 for 4, and Sky ended their coverage with an interview with me. 'The 15th of July is St Swithin's Day – though it might soon be renamed Ed Smith day after today's play: a double hundred, the first man to a thousand runs this season, his personal best.' Charles Colville is good at making you blush.

Did I think I would be picked for the next England Test? How quickly things have changed since that desperate pair at Chelmsford.

Kent 384/4

16 July

Kent batted on today, trying to win the game the hard way: bat once, bowl Lancashire out, enforce the follow-on, then try to bowl them out again. The bad news is it will be very hard to get twenty wickets on this surface. The good news is, I can have most of the day off while we get the rest of the runs.

Rod Marsh, legendary Australian wicketkeeper and now new England selector, is here. He came into our dressing room during a brief rain break and talked to Dave Fulton and me. When my name came up with regard to the England team, I walked outside to leave them to it. Half an hour later, Rod came outside and sat next to me. We talked for twenty minutes or so, but avoided the only issue that is really relevant: am I going to get picked or not?

After lunch, Sky asked me to commentate for half an hour on the Kent innings. In fact, it was more of a lifestyle interview. It went something like this:

CHARLES COLVILLE: So, Ed, you've written this bestseller – tell us about it.

ES: If *Playing Hard Ball* was a bestseller, which it wasn't, I wouldn't mind seeing some royalties from my publishers.

CC: Well, you have got a double first from Cambridge, you're the leading run scorer in the country, you've scored four hundreds in four innings and five in six – life's pretty good at the moment. What do you do to switch off?

ES: A combination of reading, writing, socializing [Christ, this is a terrible answer], going to the theatre . . .

CC: You sound like a candidate for Miss World.

ES: It was a nightmare question, Charles.

County cricket takes you to unusual places, and I try to get out and see them. Blackpool, I have to admit, was not high on my list of holiday destinations, but I have warmed to it. The evening before the first day's play I gave a different television interview from the beach, just in front of the pier. 'So what do you make of the Blackpool coast?' was the surprising first question.

'A bit like Brighton,' I blurted out, which is, of course, plain wrong. Blackpool, unlike Brighton, is firmly rooted in working-class culture. It is the real thing.

A friend, up north on a business trip and curious about Blackpool, visited for dinner. We walked along the beach, while the low tide revealed yet more acres of mud-brown sand. It wasn't exactly pretty, but that didn't seem the point. We ducked into a bingo hall and took a ride in a rocking horse carousel. Initially, I thought we were the only customers, and that the wheel had turned just for us. But then I noticed an octogenarian couple struggling cheerfully out of their chariot. How much longer, I wonder, will all this survive, this nostalgic reminder of a different England?

Kent 602/6 declared, Lancashire 130/2

18 July

A resolute innings today by Carl Hooper, a favourite Kent player when he was our overseas pro in the mid-1990s, deprived Kent of a win today. He made 128 calmly accumulated runs, saving his top gear until the very end, when the game was safe. His early-evening sixes thrilled the Blackpool crowd, but it was his defensive shots that hurt Kent the most. He went about his business with no fuss and few flourishes, just a thorough relentlessness.

Along with Hooper, the rain breaks in this game also conspired against us. With a full four days of uninterrupted play, we might well have made it three wins in a row. If that doesn't sound like much, it wasn't so long ago that we were looking for a sequence of one win in a row.

We are playing with spirit. This was a flat, dead wicket, but the bowlers – particularly Martin Saggers, Alamgir Sheriyar and Andrew Symonds – ran in hard and competed. Bowling in high summer on flat wickets is unglamorous, hard work: it is also the key to winning four-day matches. This mid-season upswing in our form relies on the bowlers staying fit and the batters staying hungry for runs.

Kent 602/6 declared, Lancashire 365 & 244/6. Match drawn

19 July

One of the messages on my mobile phone after my 203 was from the BBC asking me to commentate on the finals of the Twenty20 at Trent Bridge today. Initially I said no, thinking I needed the rest, then I changed my mind. Why? Partly because I realized that Nottingham is halfway home from Blackpool to Kent, and would be a neat way of breaking the journey. Trent Bridge is also the Test ground I know least well – I have played for Kent there only once, scoring 30-odd and crashing my car. I wanted to make it a place of happier and more recent memories. England play South Africa at Trent Bridge, incidentally, in a fortnight.

The Twenty20 has been a huge success and the ECB deserve great credit for introducing it. Over a quarter of a million people passed through the turnstiles in June to watch its inaugural year: a younger, after-work crowd, wanting the quick fix of sixes and run-outs. They got plenty of both. Nor do I think the Twenty20 will encroach on the four-day game, support for which runs deeper in the English psyche than people imagine. If anything, the Twenty-20 will make one-day cricket fight harder for its market share.

The semi-finals and final were all played today. Leicester lost to Warwickshire, and Surrey beat Gloucestershire, leaving the Lions as strong favourites for the final. I commentated for Radio 5 Live on all three games, alternating with Notts and England keeper Chris Read in the summarizer's chair.

I enjoyed the commentary, trying to add value, as they say – to give a player's perspective without being an uncritical member of the players' club. Of course I looked to praise, but I also tried to be honest.

Most interesting for me was being at a major cricket event without playing in it. There are players, there are the spectators, and then there are those who bring the game to the people – the media. I am usually in the first category; today I oscillated between the second and third. Up in the back row of the top tier of the stands, during breaks in the commentary I tried not to watch as an off-duty professional (a very long long-off, a distant fielder, completely frozen out of the action) but as a fan. I warmed to it, gradually switching off the side of me that says, 'Actually, that wasn't a great shot, it was a dreadful ball.' I started to roll with the emotion of the crowd, the spectacle of bowling, slogging, diving. Four! Six! Out! Many fans aren't there for subtleties; they are there to escape.

The commentary box is high above the bowler's arm, appropriately directly opposite the players' dressing rooms. I felt almost no nerves before going on air in the semis and expected the final to be the same. But as the lights came on and the walk-ways in the open stands and the corridors of the media centre filled with urgently moving bodies, I felt suddenly part of something: a participant, albeit a different type of participant, in a major sporting occasion. My words, my tone of voice, my degree of involvement with what was happening on the field – the way I described what people like me do for a living – would directly affect the way the match was experienced by the listeners. I was performing as a different strand of the sporting triumvirate, and I was nervous.

As Ian Ward eased Surrey to victory with essentially correct, old-fashioned batting, I allowed myself one pointed remark: 'Ian Ward has shown how batting normally, with a decent method and a cool head, can win any game of cricket, no matter how abbreviated.'

I popped up to see the players after the final. Even the losing semi-finalists had stayed to watch, so I bumped into my old colleague Paul Nixon. Still in cricketing evangelist mode after my commentary, I almost said to him, 'Great spectacle, don't you think!' before I remembered that Leicester had played dreadfully in the semi and now had no realistic chance of winning a competition this summer. 'We were poor,' he said with an uncharacteristic lack of bounciness, 'very poor.'

I saw Phil DeFreitas and gave him room to ignore me if he wished. We have never been the best of friends on the field. I didn't see any point in insisting on banal niceties. But he took a step in my direction and said warmly, 'Very well played this year, Ed.' Along with Martin Bicknell, 'Daffy' has been county cricket's most prolific bowler over the last decade. Even now, nearer forty than thirty, you know he is always trying something with the ball, always setting you up. I've enjoyed facing him, without always coming out on top.

As I left the ground, Trevor Ward, whose time at Kent drew to a close as mine began, pulled me by the arm. 'Let me touch this arm,' he said mischievously, 'I could do with some of your form rubbing off on me!' Trevor is a keen carp fisherman, and I sometimes think his down-turned mouth has started to resemble his favourite prey. But he isn't always gloomy and he lights up with an infectious warmth. 'Seriously, well done, mate.'

What a strange moment. Trevor was one of my Kent heroes. As a kid, sitting in the green seats at Canterbury, I watched him dozens of times. He was in his mid-twenties, fully in his prime, with a dazzling array of shots. He could pull or hook anybody, which he often did first ball of the day; he could drive on the up, cut with the best, go over the top against spin, score lightning 80s and big double hundreds. He really was in the very top category as a talent – Trevor at his best would lose little in comparison with world superstars.

When we played together, he was still not much over thirty and he had lost some self-belief but none of his extravagant gifts. If we netted together, I would glance into his net and watch the bowlers collect their balls from all parts of Canterbury. 'That's in the Frank Woolley stand, Ed!' he'd say, imagining he had hit it over long-on in a match.

The gap between what he was capable of and how he was playing in the middle hurt him terribly. I honestly don't think he ever realized how extraordinary he was. He heard it plenty of times – he knew the words well enough – but I wonder if he ever believed them.

Passing all kinds of ex-colleagues and opponents in Trent Bridge, I felt something I have never quite experienced before today: genuine respect and warmth from my contemporaries. Once, they felt my reputation exceeded my performance; then I felt my performance exceeded my reputation. Today, they were happy to give me encouragement, and I felt humble to be so generously treated.

Today was my twenty-sixth birthday.

23 July

The balance between rest and stimulus is a difficult one. A month ago, when I was feeling a little restless and under-stretched, agreeing to record a programme about nostalgia for the Radio 4 show *Off the Page* sounded like a very good idea. Now, after five hundreds in six innings, I feel fully stretched and insufficiently rested. A day at home looks more attractive than driving to Bristol to record a radio programme.

Off the Page is presented by Matthew Parris and features three different writers each week. Each writer reads out his or her own 500-word essay on a chosen theme – it might be memory, or superstition, or, in this instance, nostalgia – then Matthew leads a broader round-table discussion.

Amazingly, my father was also invited on to today's programme. He explained to the producer that there had been a mistake, and that they had confused him with me, and that I had already agreed to go on. The producer, who had no idea we were related, confirmed that he did indeed want us both and was surprised to hear we were father and son.

So Dad drove me to Bristol, where his twenty-odd radio plays were recorded in the 1980s and '90s, and we arrived early enough to walk around Clifton village before the show. Anyone who doubts that London is not the only serious cultural centre in England should visit Clifton: it is elegant, busy, bohemian and sophisticated.

Dad and I had different attitudes to pre-recording preparation. Dad wanted to get to the studio early and meet the other guest and the producers. I wanted to sleep in the car until the last minute. Chit-chat before a performance just dissipates my psychological energy. I viewed the day as no different from a gentle day's cricket: at some point I would be called upon to bat, and when I was, that would be the time to concentrate, not before.

If I viewed the performance as a bit like another innings, I would like to come across some other bowlers as helpful as Matthew Parris. He bowled a succession of gentle and well-signposted half-volleys so skilfully that the untrained ear might think the skill lay with the batter and not with the generosity of the bowler.

Ironically, I am now feeling considerably less nostalgic than when I wrote my essay, a few weeks ago. Perhaps success, particularly the promise of continued success, is a great antidote to nostalgia. When the future looks full and colourful, we are less likely to live nostalgically in the past.

Thinking about nostalgia today made me appreciate how the past and the future are to some extent pistons in our personalities: when the past is up, the future is down, and when the future is central, the past recedes. Perhaps that is why performers are so needy of company, to jolt them out of too much introspection and the nostalgia that can bring. '1997 . . . those were the days . . . sunny all the time . . . I seemed to get runs all the time' – that is not a great attitude to bring into a match in 2003. Friends who can fill the present and future with fun and possibility help us to look forward not back, and it is forward, of course, that the sportsman should be looking.

24 *July*

It is a fine summer's day, I am in a generally good mood, am in the form of my life and am practising the game I love. What could go wrong?

Actually, quite a lot. Since I commentated on the Twenty20 last Sunday, Kent have had the first half of the week off, which almost never happens in the middle of the season. I have enormously enjoyed getting off the merry-go-round of travel–perform–travel–perform for a few days. I will play better in the last third of the season for having had a few days' rest.

What I do not need to do is spend Thursday and Friday practising. Usually, I am an obsessive practiser: sometimes I will even come into the ground and hit balls on my one day off after ten straight days playing. If I don't feel comfortable with how my game is functioning, I work at it until I feel it's resolved.

The flip-side is that when I am in a sustained period of Ideal Performance State (apologies for the psycho-chat) that is all I want to do: perform. If there is no performing to be done (i.e. no games), I don't want to waste my competitive fire by trying to fix things that ain't broken.

Today, I would much rather not have had a net. In fact, I netted badly and walked out to let someone else have the practice time. I rarely do that – I like batting too much – and when I do, it will always be because I feel that meaningless practice is starting to hinder, not help, my game.

The team, of course, comes first, and if we need to practise as a unit then we should. I bring up the topic not to complain but explain: we are all different and not even consistently different. Two people might both be practising below par: one because he is busted and out of form, the other because he is already in match mood and knows this isn't the real thing. It is the responsibility of the man in form not to ruin everyone else's practice by messing around. But his needs, just like those of the worried struggler, also need to be understood. I should know: I've been in both camps.

Today, I also met Muttiah Muralitharan, the world's leading bowler and smiliest cricketer. He exudes a playful intelligence and a self-effacing self-belief. As well he might: he has taken over 400 Test wickets. He looks like he has enjoyed it all.

He is joining us from now until the end of the season. My prediction is we will win almost every championship game he plays in, and more than half the one-dayers. His record in the championship is phenomenal. I watched carefully – sometimes from the batting crease – what he did for Lancashire and can see no reason why he won't do the same for us.

26 July

Recently I have been thinking a lot about timing. Cricketers use the term 'timing' a great deal – 'He's a sweet timer of the ball' – without often analysing exactly what it is or how you can do it better.

Put most simply, timing is making the ball leave the bat faster than it ought to. Good timers hit the ball hard with a minimum of force and effort. Timing is what Colin Cowdrey, David Gower, Mark Waugh and Sourav Ganguly all have in common.

Because timing creates the illusion of effortlessness – a graceful swing of the bat, and then the ball whistles away – it is often assumed to be an entirely God-given blessing. To an extent that is true. Some people were given at birth a special hand–eye coordination that enables them to locate the middle of the bat more often than most.

But timing cannot be all talent, otherwise you cannot explain how some days you time the ball better than others: some innings you don't try to hit the ball hard at all and it flies to the boundary; other days you put everything into your shots and the ball limps to mid-off. Even within the same innings, timing comes and goes. You might start in sync and time the ball well, then you get tired and lose your technique and timing as you weary.

There, I've said it. Technique. It isn't a word often associated with timing. But it is the other half of the story. Talent is one-half of timing, technique is the other. It is your technique that enables a full expression of your talent. You can be the best potential timer of the ball in the world, but if your technique is dreadful then you don't time the ball well very often. In other words, timing is a skill (an underused term in cricket – think how we talk of *skilful* footballers), and skills can be honed.

So what is this technical aspect of timing? Which parts of your technique affect your timing? To a degree, all of your technique (your grip, body position, footwork) affects your timing, though that is an unhelpful answer. Anyway, we know that some very good technicians are not particularly good timers – so there must be some strands of technique that are more closely connected to timing than others. I have been trying to work out which ones.

Three come to mind. The first must be your bat swing. Given that the business of being a batsman is primarily concerned with swinging a bat, we talk about the bat swing less than we might. Think how much attention golfers give to their golf swing. It is the talk of their profession for the simple reason that it is the essence of their profession. All golfers know their swings come and go. When they are swinging well, the ball basically goes straight; when their swing is off, they struggle with the basics. That doesn't mean they cannot win when their swing is out – a host of things (like mental strength, canniness and good putting) might get them through. But they will still be searching for that good swing. They want their natural, regular golf swing to be perfect.

In cricketing terms, good timers of the ball nearly always have a free, fluent – and usually longish – bat swing. The bat swing has two simple components: the back-lift and the follow-through. They are separated by contact with the ball. Brian Lara, of course, has both the highest back-lift and longest follow-through of them all, and is one of the best timers of the ball in the world.

So how is bat swing associated with timing? Timing comes from the acceleration of the bat swing through the hitting area. Great players with even the highest back-lifts don't usually 'swing hard' at the top (beginning) of their swing. That would be inflexible: they would have no capacity to decelerate the swing and play defensively. Instead, the acceleration of their swing is perfectly in sync with the arrival of the ball. They time their swing, and this enables them to time the ball. The later and more imperceptible the acceleration, the greater the illusion of effortless timing. Colin Cowdrey appeared not to swing the bat very fast in those famous cover-drives. But if you study his swing at the point of contact, he suddenly accelerated his bat through the hitting area when he needed to. That is where the power came from.

The second component of timing is the uncoiling of your wrists. It is really all part of the first point, the bat swing, but it is easier to deal with separately. At the point of the swing when the bat is moving fastest – just before contact with the ball – good timers often gain extra power from uncoiling their wrists. This wristiness adds 'snap' to their swing. The Indians do it particularly well. When Rahul Dravid hits a cover drive, he gains extra power at the last second by uncoiling and flicking his wrists at the ball – almost like a hockey flick at goal. It is also what Tendulkar does in those unbelievable flicks to leg off his hip. He does not need to swing the bat fast at all for that shot; he simply flicks his wrists at the last minute. He almost appears to 'turn over' his hands – flipping the bat over as he hits the ball. If you do that a fraction early, the ball balloons to mid-on off the leading edge. Ditto Mark Waugh's front-footed clip through midwicket. It is not something for mortals to try at home.

Not all good timers of the ball are wristy. Some of them don't uncoil their wrists at all but leave the bat fully 'square' (leaving the old 'maker's name' showing all the time). But I think nearly all great timers grip the bat tighter at the point when they hit the ball. Gripping the bat tighter on impact by definition means that they don't grip the bat hard throughout their swing. It is often said that you should easily be able to slide a golf club out of someone's hands when it is set at the top of their swing. It is argued you should be gripping the club loosely at that point, only tightening later. The same is true of cricket. If you watch good timers in their stance and set-up, as the bat sits in the hands, the grip often looks quite loosely held and relaxed. People who 'choke' the bat in their grip, grabbing it as hard as they can throughout their swing, might be able to club the ball hard occasionally, but they cannot have the flexibility required to time the ball consistently.

('Choking the bat' is one of the first things to watch out for when you are nervous. Instead of trusting yourself to time the ball as normal, you tense up and choke the bat. Often, the result is that the bat is closed towards the on-side at the point of contact, squirting the ball to leg and making it hard to get sweet contact. The solution, if you can do it, is usually to relax your whole top half: shoulders, arms, wrists, hands.)

Back to timing. The last thing good timers of the ball do is to transfer their weight into the ball. This used to be called 'leaning on the ball', the late lean of the torso in the direction of the ball just before contact. It is what helped Colin Cowdrey and Tom Graveney to be such exquisite off-side players. Now we call it 'transferring weight into the ball'. The front-foot off drive is prob-ably the clearest example of how transferring weight into the ball can make a huge difference. Try swinging the bat hard without any weight transfer, and see how hard the ball leaves the bat. Then try a late transfer of weight just before the point of contact, and see how the ball goes faster with less effort. On the front foot that is obvious. Less easy to see (let alone do) is to transfer weight into the ball on the back foot. Of course, you have to transfer back first. But if you watch people execute the hardest shot in cricket – the back drive, straight past the bowler's stumps – I think there is a late transfer of weight back in the direction of the ball. Tendulkar and Ponting are the only players I can think of who can play the shot regularly. I think, at the very last minute, having already moved back, they transfer back in the direction of the ball.

If you're still with me, that makes four components of timing.

1. Accelerating the bat swing in sync with the arrival of the ball.

2. Gaining extra power from uncoiling or snapping the wrists.

3. Gripping the bat tighter on impact than in the rest of the swing.

4. Transferring weight into the ball – or 'leaning on it'.

There's no reason why you can't practise all those things.

Now here's my argument: really perfect timing derives from doing each of these things in sync with all the others. You can score runs with one or two or none of them working well. We all know that. But that doesn't mean you shouldn't try to get them working together. And when all those skills do work together, when they are perfectly synchronized – then the ball really does fly to the fence.

That's the best I can offer.

27 July

Blackpool one week, Scarborough the next. Scarborough is a classier, more moneyed northern resort, with Victorian squares, grander hotels and fewer cheap B&Bs. We are here for just a one-day game, so the club have organized a coach rather than the normal system of driving in pairs. Instead of fearing boredom, I was happy to have enforced inactivity for the whole afternoon.

I like Scarborough. Last night I walked along the cliffs before dinner, and this morning – a bright one – I made a point of checking out of the hotel half an hour early so I could lie on one of the benches above the beach. With my kit bag as a pillow and the warm morning sun on my face, I could have stayed there all day if I hadn't heard the coach's engine start. Those snatched moments of solitude are precious to me during the season. I think I play worse without them.

Blackpool is a good ground, Scarborough is a great one. Carved into a densely populated suburb of Victorian terraces, and surrounded by stands on all sides, it is the best amphitheatre in England. It has the feistiest crowd, too. In 1999, trying to save the game for

Kent, I made 55 in four and a half hours here. 'You wouldn't get in our second team!' they shouted. Eric Scarbrough was there that day, the penultimate time he saw me play. I imagined him terribly torn between joining in with the Yorkies and shouting back at them, 'He's my grandson!'

I disagreed with the selection today. Unless there are extraordinary circumstances, you should never play more than five front-line bowlers in a one-day game. They cannot all bowl their full allotment of overs. All you are doing is creating a get-out clause for a bowler who bowls badly – someone else will bowl my overs for me. It fosters weakness. Not so playing the extra batsman: there are no restrictions on the number of people who can bat in a one-day game. I should have argued harder when we discussed the team.

The details: Yorkshire got 197 (30 too many); Kent 179 (20 too few). I made a fluent 36 before Craig White took a diving catch at gully. It is the first time in 15 days and five innings that I have been out for less than a hundred. Dave Fulton batted very bravely at the end for 48, but we couldn't quite find the big hits when we needed them. We could have done with a pinch hitter at the end – that is, a normal batting order.

Much more importantly, when I was speaking before the game to Dave, I thought I was facing his good (left) eye. Then I realized I was sitting to his right and that I was looking at his injured eye. It is the first time it hasn't been obvious. The scarring on the lower eyelid has receded, and the pupil has shrunk to a more normal size. Previously, as the eye tried to take in as much light as it could, the pupil took up nearly all the iris. It is now about halfway between the size of his left eye in normal light conditions and the size it was before. Progress, even slow progress, will keep his optimism alive. That and runs.

Yorkshire 197/8, Kent 179. Yorkshire won by 18 runs

30 July

I am interested in statistics only up to a point. But I don't deny part of the appeal of sport is the fact you cannot fake being good at it – and statistics are part of that scientific rigour. The score goes on the board. You can have the emperor's new clothes in art; the art of spin can rescue ineffectual politicians; even academics can write so obscurely that we imagine them much cleverer than they really are. But sport is unspinnable. The results are there in black and white.

The paradox of modern sport, then, is that it seems silly and unsophisticated, but it has an essential integrity that is often missing elsewhere. Sport is accused of being childish. But, like a child, it speaks plainly and truthfully because it has not learned to lie.

To that extent, I am interested in stats. They can help move away from opinion and towards fact. But when people start pretending that statistics aren't often misleading, or comparing one generation with another, I lose interest. An over-involvement with your own statistics also rarely helps. The best philosophy is to play as well as you can and try to win, and then the statistics will follow accordingly.

So I haven't paid much attention to the glut of statistical analysis that has followed my recent sequence. But I did take note when I read today that I needed one more hundred against Essex today to equal the great Frank Woolley's record of four consecutive first-class hundreds. His Kent record has stood since 1929. The biggest stand at Canterbury is the Frank Woolley Stand. I play literally in his shadow. A great six in the nets is termed 'in the Frank Woolley' – that is where it would end up in a game.

I got that fourth hundred and equalled the record – 108 off 112 balls out of Kent's total of 189 in 40 overs. The ball swung and seamed all day. The next highest score was 12, shared by Dave Fulton and Amjad Khan. In terms of match significance, it was easily the best of my recent hundreds. Only my 175 at Chester-le-Street in 2000 contributed a similar percentage of the Kent total.

I wish I could write some profound secrets about today's innings, insights as to how I got 108 out of 189. There are none. I started a bit loosely, needed a little luck, got going in the twenties, played nicely to fifty, concentrated harder when the game situation moved away from us, and played my shots with the tail. I am not sure I would have got a hundred today if Kent had been cruising to a high total – like in the second innings at Maidstone. I fed off the game's low-scoring tension today. That is not admirable – in fact, I should take note and put it right. I should have enough hunger to go on and on, regardless of the match situation.

My most memorable internal conversation was on 96 when I was facing the off spinner James Middlebrook. James was also in Bombay with me this winter, and in the nets there I often used my feet to him. We all do when there's no pressure. With eight wickets down and Murali – always unpredictable with the bat – at the other end, I said to myself, 'If you don't go down the track now, what exactly are you waiting for? A few weeks ago you used your feet against Azhar Mahmood bowling at 80-odd m.p.h. You should be able to do the same against an off-spinner when you've got 96 and there's eight wickets down.'

I hit it well enough, two bounces and into the lime tree at Canterbury, giving me a hundred out of 174. It wasn't the only statistic of note today. Tony Palladino, who had played only a handful of first-class games, took 6 for 41, mainly by pitching the ball up and swinging it away, not unlike the way Mark Ealham does for us. Ealy, in fact, quickly reciprocated with wickets of his own. With Essex on 164 for 7 at the close, the game has certainly moved forward.

It is Canterbury week – marquees, brass bands, straw hats and club ties – and after play the team had a drink in the President's tent. I talked to Derek Underwood. 'Above all,' he said, 'I hope you get a place on the England tour this winter. I always enjoyed touring – somehow there's less pressure than in home Tests.'

Either would be just fine with me.

Kent 189, Essex 164/7

31 July

Some games develop an inexplicable momentum of their own. Another fourteen wickets fell today, to go with seventeen yesterday. I don't think it's that bad à wicket, nor has either side bowled brilliantly. Batsmen, I think, get sucked into a 'low-scoring game' mentality that works against them feeling secure at the crease and making big scores. Low-scoring games exert a kind of mental block on batsmen and the wickets continue to tumble.

I made 32 today and played nicely enough. Maybe I, too, despite lecturing myself about the 'low-scoring game' mentality, didn't value my wicket as highly as I should have. I was caught at slip off Joe Grant, playing a loose defensive shot. So Frank Woolley's record of four consecutive hundreds has not been surpassed.

In fact, today did throw up a phenomenal statistical fact, but my sequence-ending 32 wasn't it. Today was the first time in two years that Murali has completed a first innings in the field without taking a wicket. Think about that for a moment. In all the dozens of games he has played for Lancashire, Kent and Sri Lanka, he has never failed to take a wicket in the first innings. He finished today with the not very disastrous figures of 0 for 41 off 22 overs – and he couldn't believe it. 'No wickets!' he kept saying.

Kent lead by 290 and Essex are 24 for 1. 290 should be enough.

Kent 189 & 284, Essex 183 & 24/1

August 2003

1 August

Normal service was resumed today: Murali took 6 for 61 in Essex's second innings. We have now won two of the last three championship games – we might also have won at Blackpool but for the rain – and there is an entirely different atmosphere around the whole club. The most alarming danger, relegation from the First Division, has receded and we are enjoying our cricket again. It is as if a huge weight has been lifted.

Today wasn't without alarm, but I was never properly worried. Andy Flower showed what a brilliant player of spin he is during a typically composed and assured 83. But when he played on against Alamgir Sheriyar, we were always strong favourites. James Foster also played neatly and confidently. With Chris Read, James Foster and Kent's Geraint Jones – there may be others, too, in the Second Division – England have several talented keeper-batsmen to replace Alec Stewart when he retires this summer.

Kent are finally playing with self-confidence. We must enjoy the self-belief without becoming complacent. The hardest challenge about form is to combine the hunger you have when you are out of form with the confidence you feel when things are going well. Teams, no less than players, have to know when to cash in.

Kent 189 & 284, Essex 183 & 235. Kent won by 55 runs

2 *August*

Having had a bit to do with beating Essex inside three days and thus earning ourselves Saturday off, today I rewarded myself with a day at the beach, in this instance Camber Sands on the south coast, about an hour's drive from home.

The weather continues unceasingly sunny and hot, just as my friend had predicted in March. 'It looks like God has turned off the taps,' he said. Certainly this July has been the most prolonged spell of fine weather I can ever remember. I missed the summer of 1976, the only other contender, by one year.

Romney Marsh, haunting at the best of times, looked eerily parched: a mass of rusting farm machinery, dried-out lowlands and satellite dishes. Here was a different Kent again, neither rural Arcadia nor plush commuter belt.

Camber Sands, just the other side of the Marsh, still serves up old-fashioned beach fare: fish and chips, noisy families arguing about games involving inflatable balls, asymmetric sandcastles, and flabby English men and women turning sunscreen-less pink. Though it was packed, I dozed happily enough, part reflecting on the past fortnight, part looking forward to tomorrow's game.

Having written in the Introduction that I like to 'walk by the sea', I must confess that walking was not a big part of the agenda on my day off. Nor was swimming. But I did manage two submersions in the sea. Drying off in the sun, with scarcely a shiver, I wondered if this was really England after all. 'Come on, Mum,' someone shouted as if in answer, 'give me my effing phone back!'

Rye is only a few miles from chaotic and crowded Camber Sands, but it exists in another universe. Picture-postcard pretty, Rye is England as Anglophile American spinsters might imagine it: cobbled streets, tea houses, bookshops, art galleries, small hotels, overhanging precincts and walkways, the general impression of quietness and cosiness. I enjoyed the prettiness but also felt slightly claustrophobic. A really loud and spontaneous laugh, I imagined, might bring the most disapproving looks in Rye.

Henry James, an Anglophile turned Englishman, lived here at Lamb House in Rye for the second half of his career. It is a good trick that famous writers play on their readers: we imagine them much grander and richer than they really were. Lamb House is a perfectly proportioned but by no means huge old rectory. The New York ballrooms of *Washington Square* and elegant country estates of *Portrait of a Lady* belonged to others. James owed even Lamb House to the financial support of his London admirers. It was only the emergence of the mass media, the winner-takes-all world of global cultural products, that could inspire J. K. Rowling-style artistic fortunes.

The same is even truer of sport, of course. Had Michael Jordan been born in 1880, even with exactly the same degree of talent and determination, the biggest stage he could have graced would have been his assembled home town. He would have been paid accordingly – in other words, not very much. Champions were indulged, spoilt and petted, but were never wildly rich.

It was technology, that headless horseman of history capable of changing everything without intention or care, which turned sport on its head. With the emergence of TV, sport became a branch of the mass-entertainment business, and entertainment sells. For those of us who earn a good living from sport, and sometimes complain about having to give media interviews, it is worth remembering how much we owe to television.

3 August

Today was a great one-day game that we should have won; it ended as a tie.

Before the game, while I waited for the Kent bowlers to come over to the nets, I had a brief chat with a few of the Essex players. Usual stuff – where are you guys staying? Is it any good? 'Well, it can't be worse than the hotel where we stayed in Brentwood during the Chelmsford game,' I said. 'My bedroom was an island in the middle of the M25 – what a place to get a pair!' When you're scoring runs, people laugh at your stories. Success, in that way, is very nice: you don't have to try too hard.

But the game isn't about you having a nice day. I don't play cricket wearing anti-social blinkers, but nor do I seek to have unnecessarily matey chats with opponents. When I was starting out in the Kent side, I sometimes thought one or two of our senior players spent more time being nice to the opposition than they did to their own team. The broader community thinks, 'Great bloke Smudgie/Thommo/Robbo/Matty'; your team mates think, 'Stop talking and just get the job done.' So I was glad when the other Kent players arrived and we could get on with practice not chit-chat.

Out in the middle, we batted first and I faced the first over without alarm. (It was bowled by the Pakistani Mohammad Akram, who is apparently 'now English', but that's another story.) I thought: hot day, dry wicket, white ball, big crowd – it doesn't get much better than this. Next ball – bowled for one by Tony Palladino.

The frustration of getting out when you feel good and are in the middle of some great form is equivalent to the despair you experience during a run of failures. The paths that lead to torture are much more numerous in this game than those which lead to self-satisfaction.

We took control of the innings only when Mark Ealham and Geraint Jones got together, Geraint continuing his brilliant first season with 58 and Mark hitting a fantastic 73 off 56 balls. He hit 3 sixes, one of them as big as any you'll see this year. We often say to him in the dressing room, 'You should bat with that positive intent in all competitions, all the time.'

'I know, I know,' Mark says.

After he played similarly brilliantly at Maidstone, I spoke to Glamorgan's Matt Maynard. 'Ealy used to bat like that *all* the time.'

254 – with Murali up our sleeve – should have been enough. But Andy Flower made a masterful 100 off 89 balls. In terms of making the most of his ability, knowing his own game, using his head and pacing a run chase, Andy Flower is a model of how to

bat. But when he was stumped off James Tredwell for exactly 100, Kent looked – and stayed – firm favourites.

A word about ambition realized. We have been struggling to find someone to bowl accurate yorkers 'at the death' late in the innings. Martin Saggers, who was initially left out of our team to play at Scarborough last week, desperately wants to do it. He asked me to come in early this morning to practise bowling yorkers with an old ball, so we had an extra net before warm-ups. He charged in, cursing himself for every mistake, asking questions: 'Too full? Too wide? Was that one about right?' He left the net pouring with sweat, saying, 'Better, don't you think?'

Dave Fulton threw him the ball today to bowl at the death. He took four wickets in the space of a handful of balls, three of them bowled with inslanting yorkers. He did what he has always said he could do.

It also meant we looked almost certain to win, going into the last over – bowled by Muralitharan. Essex got down to needing 9 off three balls, with the number eleven Mohammad Akram coming in. He reverse-swept his first ball for four, missed the second, and hit the last ball of the game, which bounced once over the 5 foot 6 inch Matt Walker at long-on for four. I paused for a second. Hang on a minute. If they needed five off the last ball . . . and hit a four . . . no way . . . they've tied the game. It was only then that I noticed Aftab Habib shaking his fist and celebrating.

I had been thinking so much about fielding well – go for anything in the air, make yourself as big a target as you can – that I'd scarcely considered they might get 9 (or even 8) off Murali's last three balls. We all walked off a little dazed. Did that really happen? It felt surreal, like something had gone wrong with the script or the sequencing.

Incidentally, I had enjoyed being in the field today. You have to enjoy tense, close games. Perhaps because I am batting well, perhaps because I may be on the brink of playing for England, my thoughts were positive in the field today: 'Want the ball to come to you, want to be challenged in the field, use today as an opportunity to practise being under pressure.' Not much came my way, but I enjoyed hoping something would. The real challenge, of course, is keeping that positive mindset, not retreating into fear, even *after* you have made a mistake.

More importantly, however, we are now in serious danger of being relegated from the First Division in the National League. We aren't in a position to shrug off losing two points in one hit.

The players and their wives and girlfriends stayed behind after the game for a team dinner. Murali was still in shock. 'Eight off three balls! It's never happened to me. Never! Eight off three!'

Dave Fulton got engaged today. Martin Saggers produced a glass of champagne for everyone and told me ('as the writer') that I had to propose the toast without a second's notice. Let me take back what I just said about him bowling well today . . .

Kent 254/9, Essex 254/9. Match tied

6 August

Dave Fulton is resting this week and I have been made captain for tomorrow's game against the South Africans at Canterbury.

It all happens at once, doesn't it? While I am nearer to the England team than ever, as if to sharpen the issue I am about to play England's current opponents. Talk about shop window. Now I have also been made captain (albeit temporarily) of Kent, the team I have supported for over twenty years. One of those things would be a lot to contemplate. The two happening together means I am experiencing total psychological engagement, with no slack in my reserves.

The Kent team for this game lacks its four most experienced senior players: Mark Ealham, Andrew Symonds, David Fulton and Matt Walker. That is understandable, given that we are into the second half of the season. But those who do play can still play as hard as they can. And I have always hated the idea that tourist games don't count. They are first-class fixtures, and you are still wearing a Kent cap.

I asked to speak to the team after practice today. With South Africa 1–0 up in a five-match series in England, I said simply that it was a great opportunity for Kent to play not merely for ourselves but also as representatives of English cricket. If an England touring team was one match up in an Ashes tour, and due to play Western Australia during the gap between Tests, you can be sure the WA side would think, 'We have to stuff the Poms here and ruin their momentum.' That's how I want Kent to play over the next three days. Beyond that, I understand that we have a young, untested team and are distant second favourites.

7 August

The first thing to say about captaincy is that it isn't easy. I knew that already. But knowing in the abstract is different from feeling in the flesh. Today was a reminder that 'reading the game well' is different from getting everything right as captain.

We started well. Alamgir Sheriyar and Martin Saggers did what captains all ask for: they bowled a tight line outside off stump. It was a flat wicket, and we did well to restrict the South African top order to scoring at around two an over for the first hour.

In the slips cordon, while we switched off between balls, I had an interesting chat with Rob Key about bowling strategy. He spent the winter playing against Australia, where McGrath and Co. bowl relentlessly – and with huge success – outside off stump. Rob thinks English bowlers get bored too easily and 'come inside', allowing batsmen to alleviate pressure with easy shots to leg.

I agree. But I think there is a difference between bowling wide of off stump and *just* outside off stump. As a batter, particularly when I am starting out, an easy leave is a victory for me, not for the bowler. What I ask of bowlers I play with, and fear from those

I face, is a relentless examination in which I am forced to make difficult decisions every ball: forward or back, play or leave? The more regularly those questions are asked, the quicker a batter makes a potentially fatal mistake.

That is why I believe fielding sides sometimes take too much interest in maidens and scoring rates. Keeping the opposition's scoring rate down can be evidence of bowling well – but not always. It might just be that you are bowling too wide, offering no threat to the batsmen, who are simply waiting for easy pickings as the day progresses. Not many bowling sides bowl as well after tea as they do in the morning session. Time matters in cricket.

I also think there is a difference between McGrath-style bowlers – tall, back of a length, more reliant on seam movement and accuracy than swing – and English-style swing bowlers. I would love England to unearth a Glenn McGrath (Steve Harmison has the tools to be one) but if we don't, there is no point telling English swing bowlers to bowl in a way they can't. Shorter bowlers who get less bounce and usually rely on swing have to threaten the stumps – not necessarily bowl *at* the stumps, but *near* them. A swing bowler who bowls wide of off stump with a swinging, new ball on a flat wicket is wasting the one time in the day when the odds are in favour of the bowlers.

That was what Rob Key and I were talking about, in abbreviated form, while we clapped or didn't clap balls from Martin Saggers and Alamgir Sheriyar which were left alone by South African batters. This morning they generally bowled well: Sheriyar had Gibbs caught at second slip by Matt Banes, and Saggers, though wicketless, forced Gary Kirsten to retire with a blow on the elbow.

The problems came after the new-ball spell. Our third seamer, Ben Trott (who is very much in the McGrath mode, incidentally), started well, claiming the wicket of Boeta Dippenaar, but then struggled. I desperately needed a fourth seamer, someone like Mark Ealham, to provide accuracy and control while I tried to provide an attacking threat at the other end. But there was no fourth seamer, only the spinners Rob Ferley and James Tredwell, both very young and still learning with each game. Jacques Kallis and Neil McKenzie played both of them extremely well, proving that if you use your feet to finger-spinners when the ball isn't turning much, there is little or nothing the bowler can do about it except retreat to negative, leg-side fields.

The result was that South Africa cruised to 325 for 4, with McKenzie 105 not out. In an expression of positive intent, McKenzie immediately declared, leaving us about half a session to survive before the close.

When Michael Carberry nicked a widish ball, I walked to the crease knowing that – with the Test team to be picked imminently – I was in the spotlight. A big score now might not be as important to Kent as a hundred in the championship. But in terms of personal significance, it was out on its own. I try to believe selectors are too thoughtful to be swayed by last-minute fancies. But I also know that timely runs count double.

Going in to bat late in the day is never easy, particularly after a day in the field as captain. But self-pity is the most disastrous of sporting excuses, and I silenced any negative voices by saying to myself, 'If you're going to complain about batting late in the day at Canterbury with a few thousand watching and the Test team being picked tomorrow, you don't deserve to get picked for England in the first place. It's another innings, that's all. Just bat.'

I started OK, scoring 7 off my first 7 balls. But the eighth, bowled by the young opening bowler Zondeki – who looked as if he could bowl any sequence of good balls, bad balls, wides and no balls – pitched on a length on off stump and seamed away. I nicked it to Mark Boucher and trudged off in the evening sun – chance missed, words meaningless.

My team mates said all the sensible (and true) things in the dressing room. Not much you could do about that one . . . came from nowhere . . . always worse when the bowler's spraying it, then suddenly bowls a jaffa. I sat quietly on the balcony, thinking, 'The selectors can't read too much into *that*, can they?'

It was the most reflective I have felt in a cricket shirt for months.

I was glad of the distraction of watching Rob Key and Matt Banes battle hard through to stumps. Rob has not played as well as he can this year, and Matt is getting a rare chance in the first team. Watching the game with their careers in my mind, not my own, actually helped me to stop moping around.

But I left the ground tonight wondering if the England team will be picked tomorrow or the day after, and which – if it makes any difference – might work in my favour.

I had dinner after the game with Alex Loudon and Matt Banes. After a while, I must have looked sufficiently relaxed for them to bring up the subject of my captaincy.

Alex said, 'Not bad in general, though you might try not to look at your shoes when the ball goes for four.'

Matt added, 'And it was pretty funny when you had that big debate with Saggs about where you should stand at cover, and then Kallis hit it for four exactly where you were standing before you moved.'

Aside from amusing themselves about my captaincy, Matt and Alex have a lot on their own minds at the moment. For Matt, this game may be his last chance to make it as a professional cricketer. He has played only a handful of first-team games over five years with Kent, never getting established, not even ever becoming clearly the 'next man in'. Everyone agrees that he is gutsy and battles hard. The management have been less certain as to whether he is good enough. He battled typically to 10 not out this afternoon. This evening, he was probably trying not to over-rev with this-is-my-last-chance thoughts. In fact, he is probably as glad as me to have some company.

Alex is a more natural player, a sweet striker of the ball who also bowls off-spinners that actually spin. He is not in the last chance saloon, and it shows. Cricket hasn't yet driven Alex to the same degree of despair that both Matt and I know well. Though he is a year younger than Matt, this season he has probably leap-frogged over him in the Kent pecking order. They are close friends, supportive of each other even as they jostle for the same spot. The criticism of Alex tends to be that he looks too casual and insufficiently hungry.

Perhaps some people misread his self-effacing and undemonstrative style, both as person and as player, as a lack of ambition.

Appearances this evening might have suggested light-hearted fun. But beneath the bonhomie, there was a lot going on in the minds of these three cricketers, each at some kind of a crossroads, a different moment of truth.

Matt, though he is far too proud to admit it, must be dreading failure tomorrow. He has been in good form in the second team. It is a flat wicket. There's nowhere to hide. He not only has to get runs, but get runs convincingly. Time, he will be certain, is running out.

Alex will want runs, though perhaps not so desperately, which itself may be no bad thing. He knows with equal probability that this will not be his last chance. He is still maturing as a player, and the world of second chances still exists for him. But that, too, can be a dangerous place. People offer excuses for you; the temptation is to take them – and then get stuck with them. I hope he is saying to himself: this is a great opportunity, grab it.

And me? Today I failed in a game that matters more to me than most. Tomorrow morning, people will look in their papers to see if I succeeded against South Africa. They will not care how good a ball it was, just that I failed. Did I freeze at my big moment, they will wonder. I know I didn't. But I am not a reporter, pundit or selector. Today was a quiet reminder that it is a humbling and difficult game. But it remains my hope that, rather than returning to normality, I am about to take off properly.

South Africa 325/4 declared, Kent 47/2

8 August

Matt Banes and Rob Key must have started this morning with very different mindsets. According to this morning's papers, Rob is about to be recalled to the England side to bat number five in place of Anthony McGrath. Two days ago, Christopher Martin-Jenkins wrote that the choice lay between Graham Thorpe and me; today he suggested it is Rob who will be selected. A big score here and a Test recall, and Rob will be right back on track.

Matt will have been contemplating something much simpler: survival, at the crease and in his job. Having battled hard last night, he will have been hoping to get through the new ball this morning, then prove his point.

For a while, as they blunted the opening spells by Zondeki and Willoughby, it looked good for both of them. Just as it was starting to get easier, Matt dragged an inswinger on to his stumps. A stubborn 15 off 60 balls will not change anyone's mind. He looked inconsolable.

Rob played confidently for 47, batting with some of the untroubled authority that has impressed people over the years. Though Alex Loudon is only a year younger than Rob, they are separated by over 100 first-class games and seven Tests. Alex's 63 was his first significant score for Kent. He has scored a big first-class hundred for Durham University, but people don't remember what they didn't see.

While Alex was batting with Geraint Jones, Graeme Smith, the South African captain, bumped into me on the stairs outside the dressing room. He arrived in England as a 22-year-old captain under huge pressure from dissenting voices at home. He has responded with back-to-back double hundreds. Whatever happens in the rest of the series, his achievements are already extraordinary. We said only a few words to each other – I said, 'Well batted,' he replied, 'Well batted yourself' – but he was courteous in exactly the right way, as if to say: this is now, while we are not competing – things will change when we are competing, and we both understand that, don't we?

On the field, we deserved more than 235 with the bat, and we bowled better second time round. Martin Saggers, in particular, bowled excellent lines – not too wide – and picked up the scalps of Gibbs and Kallis.

After the day's play, Ivo Tennant interviewed me for the *Sunday*

Times. Did I think I was in the Test side? No, I thought Rob Key was in – on the basis that the press are usually right.

I had dinner at home with my family and a few friends and tried not to talk about England selection. Next time. Maybe.

South Africa 325/4 declared & 145/4, Kent 235

9 *August*

Just after setting off to drive to Canterbury this morning, about two hundred yards from my house, my mobile rang. I didn't recognize the number and thought about forwarding it to my voicemail. But I took the call. It was Geoff Miller, the England selector.

> GM: I'm calling on behalf of David Graveney, the Chairman of Selectors, who is ill in bed . . .
>
> [Was I close, I wondered, and Geoff Miller was ringing to say, 'You're not in, but don't lose heart.']
>
> GM . . . and I'm ringing to give you the good news . . . [not close! – in! in! in!] . . . that you've been selected to represent England in the third Test [in! in! in!] at Trent Bridge against South Africa. I've spoken to Paul Millman [Kent's Chief Executive] and he's got all the administrative details – congratulations.

That final sentence – 'administrative details' – gave me just enough time to slow my heartbeat enough to speak calmly.

> ES: That's good news. Thanks.
>
> [There was a pause, as if one of us was not hearing right.]
>
> GM: Did you get that, Ed? You've been picked to play for England against South Africa in the third Test.
>
> ES: Yes, I got it. That's good news. If I don't sound as ecstatic as I might, it's because I'm driving and I don't want to crash my car.

GM: That's fine. We'll be in touch with more details. Well done. Drive safely.

In! In! In! An England player! I have been telling people since I was three that I would be an England player. Now I will be. In! In! In!

I rang my dad. By then, perhaps three minutes after hearing the news, my initial feeling of light-headed elation had receded. I had a game to play that day – and a car to drive. I recovered a little perspective, a yes-that-is-rather-good-news-isn't-it tone in my voice.

Dad hadn't. He sounded like he might faint. 'No, it's not "good news" – it's amaaazing, Ed, amaaazing. England. My God, let me sit down.'

By chance, my sister was staying with my parents last night, and I could now hear her screaming in the background. She was jumping up and down shouting, 'He's in the team! [scream] In the team! [scream] In the team! I always, always, said he would do it!'

It was lovely to think of my refined, urbane older sister being as silly as an irrational schoolgirl. In fact, even though she knew I was on the phone to Dad, and her call would inevitably go through to my voicemail, she shouted, 'I'm calling you now from my mobile!'

The longer this went on – my sister screaming and jumping up and down, my dad sounding like he'd just seen a miracle, my mother a quiet voice of sanity in the background – the more I recovered a sense of balance. It was almost as if my family was living out the hysterical elation for me, and I could get on with refocusing my mind on performing well – first of all today for Kent, then next week for England.

Of course I was thrilled – for my family, and for me. I knew that my friends, even those who don't understand cricket, would also feel the elation of my happiness. I thought about all the coaches (in England, Australia and India) who had seen something in me, run the extra mile, stood up in selection meetings, given up their time, taken a close interest in my game. Now I had the chance to pay them back by performing well.

But after that initial, soaring elation, I quickly recovered a degree of level-headedness. I have prepared for this moment, and I have a definite plan. My ambition has always been to excel for England, not just play for England. You cannot excel for England without first getting picked – that is obvious. But I think my best chance of playing well is not to use my full emotional range celebrating the first bit.

Once, a great ambition had been to go to Cambridge. When I read the admission letter [in! in! in!] as a seventeen-year-old, I remember thinking almost immediately, 'Now I want (need?) a First.' The difference, of course, is that I had three and half years between being admitted to Cambridge and sitting Finals. I will join the England team in three days.

So much for self-controlled ambition. After putting the phone down to my dad, I reached for my CD of Bruce Springsteen's *Born to Run* and played the title track at full volume.

By the time I got into the dressing room at about nine o'clock, most of the team knew I had been picked. There were hugs from some, handshakes from others. Dave Fulton wasn't there (he was seeing an eye specialist) but he happened to be on the phone to Ian Brayshaw when I arrived. 'Ed's been picked,' Ian explained, 'I'll pass you over to him now.'

'Ed, I just found out literally one second ago,' Dave said. 'I haven't had a chance to think yet. But just put your "A" game out there and be yourself.'

It should have been him, two years ago, when he was in the middle of a streak like mine now. Now he is wondering if he will ever see properly again.

As captain, I said a few things while the team went through our stretches on the outfield. 'It's emotional when team mates get picked for England, and thanks for all your support, but let's remember that Saggs and Keysey missed out in the England shake-up. And if you really want to make me happy, you won't get distracted by the England stuff, but simply focus on competing hard today and coming out of the game with some credit.'

The good news for our bowlers was that the wicket started to turn prodigiously. James Tredwell, who has a very balanced, calm temperament, bounced back from taking some stick in the first innings and took 3 for 75. Rob Ferley chipped in with 2 for 35, and South Africa declared on 243 for 7, setting us 334 in two and a bit sessions.

At lunch, rather than endlessly having to repeat the same story to different papers, I agreed to give a brief press conference for all of them. I tried to answer the questions honestly but undemonstratively. I was about to bat in a first-class game, and, anyway, hasn't everyone tired yet of the 'lost for words/best day of my life' stuff?

What had revolutionized my batting? I said it hadn't changed all that much actually. Was I too old to be making my test debut? I was tempted to say, 'Yes, three weeks ago I was twenty-five, which is OK, but now I've turned twenty-six I'm definitely too old,' but settled for plain 'No'.

Kate Laven of the *Sunday Telegraph* asked me whether I would be intimidated by sharing a dressing room with Alec Stewart and Nasser Hussain. When I said 'No', she asked me to explain what sort of person I was.

'I think that's for other people to say, don't you?'

'But I don't know anything about you at all! Tell me something!'

'Well, I've published a partly autobiographical book, so that might tell you something.'

My primary thoughts were about batting.

When I did, after Rob Key was out for 49, Herschelle Gibbs greeted me in the middle with, 'The coach has got his notebook open, let's give him something to write down.' I wouldn't say there was any sledging in this game (I have no idea, of course, what they were saying in Afrikaans), but the level of competitive chat definitely rose during my second innings. That was to be expected. Today was a chance for me – and them – to win an early psychological battle.

I survived a big appeal for caught behind first ball from Paul Adams. It was given not out, but I realized that Adams was enjoying the turning pitch as much as our spinners had. I started as fluently as I have throughout this spell, hitting 6 fours off 20 balls – mostly off Adams, but also including two hooks off Zondeki. But on 27 I chipped a check drive back to the left-arm spinner Robbie Peterson. One of those frustrating cameos. 'Hard hands [meaning I go 'at the ball'], eh, that's in the coach's notebook,' Gibbs added as I walked off.

In fact, though I was disappointed to fail and disappointed not to help Kent save the game, I wasn't too upset not to bat all day against South Africa. I quite like the idea of being an unknown quantity. They have seen I can bat, but not for long enough to know the total package.

At the outfield gate, in an ironic moment novelists would like, Matt Banes passed me on the way to bat. It will probably be either his last innings for Kent or the first in his reincarnation as a first-team player. He made another attritional start, but fell for 24, on the brink – once again – of being able to express himself.

Despite 75 from Michael Carberry and 30 not out by Alex Loudon, we struggled to master the turning conditions and were all out for 232. Mine was the only wicket, in fact, not to fall to Paul Adams, who goes into next week's Test with a career-best 9 for 79 behind him.

Almost every member of the South African team said, 'Well done on getting picked,' as they shook my hand at the end of the game. I think it was one of their selectors who added, 'I can't really say good luck, but you know what I mean.' They have been a model touring team all week: courteous, hard working, together.

I gave an interview on the outfield with Sky TV. 'Apparently your parents had booked a holiday in Italy next week. Do you think they'll cancel and come to watch your debut?' I didn't know. 'Well, in that case I can be the first person to tell you that they've cancelled and are coming to Nottingham!' Gossip obviously travels quickly when you are in the England team. It also looks as though not only you, but also those close to you, become public property.

Heading back to the dressing room, I saw Alan Samson, who published *Playing Hard Ball* with Little, Brown. I got us both a drink and sat outside the famous members' stand at Canterbury. 'Cheers, you're the first person I've had a drink with to celebrate!'

'What are you celebrating?'

'Getting picked for England.'

'Christ, I didn't know. I feel privileged. What a day to choose to come and watch you!'

The pile of administrative pieces of paper above my seat in the dressing room has tripled in one day. Call this number, read this message, send these details, reply to this person. Now would be a good time to have a manager and a secretary.

Then there is the phone. I am already associating my mobile ring-tone with a sinking feeling: obligation, politeness, the dissipation of emotional energy, happy voices getting short-changed by my short answers.

I would leave my phone permanently off – but for the happy moments it brings. Rahul Dravid, for example, sent two text messages. I read them after today's play, sitting on the players' bench outside the dressing room. It was on the same bench, when I was in despair at my poor form in 2000, that Rahul sat with me and said quietly, 'Don't get desperate – it will come.' The runs came, and I have never felt desperate since.

By chance, Richard Ellison, the former Kent and England swing bowler (and fellow Old Tonbridgian), was watching today's play from the dressing room. I have known him since I was a boy, when he was a hero of mine. In those days, imagining myself a future England fast bowler, he used to let me bowl at him in the nets. Now, twenty years on, he just said, 'Express yourself, Ed.'

Back in Wye, I dropped my kit off, switched off my mobile and went to Alex's house to escape my landline ring-tone. I didn't have to talk too much about cricket, but instead listened to snippets of other people's conversations while receding into happy anonymity on the sofa. I didn't want to talk about selection, or celebrate, or even be congratulated. I wanted to come down slowly from the day's extreme emotions, to return to a normal psychological tempo, to enjoy the calm before the storm. I needed a warm backdrop, nothing more.

At midnight I walked home, knowing that, no matter what follows, life will never be quite the same again. Tomorrow I will wake up an England player, not an England hopeful. I feel shaken to my shoes, exhilarated, scared, happy, ready, unprepared, controlled, emotional, grateful, determined. I plan to answer any negative voices with, 'If not now, then *when*?'

But now I have to sleep.

South Africa 325/4 declared & 243/7 declared, Kent 235 & 232. South Africa won by 101 runs

10 August

I thought I would wake up this morning with the simple, happy thought, 'England player.' In fact, my first thought was, 'For God's sake, go away and leave me alone.'

Last night I remembered to leave my mobile off overnight, so it didn't wake me up. There are still plenty of messages on it that I haven't even listened to. Like most cricketers, I give out my mobile number to journalists, reporters, other people who might want something. If I want to get away from that stuff, I just switch it off – something I do very rarely.

My home landline is different. Only my family and friends know the number and I always answer when it rings. So I was a bit surprised that it rang twenty times this morning between 8 and 9 a.m. No one I know well would ring me relentlessly at eight in the morning the day after I got picked for England. Eventually, worn down and woken up, I took the cable out of the wall socket.

A few minutes later, there was a loud knocking at the door. That is even more unusual at 8.45 in the middle of the Kent countryside. I went to the door groggily. It was a neighbour who had been listening to Radio 5 Live all morning. 'They said on the radio, "If anyone knows Ed Smith, can you please go and wake him up because we're really keen to interview him on the phone," so I thought I'd pass on the message.'

'Thanks, but I'm trying to sleep.'

I later found out, when I braced myself to listen to all my messages, that Radio Kent had somehow got my home number and distributed it to the rest of the organization, including Radio 5. They rang home twenty times and my mobile twenty-five times. One of their messages said, 'Where are you? You're like the Scarlet Pimpernel you are, Ed [a reference beyond me]! We've *seen* you on Sky Sports, we've *read* your quotes in the paper, it's Radio 5 here, we'd love to talk to you.'

The implication was that I had badly let them down. I had favoured television and the press, but snubbed radio. Nothing could be less true, not least because I love radio. In fact, Sky TV, as I wrote yesterday, turned up at Canterbury and pointed a camera at me on the outfield. I dealt with the newspapers in one short press conference outside the press box at lunchtime. Beyond that, I have given no interviews to anyone. I would have been more than happy to speak to someone at BBC radio, but not at 8 a.m. on Sunday morning.

I hope this doesn't continue. I don't enjoy making enemies, but I do value my privacy.

I wanted to practise today. I might be in good form, but there are one or two things I want to work on before joining the Test team. No matter how single-minded I am, it will be hard to rise above all the distractions during the two days' practice before the Test. Alex Loudon – guessing as much – offered to give me some throw-downs. 'My turn to throw,' he said, 'I'm not even bringing a bat.'

On the hottest, most unpleasantly humid day of the year, we met up at the nets in Canterbury, where the temptation to sit under the sprinklers was sometimes greater than the urge to hit cricket balls.

I wanted to re-create some of the angles of delivery of the South African bowlers, particularly Makhaya Ntini. He bowls from very wide of the crease, almost impossibly wide, proving you can 'fall away' and still bowl at 90 m.p.h. I've heard this unusual slant makes him awkward, particularly when you aren't used to it. I am trying to get 'my lines right' in practice so it is less alien in the middle. So

I tried to get Alex to throw the ball from exactly the right position on the bowling crease.

Then Pollock. Ntini and Pollock have bowled well in tandem this series because they are so different: Ntini attacking, brisk, charging in from wide of the crease; Pollock, metronomic, relentless, classically close to the stumps. Against 'Pollock' throw-downs, I wanted in particular to practise leaving the ball. He constantly asks difficult questions (to return to my conversation with Rob Key), and it is essential that you feel confident where your off stump is, not get 'drawn', playing defensively wide.

It is, of course, much easier against throw-downs with old balls on an Astroturf wicket than against international bowlers out in the middle. But I told myself that I was not only practising technique but also good, disciplined clear-thinking. We use the term 'Test Match throw-downs' to mean practising with match-like intensity, not just enjoying the pleasure of striking the ball well. 'We should do Test Match throw-downs, don't you reckon, Ed?' 'Probably appropriate, yes!'

All the time we were trying to re-create facing Ntini and Pollock, I was batting as if I was at the start of my first Test innings: precise, watchful, low risk. After a while, I wanted to practise expressing myself too, and we laughed about changing the match situation. 'Right, I've got a big score now, and I'm playing well, do you want sweepers out on the boundary or are you sticking with attacking fields?'

I didn't spend too long practising in top gear – just long enough to remind myself how great it feels to be on top as a batter. I don't want to turn up at the England camp batting fearfully or differently. What I do want is to be well prepared and thinking clearly.

I wanted to practise fielding specifics too. England new boys tend to field at short leg. I don't field there for Kent, so I caught 40 short-leg catches after my net. In some ways, catching is like batting: 'Stay still, trust yourself, don't guess, just react.' Fielding well, like being a positive force in the dressing room, will be one way of making a contribution in the Test.

Today was more unpleasantly hot than any day I have known in Australia, India or South Africa. Maybe that is why my legs feel weak and tired and my whole body feels un-dynamic and lazy. Or maybe it is a skilful subconscious device for preserving energy until I really need it. Or maybe it is nerves, and I will stay like this until (and maybe after) I've faced my first ball in Test cricket.

When will I start to feel normal again? I'd love to know the answer.

11 *August*

Anxiety makes us risk-averse, risk aversion means we arrive early – can't afford to be late! – being early means having dead time on our hands, dead time fosters anxious introspection. It is the vicious cycle of concern.

So before the dinner date with that beautiful girl who you've finally had the nerve to ask out, instead of allowing an absurd amount of time for extra traffic, then arriving so early that you've nothing to do other than memorize the wine list, choose a dessert, and generally look lost and like you've been stood up – you'd be far better off going to a gallery, cleaning the house, going for a run, rushing a bit. You'll have more to say and say it more naturally.

All this I know well. So how much time did I allow for the drive from Kent to Nottingham, where I join the England team tonight? Oh, not long – only about eight hours. I mean, what's the worst that can happen? I could break down on the M25, injure myself trying to fix it myself, then get lost trying to find a garage. Guessed it in one.

I am running out of ways of writing 'it was another very hot day', but it was. Cars dehydrate in hot weather. So somewhere on the Kent stretch of the M25, I noticed my engine thermometer was pointing at the red danger zone. I stopped at a service station and opened the bonnet. There seemed to be a great deal of hissing and unnecessary hotness. More water, I decided, was the cure.

Using a rag to open the water coolant tank, after half a turn I realized this might not be such a good idea. It felt like unscrewing a Coke can that had been vigorously shaken and then heated to just below boiling point.

Boiling water sprayed out, most of it on to the rest of the engine, a little on to my hand and shirt sleeve, the rest on to the pavement. Mistake. First thought: I am going to get burned. Second thought: that could have been much, much worse. Amid the mess, I wasn't entirely sure how badly I had been scalded. I managed at least to screw the top back on, close the bonnet and decide to pursue professional help.

Was there a garage near here? My car should be able to make a few more miles without exploding. Oh sure, someone explained, just round the corner, first exit off the little roundabout, then third exit off the big roundabout. Anyone familiar with Thurrock, a vast complex of roundabouts, warehouses and super-stores, might sympathize with me: what is the difference between a small round-about and a large one? After forty minutes of seeing the same signs for 'Huge Discounts!' and 'Kids Eat Free' coming round and round, I admitted that I seemed to be going around in a circle. I rang the garage and asked them to stay on the line while they directed me to the parking lot. 'No need to do that, sir, it's easy: first exit off the little roundabout, then third exit off the big roundabout.'

'Perhaps you could just stay on the line? Thanks.'

When I arrived, the receptionist asked, 'Do you have a service appointment, sir?'

'No, I've broken down unexpectedly.'

'Sorry, nothing until next Thursday.'

'I think I just need someone to take a very quick look at it – might be curable in seconds.'

'Eleven on Thursday any good?'

'Not ideal. I'll be playing against South Africa in my first Test Match.'

'Friday afternoon then?'

This wasn't working. I walked from reception on to the work floor and asked around for a mechanic who liked cricket.

'If you can fix my car, it'll be a patriotic act – by getting me to Nottingham on time and reducing my stress level, you'll increase the chances of me getting some runs!'

He agreed to have a look and walked to my car. He peered under the bonnet and grabbed a couple of plastic tubes. 'Nope, no chance of getting to Nottingham – better call the AA and get towed. Sorry.'

'Are you absolutely sure – there's no chance it might just need more water?'

'Well, we *could* try that, I suppose. I'll get a watering can.'

A few minutes later he was pronouncing a miracle.

'The temperature's gone right down again! She just needed a little water! Amazing. Good luck on Thursday.'

I tipped him heavily, bought two bottles of water – one for the car, one for me – and felt grateful for the extra time I had allowed. I must remember to anticipate terrible traffic next time I have a date with a beautiful girl.

I checked into the hotel at about eight. Walking towards the lift, I bumped into Marcus Trescothick, who stopped and said simply, 'Congratulations, mate.'

Of all the England players, I know Marcus least well. We have never, so far as I can remember, had a conversation. It would be harder for him, I guessed, to say the right things to someone he hardly knew. He had scarcely seen me play, let alone had time to form the opinion of whether I 'had it'. I was keen to avoid the impression that he ought to stand around saying things he didn't believe when he would probably much rather be getting some rest and privacy before the pressure of the Test.

I said: 'Thanks. There's nothing we're supposed to do with the England set-up tonight, is there? [I knew there wasn't.] See you tomorrow.'

Upstairs in my room, unpacking felt odd. I shouldn't really have much to unpack. Tomorrow, I will be given England shirts, sweaters, tracksuits, T-shirts, waterproofs, shorts, training tops, sweatshirts, baseball caps and (hopefully) a real England cap.

Why, then, have I brought most of the above, only in their Kent incarnations? Well, the entire reserves of England kit might have been lost. You just never know. You could break down on the M25, burn yourself trying to fix it, then get lost trying to find a garage.

Kent versus Worcestershire was on Sky Sports. As I watched Michael Carberry and Andrew Symonds bat brilliantly, I found myself thinking: 'Good old Canterbury, what a lot of happy memories! What a great ground. Look, they're screening the Kent dressing room – Walks . . . Alex . . . Keysey . . . they all look to be having a fun, relaxed time up there. What a great bunch of lads! We're winning too. I wish I could be . . .'

Well, of all the sentimental, backward-looking, unhelpful trains of thought, that one just about takes the cake. I quickly replied: 'You've been there plenty of times, and you will be again. While you *were* there – much as you enjoyed it – part of the plan was to get to *here*. Now you're here, for God's sake be fully present. You can't do anything to help the Kent team by nostalgic over-attachment. The best thing you can do for them, yourself and England is belong here and play well.'

I have felt nicely at home here ever since.

So much for me. Anyone reading this book will realize that I come from a close family. What will Mum, Dad and Becky be going through when (hopefully) I play for England on Thursday?

Dad will certainly be the most worried. He knows better than anyone how much it matters to me, how hungry I am to do well. He has thrown more balls at me, watched more innings, made more suggestions, listened more than anyone else. That is normal. Less normal is that his greatest gift – as a novelist and teacher – is the ability imaginatively to inhabit the lives of others. He often understood what I felt without being told.

But now he will be wondering how he and I can be so alike in some ways and yet so completely different. He would freely admit that he wouldn't have liked the pressure of playing for England. Yet he knows that I probably will. He may well end up being more nervous than me.

My mother will be trying to explain to him that I am me, and

Dad is Dad. Ed's wanted this all his life, she'll say, so there's no point worrying about him now. Mum's big fear will be typically motherly: please don't let him be humiliated! So long as I don't slip over under a sky-er at long on, or run out the captain, or collapse in a heap and get bowled playing a reverse sweep, she will take whatever success or failure that comes my way with an even-handed sense of perspective. She wants me to do well, of course she does. But she has never confused – as it is easy to do – how much people achieve with how well they behave as human beings. She is also the only one of my immediate family who fears, deep down, what the inevitable toughness needed to make it at the top might do to me. She wouldn't think I suspect as much – still less ever say anything. But I think she believes running other races will matter more than playing for England against South Africa. Strangely, I have found that a nice philosophy to be around recently, no matter how much – for now – I disagree with it.

Where parents start out as protectors, siblings get to know each other as adversaries. Having known me first as an opponent, my sister will have a more straightforward attitude to my Test career: kill them! You've been telling me how good you are for twenty-six years. It's about time you showed everyone else. Show off! Sod the critics! Take it out on someone else! Don't listen too much, for God's sake don't intellectualize, just get out there and play. Worry about Ed? You must be kidding. I know him. I mean, I've *seen* him. Always had an unbearable expression when he won, which was far too often. Then he'd call me a cheat. *Unbearable*.

Beneath the broadsides – which I enjoy – she also will be the most emotional and, should I do anything very good, the most likely to cry. I hope she will forgive me for giving the game away, but beneath the cashmere this Kensington girl has a strong Celtic streak.

They will sit together at Trent Bridge, each knowing different sides of me, each thinking they know what's inside my head. What sort of conversations will they have? [This is making me laugh.]

DAD: He looks nervous.

BECKY: No he doesn't.

MUM: It's his first Test, of course he'll be a bit nervous.

DAD: Speak quietly, by the way, you never know who's sitting around us.

BECKY: I know, I wish that awful couple would move.

MUM: That poor South African has been bowling all morning – he must be exhausted.

BECKY: That's the whole idea, Mum, *exhaust* them.

[And so on for seven hours.]

12 August

I am one of the first to go down to breakfast. Duncan Fletcher arrives soon after. 'It's Ed, isn't it? Duncan Fletcher. Welcome.'

Ashley Giles sits next to me and says, 'Congratulations – great effort.'

Mark Butcher, yawning while ordering Earl Grey tea, is next to arrive. 'It's unbelievable – you get here a day early, go to bed early and then can't sleep because the bed is the most uncomfortable thing ever.'

'I feel exhausted,' he adds, coughing. 'I think I've got some flu bug as well.' He settles into the T2 arts section of *The Times*. 'Just your sort of thing, I reckon Ed, T2? The essential guide to what's going on. God, sorry, old boy, forgot to say congrats.'

I don't mind at all.

While the others have a quiet morning, the potential debutants – James Kirtley, Glen Chappell, Gareth Batty and me – have to go through an individual medical examination. Apart from finding out whether I am in one piece, the medical is necessary for insurance purposes, in case of injury. So my first official duty as an England player is to lie on a hotel bed being examined by the England team doctor.

I am expected at Trent Bridge before the rest of the team. The England press officer, Mark Hodgson, has organized a press conference so that I can deal with all interview requests in one go rather than spend the whole day being followed around by journalists who are all asking the same questions.

But I wasn't the first into the home dressing room as I expected to be. Alec Stewart has already set up camp. His bats, all five of them, are already lined up by the table in one corner. His three different pairs of cricket shoes, each of them scrubbed and pristine, sit on the shelf above his clothes pegs. Both his batting and wicket-keeping pads, buckles fastened at the back, are standing up on the floor next to his bats. So it's true what they say about Mr Immaculate. 'Congratulations, Ed! Well done. I think your box of kit is here next to me,' he says, without any suggestion in his voice that he has said those words to about fifty different people.

Nasser Hussain is in residence as well, sitting in the opposite corner of the dressing room from Alec and me. He walks briskly over when I arrive. 'Well done, it's a great achievement and you deserve it.' Sometimes it can be difficult to tell when Nasser is taking the piss, but this time he isn't. 'Talk about funny old game, last time I saw you, you'd just got a pair at Chelmsford. What odds would you have got then on us two playing a Test match together later in the season?'

I laugh. 'Twenty to one?'

'More like twenty thousand to one! Who would have guessed it, me playing in a Test match with a jazzer like Ed Smith?' (A jazzer is a synonym for posh cricketer – named after the jazzy, striped caps of public school cricket teams.) 'I've seen it all now. Ed "the jazzer" Smith . . .'

If Nasser sounds direct, he is. But my guess is that he thinks I am fairly confident and couldn't care less about being called a jazzer (misleading as it might be). He is absolutely right. In fact, sometimes people who dish out jokey abuse like that help you to settle in.

I should say at this point that I have one very simple approach to dressing-room life: be utterly thick-skinned and insensitive about yourself. I try to be completely indifferent to barbs, mickey-taking, criticism, cliques, opinions – indifferent even to 'not being rated'. Let people think what they like. You cannot change their minds with words or thoughts, only with actions, only by run-scoring. Whatever preconceptions my new England team mates may have about me will soon disappear if I bat well in an important Test match. This is a very important Test match. One hour's good batting under pressure on Thursday or Friday, and most people won't even remember what they thought about me before the game – so let them think what they want. I just want to play well.

I attempt not to look too excited as I put on my new kit, my new England kit. I try on all the different tracksuits, T-shirts, training tops and white shirts. The only thing I leave in its plastic pack is the England sweater, that plain white sweater – no stripes – with just three navy lions and a crown. I won't touch that until I have been officially picked (touch wood) on Thursday morning.

Downstairs from the dressing room, the same stairs I will walk down on my way out to bat in the game itself, one of the reception rooms has been set up for a press conference. The three chairs at the front face an auditorium of about forty journalists. I think I am the only player – probably because I am both completely new to the England set-up and am likely to play – who is giving a press conference.

Most of the questions – about form and nerves and the 'step up' to Test cricket – were standard, but others were a bit more complex. How did I explain the fact that I was a late developer? Well, am I a late developer? I thought most batsmen were at their best in their late twenties and early thirties – I have just turned twenty-six.

Richard Hobson of *The Times* asked if I saw myself as a standard-bearer for county cricket. That was a good question, inviting me to set myself up as a defender of county cricket against the fast-track system of picking players straight from the Academy. A controversial answer would make good news copy. But, in truth, I am neither 'against' the Academy nor has anyone appointed me to be a standard-bearer of county cricket. I said I am just here to play as well as I can, for myself and for the England team.

Then they moved to my off-field life. How did I find the time to write books and write for newspapers? I sensed the implication was that my dedication to the game was half-hearted and that only this year had I buckled down. The *Sunday Telegraph* wrote as much a few days ago. Sadly, it isn't true. I wish I could blame moderate form in some previous years on a wild past or indifference to my career. In fact, I have always been obsessively focused. The reasons for success and failure – in my case, anyway – are more complicated than simply giving up distractions and trying harder.

As for finding time to write, there are sixteen waking hours in a day, and even I can't spend all of them in the nets. Some people go fishing, some watch films, some play with their kids, I write. I write, I explained, partly because I enjoy writing, but also because getting away from cricket for an afternoon during the season or for a month in the off-season actually helps me to play better. It is my restorative balance. I always wanted to be a professional cricketer. It wasn't a difficult choice for me, despite the myth that I was tempted by other careers. Having decided to play cricket, I play it all out, as fully as I possibly can. Writing has to fit in around my ambition to be as good a cricketer as I possibly can be – not the other way around.

Did I consider myself an oddity 'as an intellectual' within the community of professional sport? I said that reports about my intelligence were unreliable. On Sunday a newspaper wrote that I had a brain the size of a planet; on Monday a newspaper wrote that I had a brain the size of the Isle of Wight – my brain was obviously shrinking at such a fast rate that by the time the game started on Thursday, it would be the size of a pea. That got a laugh and was the end of the press conference.

Duncan speaks briefly to the squad in the dressing room before practice. He mentions the previous Test defeat but doesn't dwell on it. 'We know what we have to put right and work on, let's do so today and take that good momentum into Thursday's game.' This week, Duncan has received more criticism than at any time in his career. Geoff Boycott, writing in the *Sun*, wrote a savage article, arguing that Duncan was killing cricket in this country.

Practice under Duncan Fletcher is organized and well drilled.

The routine today is ground fielding, then catching, then nets, then time for any extra personal practice. There is a whiteboard propped up on the outfield outlining which bowlers should bowl at which batsmen. Marcus Trescothick, who has an injured finger, does not want to net, which means the line-up is: Vaughan and Butcher, Hussain and Smith, Stewart and Flintoff, and so on.

But fielding first. After a long ground-fielding session, Michael Vaughan asks if I usually field in the slips. England dropped a few in the slips last week. I said no, but I sometimes field in the gully. 'Join in with the slip fielding group and we'll decide later.' So for half an hour Phil Neale (England manager and coaching assistant) throws to Duncan, who nicks catches to Mark Butcher, Ashley Giles and me in a gully cordon. I caught every one, which pleases me most of all from a psychological perspective: despite the inevitable nerves, I don't feel tight. In fact, I am loving the sense of a blank sheet of paper that comes with joining a new team.

While Michael Vaughan and Mark Butcher net, I pad up next to Nasser Hussain. When we walk into the parallel nets, he says with a smile, 'Now listen, Ed, don't make me look stupid in there.' Nothing could be further from my mind. In some ways, your first batting session is the most nerve-racking aspect of joining a new team. Alec Stewart, Mark Butcher and Andrew Flintoff are watching from the side; Michael Vaughan, still wearing his pads after his own net, is talking to Duncan Fletcher from behind the bowler's arm. They will be more than curious about what they see.

The bowlers in my net are Steve Harmison, Glen Chappell and James Anderson. I straight-drove my first ball and heard Andrew Flintoff shout, 'Great shot, Ted!' He repeated the shout every time I played a shot that gave him any opportunity to praise. By the end of my net, Alec Stewart and Mark Butcher are chuckling, saying, 'Look at Lord Ted!' When I walk out, Alec adds, 'I'll tell you how well you are playing: from a distance, I thought you were Mick [Michael Vaughan].'

Enough. It's games that count. Don't get carried away. No one remembers nets. No one cares about practice. Peak for Thursday, not Tuesday.

There are meetings at the hotel scheduled for this evening, then a quiet dinner. Not long after that, I expect to fall into a nicely tired sleep.

13 August

'Get done today what you need to do for tomorrow,' was Duncan Fletcher's injunction about today's practice session. For me, that means batting practice as usual and then some specific fielding practices. I have been told that I am the designated short-leg fielder and, as I don't field there for Kent, I want to work on it today.

Duncan says he has spotted some errors in the way most English short-leg fieldsmen turn to get catches over their shoulder. It concerns subtle changes in footwork, and keeping your eyes on the ball as you turn. He walks through the steps I should take both for catches over my right shoulder and then for catches over my left shoulder.

We do about twenty minutes' short-leg catching, practising turning using his method, and staying down as the ball is hit. It will be a challenge, fielding somewhere new in the biggest game of my life, but even short leg has its benefits: first, it is close to the action so I will feel central and involved; secondly, I am a left-handed catcher, and lots of good short legs (most famously Tony Lock, but also Dave Fulton, who is the best I have ever seen) have been left-handed.

After my net, Michael Vaughan asks to have a quick chat with me. We have both just finished batting and we stand to the side of the nets with our pads on, looking out at the pitch. 'If there's anything you want to ask me, feel free to do so. Above all,' he adds with a smile, pointing with a Gunn & Moore bat to tomorrow's wicket, 'if you get a bad ball out there, give it a whack.'

Duncan also has a chat with me. He likes to get to know players and the way they play before leaping in with advice, but he has a few general comments about Test cricket. I have no idea whether either Duncan or Michael thinks I should be in the team, but at this stage I don't care. I simply want to play well.

After practice, I carefully put new spikes in my fielding shoes. Alec Stewart, watching the debutant lining up new spikes on the ground, is amused and impressed by my attention to detail. 'Good lad. I never saw that other Cambridge man, Mike Atherton, doing anything like that – he was lucky to have clean socks, let alone new spikes!'

'How about lunch at Hooter's, Ed?' asks Freddie Flintoff. Hooter's, I discover, is an American-style diner with a twist: all the waitresses are wearing the skimpiest outfits imaginable. It is, apparently, a famous Nottingham attraction, particularly among sportsmen.

I turn up later than the rest, and by chance I'm wearing a recently ironed formal blue shirt. 'I don't think they get too many shirts like that in Hooter's!' Freddie laughs. Freddie, James Anderson, Glen Chappell and Steve Harmison are already tucking into a vast array of sandwiches and spare ribs and chicken wings. I order yet more food and pick up the conversation about music and films. 'That's rubbish, that film . . . this is a great song . . . no it's not . . . you've got dreadful taste in music, Jimmy . . .'

It is the first 'normal' conversation I have had since joining the England squad. It's great to get a break from the serious advice, and the 'Good lucks' and 'What do you think the team is going to be?', and being around decision makers. That is all fine too, and I am more than happy being scrutinized and talking seriously about cricket. But I am certainly ready for a spell in this environment – 1960s American music, simple food, conversation without hidden significance – especially the day before my first Test, after two days of serious practice and discussion.

It is surprising how easily unwritten rules are understood by sportsmen. This is not the context for worthy questions about cricket, or analysing the England management. Instead, we talk about Blackpool. 'Did you go out in the evening, Ed? – a bit rough, eh!' We eat, chat, tell stories, laugh – that is the understood code here. The most unlikely thing for anyone to say in this context would be, 'So which one of us is going to get left out of the team tomorrow?' Because someone is going to be: there are thirteen in the squad, and two must miss out.

My food arrives – an enormous chicken sandwich and a huge rack of ribs. There are looks of amazement from the four northern fast bowlers. 'Don't look too shocked,' I said. 'Just because I'm a batter and from Kent doesn't mean I can't eat with the best of them . . .'

While I work my way through my food, a waitress – it is funny how quickly you stop noticing they are wearing scarcely any clothes – asks us all to autograph a menu, which can then be framed and hung on the wall of the restaurant. I am still eating, in fact, long after the others have finished. I tell them not to wait and that I can make my own way back to the hotel. 'Don't be ridiculous, Ted, take your time, then we'll all go and get a haircut – there's a barber shop down the road.'

Back at the hotel, I bump into James Kirtley. 'If we're both going to get any sleep tonight,' he says, 'we'd better stay awake this afternoon!' Good advice. I have a couple of hours to kill before the team meeting tonight. I fill out envelopes into which I'll put my precious complimentary tickets tomorrow (one thing less to worry about in the morning), then lie on the floor of my hotel room, stretching and doing sit-ups. I do that before every game anyway, and rituals reaffirm the feeling of this being just a normal game of cricket.

Normal?! It is my first Test tomorrow. I could write a whole novel about boyhood dreams and how many times I have fantasized about making my England debut. But that sentence says it all: it is my first Test tomorrow.

14 August

After an early breakfast, Freddie gave me a lift to the ground. The atmosphere in the dressing room was markedly different today: quieter, more reflective, more purposeful. I suspect the experienced players get used to peaking for Thursday. They might be slightly weary or sleepy on practice days; today everyone looked alert and quietly focused. Some players complain about Test cricket having an unnervingly introspective atmosphere. I much prefer that to manufactured matey jollity.

Alec Stewart is icing his hand, trying to limit some swelling on his catching hand; Marcus Trescothick is miming some shots with his match bat; Nasser is drinking coffee; Mark Butcher still looks unwell – I guess he will try to preserve as much energy as he can for the match itself. I leave the dressing room for warm-ups feeling that my equipment (and my game) is decently organized.

England's routine on match days is similar to Kent's. A brief series of running drills to warm the muscles, then some stretching; a short, competitive ball-game (soccer, touch rugby or some hybrid equivalent) to set the tone; then the rest of our stretches. All that takes about half an hour. It is then cricket all the way. The only difference today from a typical warm-up was a brief televised presentation beforehand by Richie Benaud to Andrew Flintoff for his brilliant hundred in the previous Test.

I did all my batting and general fielding practice with plenty of time to spare. But I was keen to get some extra short-leg practice. It is where I will start my England career in the field. So I was late into the dressing room and changed hurriedly into whites for the presentation of England caps to James Kirtley and me (Gareth Batty and Glen Chappell have been omitted and sent back to their counties).

In front of the pavilion steps, half an hour before the start of play, Michael Vaughan, with a handshake and a good luck, presents the caps. Within seconds of putting it on, the symbol of so much of what I have wanted, I realize I wouldn't change one fibre of my

England cap, the most perfect-looking and -feeling thing I have ever owned. The three of us pose for a moment in front of the TV cameras and a few photographers. A proud moment? Of course. But I don't linger over it. I want to get upstairs in order to think about the game.

Just after the ceremony, on the edge of the outfield, the South African batsman Neil McKenzie runs past and taps me on the back, saying quietly, 'Enjoy, Ed' – implying the whole business of Test cricket, I think, rather than specifically today.

Upstairs, the England press officer tells me that Steve Waugh telephoned to say good luck to me.

We win the toss and bat first. Private thoughts: excellent – straight out there and bat. It is the first time I have ever batted number five as a professional. Normally, as a number three, I would be padding up with the openers in case an early wicket falls. It feels odd on a batting morning to be walking around the dressing room in whites but without wearing pads.

I am a great believer in absorbing atmosphere, getting the feel of the stadium and the pace of the day. So I sit outside on the balcony, quiet and alone. The crowd is about three-quarters full and growing. I have never been at the first day of a Test match. I want to soak it up, not for the memories but to tune in to what it is like.

I would have stayed on the balcony for the whole fifteen minutes before the first ball but for 'Jerusalem'. It is marvellous, emotive stuff. But played at full volume over loudspeakers, accompanied by dozens of St George's flags and a highlights package of great England moments on the big video screen, I found my emotional cool slipping. The last thing I needed was overblown romantic overtures. Some Bach would have been nice; instead, I settled for reading the match programme next to Alec Stewart in the dressing room.

I stayed inside while Michael Vaughan and Marcus Trescothick left the dressing room. It is a difficult balance in any team: how much to say to the opening batsmen. Openers are usually self-contained and focused about their batting, and they don't want too much fuss. But the odd 'Good luck' and the feeling of the team being behind you can help as you walk out to the middle.

In Kent games, I always sit outside on the balcony while I am waiting to bat, and I did the same today. Andrew Flintoff and Mark Butcher, the latter next in at number three, were to my right, with Ashley Giles on my left. What was most different about today compared to a Kent game was the air of expectancy in the whole stadium while we watched the first over. What would the wicket be like? What was the mood of the two teams?

When Marcus Trescothick smashed the fourth ball of Pollock's first over for four through cover, the crowd roared with approval and expectation. It really was a roar, too. A few balls later, a play-and-miss was greeted by an 'Oooohhh' from the crowd – as if to say, *that was close*. Not that close, actually, I said to myself. Forget the roars and the 'ooohhhhs', and this is just another game of cricket in which you are waiting to bat, just as you have hundreds of times before. People hit fours, people play-and-miss – don't use up too much emotional energy on what you can't control. When you are called upon to concentrate and bat well – that is the time fully to switch on.

I kept saying to myself: it is simply two bowlers – one bowling at 85–90 m.p.h. (Ntini) and the other at 76–83 (Pollock) – bowling like bowlers do. Play the ball, not the occasion, and you will be fine.

What worried all of us was the wicket. Even from the first few balls it was obvious the ball would scarcely bounce at all. Instead, there was extravagant movement off the seam. Like most batsmen, I prefer the ball to 'come on' to the bat. Today was obviously going to demand grafting batting. The closest thing I have seen to this wicket was the Truro pitch in the C&G back in May! I wrote then that Cornwall would be good practice for some point later in the season when I would be playing on another low, difficult wicket. I didn't expect it to come in my first Test.

Within the first few overs, someone asked me what kind of wickets I like to bat on. 'At the moment, it doesn't seem to make any difference – they're all Ed Smith wickets!' Mark Butcher interjected.

In Pollock's third over, Michael Vaughan edges a good ball to slip, so Mark Butcher gets up to bat, and I go into the dressing room to put on my thigh pad. Two more wickets and I am in. It feels different – much closer. I feel more nervous.

While I am putting on my thigh pad, I see Michael Vaughan sitting on the dressing-room bench watching the replay of his dismissal on television. The ball moved away from the bat after pitching. There will be plenty more like that today.

It is warm but not hot, and I can't decide whether to wear a sweater or not. I try on my England short-sleeve sweater. It feels perfect, and that answers my dilemma. There are dozens of different kit manufacturers, and some fit better than others. I really do take extra confidence from the fact that I feel so comfortable and at home in my England cap and now my England sweater.

I return to the balcony. It is clearly difficult out there. Apart from the awkward pitch, the warm, overcast conditions are perfect for swing bowling. Mark Butcher, usually a quick scorer, still has only a couple of runs after facing about 20 balls. Marcus Trescothick has started more briskly, but in the twelfth over he is caught behind off Andrew Hall for 24.

Pads on, sweater on, helmet and gloves by my left-hand side on the balcony, 45 minutes into day one and I am next man in. It feels different again, another notch more intense.

When Nasser has reached halfway out to the middle, the PA announcer says on the tannoy that 'the new batsman is Ed Smith'. There is warm, but hesitant applause. I'm pretty sure it's Nasser walking out to bat, and that I'm still sitting here, but I half seriously wondered for a second if the mistake was mine. The error is soon corrected over the loudspeaker.

I say to myself: if Nasser and Butch bat well and put on a stand, that's great. But a part of me is ready to get straight out there. There are so many steps on the way to playing for England, I'm not desperate to prolong the last one. I repeat: at some stage today, you will bat – it might as well be now. Have that mentality, not 'I hope these two get through the new ball and make it easier for me later.'

Marcus Trescothick pops his head outside to the balcony and says to me, 'It's swinging – definitely swinging.' He says that in a quiet, matter-of-fact, undemonstrative way, exactly as I would say it to a debutant in a Kent game. Michael Vaughan and Freddie Flintoff sit on either side of me on the balcony. I suspect that is not an accident but an effort to calm my nerves and make me feel part of the team.

Meanwhile, in the middle Nasser and Butch are playing increasingly well. First they get through the new ball, and then, after a couple of classic drives through the off side from Butch and a pull from Nasser, they make it all the way to lunch. A brilliant effort, given the pitch and the swinging conditions. Nasser has 14 and Butch 37. There is relief and optimism in the dressing room, expressed as heart-felt 'Well dones'. I add my own but say little else.

I go down to lunch. The two teams queue up together but rarely interact. That is fine by me. I dislike an overly chummy matiness in the middle of games. I don't find it difficult to eat a modest but decent lunch – which is a sign I am not *too* nervous.

After lunch, I resume exactly the same seat, with my helmet and gloves to my side, just as I would at Canterbury. Once every four overs, I do my usual routine: I stretch my hamstrings and quad muscles, bounce on my toes and play a few straight-batted 'air' shots. It may be eccentric to be so methodical in my preparation, but it is something I have done for years and I am not stopping now just because a television camera is pointing at me.

The stand between Nasser and Butch progresses from being promising to being match-defining. They bat very well. The wicket is still difficult – though the sun has come out, hopefully drying the pitch a bit.

The overs tick by. The post-lunch burst from Pollock and Ntini is followed by Hall and Kallis. Then Graeme Smith turns to his left-arm spinner, Paul Adams. Given the start we had this morning, it seems almost impossible that England can now be so dominant.

Up on the balcony, Michael Vaughan and Freddie Flintoff are

still around. They do not force conversation, but chat intermittently. When you are nervous, people saying 'Good luck' or 'Be yourself' or 'You'll be fine' becomes tedious and annoying after a while. I'd rather concentrate on the game uninterrupted or have a distracting, non-cricket conversation. These two judge that perfectly. They allow me to watch quietly. Then – as the stand between Butch and Nasser develops and the pressure recedes and they sense I may need a bit of distraction so that I don't over-rev – they ask me about subjects likely to relax me. What was it like being with the New York Mets when I was writing *Playing Hard Ball*? What's my favourite drink?

In among long spells of watching carefully and quietly, I tell a couple of stories, and we all laugh a bit. I may be reading too much into it, but I think the two of them realize that I don't need to be more switched on than I already am, and I may benefit from some light moments before the biggest innings of my life.

Just before tea, Butch reaches a hundred with a four off Paul Adams. Brilliant is an overused word, but this is a brilliant innings, full of perfectly timed boundaries all round the wicket. More importantly, it has come when England most needed it: in a crucial period of a must-win game.

At tea, Butch has 103 and Nasser – who has also played some brilliant shots – has 72. They have batted – and I have watched and waited! – all session.

In the third over after tea, Butch nicks a full, wide ball from Ntini. Having prepared mentally to bat at the various different stages of the match, after all that waiting, *I am in*. I walk down the dressing-room steps. *My first Test innings*. I walk through the pavilion, then down more steps towards the outfield fence, crossing with Mark Butcher, who says a loud and optimistic 'Good luck, Ted!'

On to the outfield now, I hear very warm applause from the crowd. For a moment, I think of how proud my father will be, watching in the stands. Then I silence the thought, saying, 'He'll be a lot prouder if you play well.' For the rest of the walk out to the middle, I repeat: watch the ball, trust yourself, watch the ball, trust yourself.

Paul Adams, fielding under the helmet at short leg, takes a few paces towards me as I take guard. I am aware of him saying a string of sentences, probably not ones that invite a reply. Nasser, perhaps because I am on debut, perhaps because he loves a battle, wanders down the pitch in my direction, shouting, 'Fuck off, Adams.'

I do my usual routines after taking guard, the same scratching with my spike, the same walk away towards short leg, the same movement of my left hand to the peak of my helmet, then I settle in my stance for the first ball from Ntini.

It is short, straight, and it bounces chest high, and I play a solid back-defensive shot. It's fine. I'm away. Mentally, I am away. It's fine.

I chat briefly with Nasser in between overs. He tells me about Pollock: 'A bit of swing, not much. Good luck.' I have seen enough to be sure that Nasser is very much in the zone. He may not be in the mood for too much chit-chat. He looks unbelievably focused.

He plays out a maiden from Pollock that ends with a big appeal for lbw. Not out.

My turn now, again against Ntini. I push the first one back to mid-on, then sort of glance/shovel the second ball to fine leg. An easy single. Off the mark. Really fine now. Off the mark.

I chat to the umpire Daryl Harper – not because I am nervous, but because I usually chat to umpires. I don't say much, but I introduce myself and explain to him that I usually ask, 'How many left, please?' after the third ball of every over. Crazy superstition? Probably. But lots of us have them. Darren Lehmann asks umpires, 'How many?' after the fourth ball of most overs. More rituals than superstitions.

In Pollock's next over, I get a thick outside edge that goes safely along the ground through third man for four. The crowd cheer as though it was a great shot. In reality, it was a controlled edge. Still, my first boundary in Test cricket.

With each firm defensive shot to mid-off or mid-on, with each over that passes, with each mid-wicket chat with Nasser, I feel more relaxed and confident. Above all, more normal. I feel sure that, if I can just bat normally, I have a good chance of scoring runs.

On 6, I hit my first really good shot, a back-foot drive off Kallis. That's been my best shot through this season, so it is appropriate. Later, in my teens, I play a favourite on-drive for four – again off Kallis – wide of mid-on. The cheers from the crowd make me remind myself not to get distracted or carried away. Good start, but stay within yourself. You wanted to get in, to feel at home. Well, now you're in. So go on with it and make it count.

Meanwhile, Nasser is approaching 100. On 98, facing Paul Adams, he calls me for a single, then changes his mind. The infamous sequence of calls is 'Yes, No . . . Sorry'. Thank God, I got back just before Mark Boucher's throw hits the stumps at the bowler's end – and there was no need for a 'sorry'. Run out on Test debut. That might have been difficult to shrug off.

As he closes in on 100, Nasser has been looking a bit distracted – which is understandable. In the last three weeks, he has been criticized in the media, resigned as captain, then returned to just being a player. He has been having three nets a day during the two practice days before the Test. He gave a bullish press conference about how determined he was to play well, now he wasn't captain. Now he has 99. With a glance to fine leg off Kallis, Nasser hits his hundredth run and runs past me with arms aloft. He punches the air with a mixture of joy and violence. I leave him for a second to enjoy the moment and acknowledge applause, then shake his hand and say, 'Great innings.'

Most players hug their team mates who have just scored hundreds. But that is when they have been on the same journey for a long time, sharing each other's ups and downs. That – quite obviously – isn't the case with me and Nasser. I have huge respect for what he has done today. But I am a very small part of it. I have only shared the end of the last bit of the journey. It is not my place to hug him as though we were old mates.

Three balls later, I hit Kallis for four with another back-foot drive through the covers, and Nasser and I chat again in the middle of the wicket. I renew my congratulations. I am enjoying the partnership, enjoying the rawness of the game.

After eighty overs, Graeme Smith takes the new ball. I have 20-odd and have played nicely. Ntini is the quickest of the South African bowlers. In the run-up to the Test, there has been considerable discussion in the media about whether I will get a lot of bouncers. One journalist asked me if I thought I had a problem with the short ball. I said we would find out soon enough on Thursday. He continued, 'So you think they'll bounce you?' I said, 'If I was captain, and an opposition batter was making his debut, I'd bounce him. Of course I would.'

The new ball is always different. The eighty-over-old ball is so soft that it is very difficult – though by no means impossible – to make short balls really threatening. Not so the new one.

First delivery with the new ball is a bouncer, which I hook (or pull, depending on your definitions) for four through square leg. It is the first shot I have timed absolutely right. I didn't swing that hard but caught it right in the middle. It was a great moment. An over or two later, I hit a better shot, a front-footed square drive off Ntini. But Paul Adams makes a brilliant stop and saves the boundary.

There are ten overs left tonight, five of which will be bowled by Pollock – with a new ball. I know this will be a tougher examination than anything so far. He bowls from so close to the stumps, and is always so accurate, that (on this wicket) I will have to battle hard to avoid both lbw and nicks to the slips.

I take every leave outside off stump, and every confident defensive shot, as being victories – just as important as fours or nicely timed attacking shots. This is a crucial phase of the game. We have had a great day. I have to survive to keep it that way. It will be hard tomorrow morning. But easier for batsmen who have already been in on this wicket. I have to survive and get through to stumps. If getting in was one test of character, this is the second.

I feel more secure with each defensive shot, and more likely to get through to stumps. There is one big appeal for lbw, but it is given not out. I end up facing the last over of the day, bowled from the pavilion end by Pollock. I survive the first five balls, and knock the sixth to midwicket for a single. That takes me to 40. Nasser has 108. We have put on 84 and survived to stumps. England have had a very, very good day indeed.

On the way off the field, all I said to Nasser was, 'Great character today – but I think you might have heard that once or twice before!'

He laughed, then added, 'That technique of yours is working well.'

I leave him to walk off the field first and take the applause. A few steps behind, I raise my own bat and point it for a second towards my family, whom I have now spotted in the crowd.

Back in the dressing room, there are huge cheers for Nasser and some big pats on the back for me. Michael Vaughan is the first to come up to me and he says very warmly, 'Well settled, well settled!' He looks as happy for me as I am.

Duncan – who doesn't waste words – is also smiling and says, 'Well played, big Ed, well played.'

Freddie points towards my corner. There is a large vodka-and-tonic waiting for me. 'You said when you were waiting to bat, you said that you liked a vodka-tonic on an evening out,' Freddie explains, 'so we've rustled one up for you!' The implication, of course, is that in spirit I am a still a gentleman cricketer, who likes the right drink after some hot work. I play along and take a theatrically large swig. The team laugh. It was that kind of day.

England 296/3

15 *August*

The last thing I remember about last night is watching a few minutes of the TV highlights. I got back to the hotel after dinner at about 10 p.m. and couldn't resist switching on. It is so tempting. I was on 23 and South Africa had just taken the new ball. The Sky commentator Paul Allott said, 'Ed Smith has played nicely until now, but it will be a completely different story with the new ball – they'll be looking to rough him up.' When I played that hook next ball, Ian Botham replied, 'Well, he played that one OK. They've been saying Steve Waugh can't play the short ball for ten years.' I watched five more minutes then fell asleep.

After the highs of last night, the dressing room has returned to an atmosphere of business as usual this morning. Nasser is already changed into practice kit. Alec Stewart, next man in, is tidying his already very tidy corner. Yesterday counts for nothing – that is the way we must approach today.

I try to be absolutely normal in warm-ups and practice this morning. Don't think about hundreds, just be quietly focused on batting as well as you can – ball after ball. Don't get ahead of yourself. If you start thinking about getting a hundred on debut, replace that thought immediately with 'play straight' or 'concentrate' or something you can control, rather than the abstractions of milestones somewhere in the future. The last thing I need is to put extra pressure on myself.

As expected, Ntini and Pollock open the bowling. I get away quite quickly this morning. In the first over, a ball from Ntini keeps low and I squeeze it along the ground for four through gully. Two overs later, I hit a cover drive for four, again off Ntini. I am hitting the ball well. But I think the ball is moving around more this morning than last night.

Scoring opportunities off Pollock are scarce. He is going for between one and two runs per over. He is difficult to score off, even on flat wickets. When the ball seams, he is harder still to get away. I am happy just to defend as straight as I can and leave the wider ones.

I play out a maiden from Pollock on 49. But off the first ball of Pollock's next over, I get a thick inside edge towards square leg. I pick up two and have fifty on debut. The Trent Bridge crowd has been amazingly supportive on both days, and there is very warm applause. I take my helmet off and raise my bat. I look up to the England dressing room, where the team, led by Michael Vaughan, is clapping me. 'Well done,' Nasser says to me in the middle, 'now go on and make it count.' It is also what I am saying to myself.

In the eighth over, Pollock traps Nasser lbw for 116. It has been a brilliant, match-defining innings, full not only of typical defiance, but of great shots as well. While Nasser is given a standing ovation, Alec Stewart walks out to join me.

Alec is thirty-nine, the most capped Englishman in Test history, the grand elder statesman of the team, and he is under pressure. He got 7 and 0 in the last Test at Lords (which England lost by an innings). Some voices in the media have suggested he should have been dropped, despite the fact that he has announced this will be his last summer of international cricket – which might therefore end in a swansong in the fifth Test at the Oval (his home ground).

As I greet him in the middle, he says, 'Hello, Ed – match report?'

'Not much to report – pretty much as it looks from the dressing room, Pollock is getting a little swing, but basically bowling very straight.'

It seems funny that Alec (in his 131st Test) – simply because he is on 0 and is new to the crease – might be momentarily more anxious than me in my first Test.

A few balls later, Alec hits one of his square cuts. I have watched him play that shot hundreds, maybe thousands of times – but never from the non-striker's end.

I continue to battle against Pollock. The ball is now keeping low regularly, and I play and miss a couple of times to balls that bounce two or three times before reaching the keeper. You have to accept that there is an element of lottery about surviving on a wicket like this.

On 64, Kallis bowls me a length ball just outside off stump that swings away. I push at it firmly, and get a big nick to the keeper. It is a terrible fraction of a second: the period between edging the ball and seeing it in the wicketkeeper's gloves. So much goes through your mind: maybe it won't carry, maybe he'll drop it, maybe it didn't look like an edge anyway. But it carried, he caught it, and everyone knew I edged it. It is true I might have left the ball. But with so many balls keeping low, I had made up my mind to play more balls than I usually do. The one that got me out was also perfectly pitched and it swung late.

First Nasser out, then me: a broken partnership so often leads to a double breakthrough. It is so predictable that you have to guard against it as a batsman. From a team perspective, I am annoyed with myself for allowing the momentum to shift away from England. But we are still most definitely on top.

It is hard not to feel some satisfaction when you walk off with 64 in your first Test innings. But having come within striking distance of getting a hundred on debut – and the inevitably strong position that would guarantee England – I have mixed emotions as I raise my bat on the walk off. It could have been even better.

There are plenty of nice comments for me in the dressing room, but people also sense that this is a dangerous moment for the team. Having worked so hard yesterday, it would be terrible to let it slip with a middle-order collapse. While I am taking off my pads and thinking about the ball that got me out, Andrew Flintoff is caught at slip off Andrew Hall for nought. 322 for 3 has become 347 for 6.

Fortunately, Ashley Giles gets stuck in. At lunch, Ashley has 9 and Alec Stewart, who is starting to play some trademark shots all around the wicket, has 30.

In the afternoon, while England reclaim the initiative, I sit on the balcony next to Mark Butcher. I see a Graham Greene paperback lying open on the bench and pick it up. 'I'm getting through about one Graham Greene novel a week at the moment,' Butch explains.

The Trent Bridge crowd, knowing they are unlikely ever to see Alec bat again, are loving the spectacle. Even when Ashley Giles is out for 22 off 64 balls, James Kirtley and Steve Harmison stick around as valuable partners. On 72, Alec eventually hits Adams straight to mid-off – but he has made the difference between England having a strong total and a formidable one. This is not a 445 all out wicket.

Having gone through my own ordeal of waiting to bat on debut yesterday, now I watch James Kirtley take the new ball (with James Anderson) in his first Test. He has a huge appeal for lbw against

Gibbs in the first over – not unlike the way he got me out playing for Sussex at Tunbridge Wells – but this one is given not out. Despite the nerves, he looks to be bowling very like he does day-in, day-out in county cricket.

But it is the first-change bowlers, Freddie Flintoff and Steve Harmison, who change the atmosphere. Freddie starts with two maidens, and Steve gets unpleasantly variable bounce. There are few more difficult challenges as a batsman than facing fast bowling, delivered from a great height, on a wicket on which you don't know if it is going to bounce shin high or head high. That is what the South Africans will face if Flintoff and Harmison keep getting it right and this wicket keeps getting worse.

The crowd, after an absorbing but undramatic day so far, sense the opportunity to get involved. In particular, they get behind every ball that Freddie bowls, cheering in anticipation every time he runs up, and providing huge applause when he returns to his position on the boundary at the end of his over. I have never experienced a crowd make such a huge effort to inspire a team. I feel like I am riding high on an emotional rollercoaster.

We are playing with real presence and aggression now. With South Africa on 56 and Gibbs on 19, he drags a ball from Harmison on to his stumps. Now I understand for the first time what a Test wicket feels like. It is a combination of elation, relief, noise, celebration and pure joy. As an isolated moment, it feels much more memorable and emotional than anything in my 64.

Five overs later, Freddie – who has charged in and bowled regularly around 90 m.p.h. – induces Graeme Smith to tread on his stumps, playing back to a short ball. For a while, I didn't understand what had happened. The ball had gone to ground, not in the air. There had been no appeal. And yet Graeme Smith was walking off and Freddie was celebrating. It was then that I saw the bails were off and that Smith – after a sequence of 277, 85, 259 and 35 – really was out.

'You see, it's easy,' someone joked in the huddle. 'That's the way to get him out. I don't know why we wasted so much time and effort trying to get him out lbw and caught behind!' Someone else chips in, 'Why didn't Duncan think of that mode of dismissal in his tactics meetings!'

If it was a slightly lucky break for us, it was no more than we deserved. These two have bowled brilliantly, the crowd have provided great atmosphere, and the evening session has been played at an extraordinarily high emotional pitch. It seems to me, as a new boy, that some of the anger and frustration that accumulated over the past two Tests found expression in the spirit of our cricket tonight. With the shadows lengthening, the batsmen trying to survive, the bowlers fresh from a day and a half watching the batters, only a few overs remaining in the day, and a series to be won, it was everything I hoped Test cricket would be: an extended, relentless application of pressure with the occasional moment of genuine elation.

Despite variable bounce, and several huge lbw appeals from James Kirtley and James Anderson, Kallis and Rudolph get South Africa through to stumps at 84 for 2. Tonight's 33 overs constitute the most enjoyable session I have ever had in the field.

I think the team is still on an emotional high while we pad around the dressing room after stumps, drinking sports drinks and getting some much-needed food. I have been eating small snacks often in this Test. It seems I need constant top-ups of energy rather than big meals.

I have to give a few TV and radio interviews after play, so I am the last player to get into the shower. Nasser and Alec have already changed into their slacks and polo shirts. The bowlers have had their ice baths – a torturous experience intended to relieve next-day stiff limbs and tiredness. Not having to lie in a bath full of ice for five minutes is one of the positive things about being a batter.

'We've put the ice in the bath ready for you, Ed – better pop in now,' Michael Vaughan says to me.

'What? Ice bath? I only got 24 more runs today! When did any batter have an ice bath after getting 24?'

'I said yesterday in the team meeting that we were going to embrace new ideas about fitness and match preparation. This is one of them: ice baths for every player after every day of Test cricket.

It'll give us an extra edge. I already had mine while you were being interviewed on Channel 4. Nas, you've had yours, haven't you?'

Nasser nods. 'Bloody cold one, too.'

'Alec –' Michael Vaughan continues, 'you've had your ice bath, haven't you?'

'Yes, skip.'

It is at this point that Freddie takes over. 'Look, Ed, none of us can leave the dressing room until everyone has had an ice bath, so you'd better jump in now – there's a good lad.'

'You can't be serious?'

'Serious and running late, so jump in. I'll get Nige [fitness coach Nigel Stockhill] to get his stop watch and time you.'

With half the England team watching, I slowly and painfully submerge myself into a bath tub of half ice, half water. They cheer with amusement as I swear, shout and abuse them all in turn for inflicting it on me.

Nigel Stockhill counts, 'Just a minute left . . . [about 30 seconds passed] . . . only 50 seconds to go . . . [another 30 seconds] . . . 45 seconds left, then you can jump in a nice hot shower . . .'

'Nige, that fucking stop watch needs some attention . . .'

By this point, as news of my ordeal has reached the others in the dressing room, I am laughing even in the agony.

When I finally get out and stop shivering, I say to Alec Stewart, 'I don't know how you got through that!'

'What? The ice bath? You don't seriously think I got in an ice bath, do you?'

England 445, South Africa 84/2

16 *August*

We were in the field all day today. Yes, it is different. I am exhausted. Nor is it just the fact that I am unused to it. I looked around the dressing room and saw that everyone else looked the same. It is a mental tiredness. Of course, I get like that sometimes in county cricket. But here the intensity of pressure in the field does seem different. The slower pace of Test cricket creates the impression that wickets are worth more and mistakes are more costly.

We started brilliantly. We deserved more last night. This morning, we got a delayed return on our efforts with two wickets for James Kirtley in the first over. First Jacques Rudolph was caught by Alec Stewart for 15, then Boeta Dippenaar was lbw first ball. While James celebrated his first two wickets in Test cricket, and with the crowd again at fever pitch, the momentum appeared overwhelmingly in England's favour. Neil McKenzie survived the hat-trick. But at 88 for 4 – still more than 350 behind – and batting on a deteriorating wicket, some teams might have capitulated. South Africa fought back very hard.

First it was Kallis and McKenzie, then McKenzie and Boucher. That was the one that really hurt us. They put on 129 either side of lunch, absorbing the pressure for long periods, then hitting back with occasional flurries of boundaries. Even with the wicket misbehaving, they soaked up bursts from all our bowlers.

The crucial breakthrough came from James Anderson, who had McKenzie caught at slip for 90. Though he had been patient for long periods, crucially McKenzie had also kept the score ticking. He dug in but didn't become becalmed.

At 261 for 6, Pollock came in and counter-attacked. He hit 3 fours in three balls off Jimmy Anderson, freeing his arms with full swing against anything wide, and picking up anything straight over midwicket. I have often wondered, if Pollock had never taken up bowling and instead focused entirely on batting, how good he might have been as a batter. Given he has so much natural talent and such a naturally free and correct batswing, the answer is, probably more than good enough.

For me, after initially fielding at short leg and in the infield, Pollock's hitting meant a spell at deep cover. It is a different kind of pressure fielding on the boundary when someone is hitting out. You know there is a good chance that you may end up under a sky-er in front of a stand full of people. You are further from your team mates, more isolated and closer to the crowd. The closest I came to getting a catch was one of Pollock's lofted off-drives. But it ended up going about twenty yards away from me at deep extra-cover. My father, sitting in the front row, brilliantly caught it on the first bounce, reaching out in front of my eighteen-month-old niece.

The crowd – and I keep saying this – have made this game even more intense. They have rallied at any opportunity, cheered even regulation stops in the field, chanted our names warmly. But the game was no longer so clearly in our favour. Even after Boucher's dogged 48 ended when Freddie got him lbw, Andrew Hall came in at number nine and followed Pollock's example. So for a while it was shots from both ends. Hall, of course, is an all-rounder, batting unusually low at number nine.

Then when Hall's innings of 15 ended, when he inside-edged James Anderson on to his stumps, both Adams and Ntini built frustrating stands of 28 and 25 with Pollock. When Pollock was tenth out, he had hit 9 fours in a brilliant innings of 62 off 84 balls. He showed that judicious attack is often a sensible way of playing on difficult wickets. James Anderson, who picked up the last three wickets, finished with 5 for 102. He bowled plenty of unplayable deliveries.

We were in the field for 89 overs today and 120 in all. My emotions swung from feeling we were almost certainly in an impregnable position, to worrying that it was all but a level game. My emotions were in constant flux and my mind permanently switched on. It is that combination of concentration and concern that makes days like this so tiring. What a Test match to play first up!

We had one over to survive tonight, six balls for Marcus Trescothick and Michael Vaughan to experience the worst aspect of being an opening batsman: late-night survival mode. The best you can do is a couple not out. The worst is dismissal in fading light after a long, exhausting day.

I wondered if we might put in a night watchman to open the innings. Though rarely used, it has a certain logic. The worst that can happen is one ball, one wicket: night watchman out. But in the last over of the day, no new batsman can go in to bat at the fall of a wicket. So the night watchman has – in the crude sense – 'done his job' of protecting the top order until the next day.

Perhaps that would send negative, overly cautious signals. And I am certainly not being wise after the event. But we did lose a wicket in the first and only over tonight, first ball in fact, when Marcus was given out, caught bat-pad off Pollock. I was sitting on the balcony. Not much was said. 'Can you believe it?' someone said quietly. Replays showed the decision was questionable. First ball, one wicket, another shift in momentum, yet more emotional flux and another twist in the story.

Marcus trudged back into the dressing room. 'No worries, lads,' he said as he sat down. 'These things happen. No worries. We'll be fine tomorrow.'

England 445 & 0/1, South Africa 362

17 *August*

While Mark Butcher drove me to the ground this morning, I thought about the day ahead. It has been an amazing six weeks, an extraordinary sequence, a dramatic week, a thrilling game. Today I will have to bat again. I told myself to try to find that right, balanced, calm state – not to play at the same high emotional pitch at which I have been living for the last few days. I need to be normal – not emotionally hung over from being picked for England last weekend and then making a good start on Thursday and Friday.

I spent the time before the game talking to myself about all that and working hard at getting into the right mental state. Another day, another difficult day, but just another day all the same; another innings, another difficult innings, but just another innings all the same; an important game – all the more reason to keep it simple and uncluttered.

I didn't have time to find out if any of my self-motivation made any difference. I was out, plumb lbw, first ball off Andrew Hall. The ball before, the first of Hall's spell, was a perfect inswinger that had bowled Mark Butcher. Perhaps, as a right-hander, I was thinking too much about the ball going away from me (like the one before had come in to the left-handed Butcher). Perhaps I got 'caught on the crease' and was defeated by Hall being a bit quicker than he looks. Perhaps I should have been thinking, 'On this wicket, go forward almost regardless,' Or perhaps it was just a perfectly pitched ball that kept low, came into the stumps, and would have got me (and a few others) out first ball, no matter what the circumstances.

Nought, first ball. Isn't that just like cricket, surely the greatest ever game at protecting you from conceit?

My wicket came in the middle of a dire spell for England. With Trescothick out last night, then Vaughan, Butcher and me all following in the first hour this morning, England slumped to 39 for 4 – only 122 ahead. After Alec Stewart edged Kallis on 5, we went in to lunch at 60 for 5 – the worst spell we have had all game.

I have run out of clean pairs of socks – so the cricket shop at Trent Bridge brought a pair over to the dressing room for me. When I went down to get them from just below the players' area, I heard an English supporter say, 'I wouldn't mind – but they haven't even fought at all today. No guts.' *They* means people like *me*. It is the kind of comment that hurts.

In the middle, Freddie Flintoff was starting a revival. After 0 in the first innings, he still came out positively today and, instead of pushing and poking around while waiting to get the inevitable unplayable ball, he launched Pollock over long-on, then advanced down the track and hit Kallis to the same boundary for six. The crowd, always expectant when Freddie comes to the wicket, finally got back into the game. After five cheap wickets, here was something to cheer.

Sitting on the balcony, we all held our breath – hoping Freddie might somehow stay out there long enough to restore England's dominant position. He didn't – he was caught off Pollock for 30 – but a knock like that, especially on a bad wicket in a low-scoring game, is worth a lot more than thirty. Above all, he shifted the momentum in our favour. He changed not only the balance of the match but the whole atmosphere in the ground.

The same is true of the two innings either side of Freddie's. Nasser's 30 was in the same defiant vein as his first-innings hundred. He batted for longer than anyone else in both first and second innings. Ashley Giles's 21 was also crucial in England creeping up towards a lead of two hundred.

The mood was quiet in the dressing room. We know we have let it slip. There is not much to say. We have batted badly, and we know it. But it is very, very difficult out there. Unplayable balls are becoming increasingly frequent. Even when you survive them, they eat away at your sense of security at the crease.

South Africa need 202 to win in a day and a half. Time, though, won't come into it. Runs and wickets will decide it.

We wanted five wickets tonight and we got five. At 22 for nought, with Gibbs looking fluent and dangerous, it was an absolutely level game: 180 needed, ten wickets in hand. But James Kirtley made two crucial breakthroughs, trapping both Smith and Rudolph lbw. With James's low, skiddy delivery, he is looking increasingly awkward on this wicket. With low bounce around, if you bowl straight and from close in to the stumps, there is every chance of creating lbw chances.

The intensity of the game today was higher than anything I have experienced. Few Tests – and this one is also pivotal to the series – go into the last innings with both sides within striking distance of victory. It has been raw, thrilling, tense cricket all day. I tried to keep wanting the ball to come to me, wanting to do something good in the field, trying somehow to make a contribution – whether with body language or simply positive belief. We will get the wickets, I repeated it in my head – we will win the game.

We really got back on top when Gibbs miscued a pull off Steve

Harmison and Ashley Giles caught the sky-er. Then Dippenaar clipped James Anderson straight to me at short midwicket. My first catch, my first major contribution in the field. It wasn't hit that hard, but it didn't go slowly enough to give me much time to think or worry. It was a nice catch to get as your first in Test cricket. I remember the roar from the crowd and thinking, 'Thank God I caught that.'

Kallis played on against James Anderson a few overs later, making it 50 for 5. We were right back on top. The bad news was that it was the sixth-wicket pairing of McKenzie and Boucher who had counter-attacked so well in South Africa's first innings.

They scored 12 runs off the next eleven overs, a taut, tense 45 minutes in which neither side yielded at all. Freddie Flintoff and Steve Harmison, cheered on by an emotional crowd, bowled fast and straight from the Radcliffe Road end. James Anderson, then James Kirtley provided swing and lbw shouts from the Pavilion end. It was all about pressure: on the batters, on the bowlers and fielders. We applied pressure well; the South Africans soaked it up and survived until bad light stopped play.

Today was completely different from the first three days. Days one and two, though not perfect, were overwhelmingly positive as an introduction to Test cricket. Yesterday was hard work, but the game was still being shaped, not being decided finally once and for all. That is what it felt like today. One mistake could be fatal. It really was a cauldron. Tomorrow will be even more like that. We need five wickets, South Africa need 139 runs. You could age very fast doing this every day.

England 445 & 118, South Africa 362 & 63/5

18 August

I think everyone was a bit nervous this morning. How could you not be? We padded around the dressing room before warm-ups, Alec icing his hand, me checking my spikes, the bowlers getting some physiotherapy.

There was a small pile of letters on my seat in the dressing room. There has been every day – some faxes, some e-mails sent via the office here, some mail. The letters might come from friends, or well-wishers, maybe from people I haven't seen for fifteen years, or affiliates of institutions I once belonged to, or the familiar autograph-hunters. One or two have been romantically intended.

It was one of those I opened first today.

'Dear Ed, I can't go on any longer without writing to you. I must say from the outset that I find you impossibly attractive both facially and physically . . .'

'Hey, listen to this, everyone! One Test match and I have love-sick fans!'

A couple of other players wandered towards the corner where Alec, Butch and I were sitting.

I continued to read out the letter, now with a larger audience. '. . . I have been watching with rapt attention while you have made your debut at Trent Bridge . . .'

Laughter, accompanied by groans of disapproval at any swelling of my ego.

Now launched, I carried on reading out the girl's love letter. 'I must admit at this point, Ed, that I am an older gay man, though all my friends tell me that I am extremely good looking and youthful in manner.'

That was not what I had in mind. The team, though, thought it was a much more amusing twist. Now everyone tuned in.

'As I live quite locally in Kent, why not just pop in if you are ever passing?'

The letter provided an address and phone number.

'Call him now and see what he says!' someone suggested.

'Not on my phone!' I said. 'Wait for the next bit —'

The next line in the letter was, 'One other thing, Ed — I am willing to pay.'

James Anderson exclaimed, 'I've had some hilarious letters, but that is an absolute cracker. Give it here and we'll pin it on the notice board.'

So, with an unusual letter pinned on the team notice board, we went out to warm up for the biggest day in the lives of many of us.

Before the game, Michael Vaughan gave a brief and positive speech. When the match situation is as simple as it is here — bad pitch, five wickets needed — there really isn't that much to say. Sometimes, the more you complicate things, the harder it becomes. So the skipper just told us to bowl the ball in the right areas, cling on to our catches, keep our strong belief and enjoy it.

James Kirtley opened from the Pavilion end, Freddie Flintoff from the Radcliffe Road end. McKenzie and Boucher continued their partnership from last night with the same approach: survive, absorb the pressure, wait for something to hit.

Six overs into the morning, McKenzie got an unplayable grubber from James Kirtley. He had faced 73 balls for his 11. McKenzie looked as likely as anyone to hang around for long periods. If he had stayed in, it would have allowed the attacking lower-middle order — in particular the danger-man, Pollock — to bat with more freedom. It was also crucial not to have to wait too long for our first wicket. With each over South Africa survived, and with each run they chipped off our lead, the tension in the ground increased and the pressure on us grew. At 71 for 6, the crowd was again sensing a quick win.

The thing about low-scoring games is how quickly the balance of advantage shifts. In the next over, Boucher hit two consecutive fours off Freddie. With only 123 needed, all it takes is a few overs like that to change the whole game. Or one wicket. That came three balls later in the same over, when Pollock got a shooter from Freddie and was bowled for 0. The noisiest parts of the capacity crowd are sitting behind where the bowler starts his run-up at the Radcliffe Road end. I have never heard anything like it.

The next over, new batsman Andrew Hall – who is having an extraordinary series, full of match-changing moments – slashed at a wide one first ball from James Kirtley and watched it land in Marcus Trescothick's hands at first slip. That is the other way of approaching batting on a bad wicket.

It was at this point I thought, 'Don't relax for a second, but I think we really are through here.' A few overs later, with Adams and Boucher building a dangerous stand, Nasser shouted at all of us, 'No letting up! Enjoy the tenth wicket! All of you stay in this game!'

It was at Trent Bridge in 1998, in the famous Test match in which Mike Atherton survived that spell from Allan Donald, that Mark Boucher dropped a crucial catch from Atherton. He looked determined to make up for it today, punctuating long periods of defence with the odd drive for four down the ground.

James Anderson and Steve Harmison took over the bowling duties, but Adams and Boucher survived. Adams started to hit boundaries at his end too. Though I never felt properly worried, the atmosphere in the ground definitely changed. The ninth-wicket partnership became easily the highest of the South African second innings. But having put on 45 runs with Boucher, and needing only 76 more to win, Adams prodded a caught and bowled to James Kirtley. It was James's fifth wicket of the innings – a debut five-for – and he had tears in his eyes while we celebrated.

Had Adams and Boucher survived until they needed less than 50 to win, I think the pressure would have shifted more on to us. But now, we just needed one more, one more.

We didn't have to wait long. Two overs later, with Boucher on 52, he edged James Kirtley to Alec Stewart. So the veteran of 131 Tests and the debutant shared roles in the winning wicket. It was that kind of game.

The first thing I remember was Freddie running towards me, wearing a huge smile and carrying two stumps. He put one in my hand and said, 'Great game, Ted!'

It was James Kirtley's and Michael Vaughan's day. The big screen showed Michael's face when the tenth wicket fell. It was pure elation and relief, the kind of joy only brought by the release of intense pressure. I felt the same. In the noisy, chaotic moments immediately after victory – a mixture of team hugs and huddles, then individual 'Well dones' and congratulations – I felt I had been part of a something very special. My first Test, obviously, had ended in a win. But something bigger and broader, too. Somehow, at 1–0 down in a home series, English cricket felt on trial here at Trent Bridge. We have a new captain and some new players. One of them, James Kirtley, will be Man of the Match. There seemed to be great generosity of spirit among the players. It is said that team spirit is an illusion glimpsed in victory. But this felt absolutely real.

I walked towards the pavilion with my trophy stump in one hand. I saw my family clapping to the right of the pavilion; I listened to the joyous comments of the England fans as we climbed the pavilion steps; I saw an iced bucket full of champagne bottles being carried towards the dressing room. So this is Test cricket, is it?

England 445 & 118, South Africa 362 & 131. England won by 70 runs

25 August

If I thought my editor would permit it, I wouldn't write a single word about this bloody Test match. It has been a disaster for England and a major set-back for me. Trent Bridge promised great things. Headingley dragged us right back down.

If I had written an entry on the evening of Day One, I might have persisted with the discipline, as I did at Trent Bridge, and chronicled my mood over the five days. But after 90 overs in the field on Thursday, I was so exhausted that I ordered room service in my hotel room, then collapsed into bed at 9.15 without opening my laptop. On the night of Day Two, having survived the last three balls of the day, I was 0 not out with a crucial innings ahead of me. The following evening, having been out to the first ball of

Saturday's play, I faced the prospect of walking out to bat on Sunday on the back of two consecutive noughts. I avoided a third zero, but managed only seven. We lost. That brings us up to today, Monday. Understand why I haven't been writing much?

This was a back-to-back Test match, meaning we had two days between the elation of winning at Trent Bridge and playing at Headingley. One day off, one practice day. On my 'day off', three of us spent all morning representing the team at an event organized by England's sponsor, Vodafone. That was in Warrington, over an hour's drive away from Leeds, on the other side of the Pennines. Then one day to prepare. Then five days of intense cricket. Even the veterans have been saying back-to-back Test matches are as tough as it gets.

First the game, then me. With South Africa 21 for 4 on the opening morning – and Smith, Gibbs, Kallis and McKenzie back in the pavilion – it seemed we had carried on exactly where we left off at Trent Bridge. Not just the match, but the whole series, was tilted in our favour. Martin Bicknell, in his first Test for ten years, got a wicket with his second ball, a perfect away-swinger to Gibbs. He finished his first spell with figures of 6–5–2–2. James Kirtley and debutant Kabir Ali also got wickets in their first overs. It was yet another very difficult wicket. South Africa were missing their key bowler, Shaun Pollock. We were running away with it.

Then Gary Kirsten made a hundred of controlled brilliance. He was patient enough to score only 15 runs between lunch and tea, but he made up for it in the evening session. Avoiding lunging forward, and happy to play watchfully off the back foot, he late-cut anything wide and clipped anything straight. He found an unlikely partner in debutant Monde Zondeki, batting at number nine, who finished his first day in Test cricket on 50 not out. From 21 for 4 and 116 for 5, South Africa had recovered to 260 for 7.

We won Day Two, but some critics said it cost us the game. In reply to South Africa's 342, Mark Butcher and Marcus Trescothick shared a thrilling stand of 142. Late in the afternoon, with both of them in dominant form, they accepted the offer of bad light. When play recommenced, the momentum changed: both fell quickly, leaving Nasser and me to play out the final minutes of the day in gathering gloom.

The press and TV pundits heaped blame on England for failing to push home the advantage and taking the light. I had other things on my mind: starting the next day on 0, with the Headingley pitch – despite the fast run-scoring so far – getting worse by the minute. 'So, it's me and thee again tomorrow,' Nasser said as we left the dressing room.

Not for long. I edged a shortish away-swinger from Kallis first ball on Saturday morning. It definitely pitched and left me late. Less certain is that I should have played at it. To say it was first ball of the day is not to offer an excuse. But it is a fact that all batsmen are at their most vulnerable first ball. Throughout Kallis's whole spell – some of the best bowling of the series – there was a huge amount of playing-and-missing. We all know, of course, that the only difference between a play-and-miss and a nick is that you got closer to middling the one you nicked. That and the fact that it ends your innings. What do I mean? I mean I was unlucky to nick it.

Nasser Hussain stood firm for his 42 and Freddie Flintoff smashed 55, but we conceded a lead of 35 on the first innings. At 128 for 2 in their second innings, with Kirsten digging in again, South Africa were cruising to a big lead. But three quick wickets, the last of which was Rudolph caught by me at short leg (it came slowly but straight out of the sun) meant we finished Day Three with a fighting chance. South Africa 199 ahead, with 5 wickets remaining.

Not so Day Four, which was theirs entirely. Andrew Hall, more than making up for the absent Pollock, crashed 15 fours all around Headingley. We had no front-line spinner and our seamers struggled. I fielded on the boundary for much of Hall's relentless onslaught and heard the taunts of a feisty Leeds crowd. I didn't mind the silly personal stuff so much as the abuse of the whole team. I have always liked the abrasive atmosphere of Yorkshire grounds, but in this game the contrast with Trent Bridge was stark.

At one point, with Hall in fifth gear, the huge television replay screen – which uses the same footage as Channel 4 – picked out the eleven England players, zooming in on the faces and expressions of each of us in turn. England were struggling, and we were each being scrutinized.

Hall finally ran out of partners after a brutal 99, and England required 401 to win. I went in to join Mark Butcher at 62 for 3. I hit a decent cover drive for four off Kallis to get off a pair. But on 7, I hit a loose drive to Graeme Smith at deep gully. He had moved himself there immediately before I hit it to him. My weight was leaning back in the shot, meaning that the ball went up. It looked bad. It was the first of my four dismissals in Tests which was entirely my fault. It is true that – no matter how many runs have been scored in the match – a huge number of balls have been misbehaving off the Headingley wicket. But to get caught at point off a loose drive? My thoughts are the same as they were when I was caught cover at Hove during a crucial phase of Kent's second championship game of the year.

Subsequently, when I watched the 'highlights' of the day's play, they showed Michael Vaughan's face when I was out. Sitting on the balcony with him and a few others after I was out, I felt I had let him down. Not much was said. There wasn't much *to* say. Freddie Flintoff and Mark Butcher – who are both in marvellous touch – lifted all our moods with a sparkling stand of 74 late in the day. But we needed miracles on Day Five to get to 401.

Exactly as with the first ball of Day Three (when I was out) we lost Mark Butcher first ball of the last day. The rest was the death rites. England ended on 209, Kallis took 6 wickets and we lost by 191 runs. There has already been talk of tiredness and the county grind. I would say the post-mortems can now begin, but they have been going on for some time and will doubtless continue.

My errors this Test will not recede quickly from my memory. I must think about what has happened, reflect on it, then move forward. I am under pressure. So is the team.

There is one other memory from this week in Leeds that I want to write down while it is still fresh. It was dinner last night – the evening of the fourth day – with Nasser Hussain, Alec Stewart and Martin Bicknell.

It might seem inappropriate, in such times of crisis, to write about a social event. But I hope to play more Test matches. What I cannot do is play many more with Alec Stewart. He retires in a fortnight. The Oval – his home turf – will be his swansong, full of the ceremony he enjoys. But somehow teams are more needy on the road. There is no one else with whom we can share success, no other human voices to soften the blow of failure. We say and do surprising things. At dinner last night, I felt conscious of a different, less public kind of final chapter.

I felt privileged that three senior cricketers didn't edit their comments in my presence. One of the reasons they didn't is because they trusted me not to scribble down the gossip in this diary – so I won't. I am more interested, anyway, not in what was said (which ranged from why Nasser resigned, to the Zimbabwe controversy, to why neither Alec nor Nasser ever picked Martin while they were captain) so much as the different types of cricketer they have all been.

Martin has been county cricket's premier opening bowler for a decade. One story sums up how he is regarded. Three years ago, on the evening of the first day of the second championship game of the season, Kent captain Matthew Fleming had dinner with Rob Key and me. Rob (age 21) and I (age 22) were about to open the batting the following day against the champions Surrey. There was some talk over dinner about who the best bowlers were in the country. The usual names came up. Matthew, as if to draw a line under our opinions, wrapped things up with, 'Yes, but there's a big difference between all those bowlers and Martin Bicknell: Bickers always, always, gets early, top-order wickets.' Rob and I started to chew more slowly. The food wasn't tasting quite so good. 'Sorry, chaps – except for tomorrow, of course.' It isn't for me to say how many Tests Bickers should have played. Most people agree it should have been more than three.

There is not much to say about Alec that hasn't been written already – Mr Immaculate, the model professional, the survivor, the gaffer, the man who never lost his passion to play at the top, someone whose lifestyle is as disciplined as it is unchanging. He hasn't changed much over thirteen years in an England shirt, the same twirl of the bat, the same brisk walk on and off, the same upturned collar, the same sweetly timed clips and cuts.

He treats new boys with an inclusive manner and helpful word, quick with a spare spike for your shoes or the number of a restaurant. He likes having fun and being looked up to, and younger players do both. I have changed next to him in the dressing room for two Tests and he has been exactly as I expected.

Some people dislike Alec's obsessive interest in appearances, the cheeky smile and wink at the camera, the readiness to say the right thing, his ability to deflect the flak. But being turned out well, not showing dissent, being a polished ambassador for the game – they are not grafted on to the main body of his personality, they are central to his conception of himself. He enjoys being recognized, enjoys the goodies, enjoys the game of cricket, enjoys the game of life.

Instead of wondering what lies beneath the surface, we might perhaps accept that he takes the surface itself very seriously. It is not difficult to imagine him fitting in well in a royal court. He has the courtier's understanding of how the world operates: he would have neither cracked if the king turned against him nor crowed when fortune and favour shone in his direction. He would have endured, though, while more reckless spirits hitched themselves to passing stars. What exactly had Alec thought of the last king? Who could be sure? He had said so much, but nothing scandalously quotable. Better have him on board, though, in the new regime: still the best man for the job – knows the ropes, and yet still fresh spirited.

Nasser's game is quite evidently lit from within. His eyes are an easy give-away: they burn with an anger that often borders on hatred. Who it is exactly that he hates might be less important than the fact of having something or someone on which to focus his determination. It is not difficult to imagine Nasser being a nineteenth-century solo explorer or mountaineer. Why take the risk and the hardship? He wouldn't be sure – except that life seemed intolerable without the tortured journey of self-discovery. Can't live with the bloody mountains, can't live without them – that's not far off his view of cricket.

For Nasser, I suspect society is secondary to his view of himself, something to be negotiated en route to higher things. 'I hate small talk,' he feely admits, as if that explains everything. In truth, playing the outsider has probably fuelled his sense of determination. Those bastards have never rated me; I'll show them again and again!

So while Alec turned up his collar and walked to the wicket simply, confidently and breezily, Nasser engaged the enemy in a battle of willpower. The cricket, at times, seemed almost a minor issue to him, a metaphor for a larger psychological battle. Cricket is not just a game to Nasser, and it can never be. If he felt his character had failed him when it mattered, it would really hurt. I do not imagine he is an easy man to console.

While Nasser fought within and without, Alec played the game. They made their debuts in the same Test on the West Indies tour of 1989–90. Two very different, very proud men, who have served English cricket for thirteen years ever since.

As for me, I got back home tonight, for the first time in fifteen days, to find an empty house and piles of letters wishing me well in my England career, alongside others congratulating me on my debut fifty. That was months ago, wasn't it?

Nothing could be further from my mind. I have ten days until the Oval Test – if selected. I have only one Kent innings in that time, a one-dayer at Bristol. Before then, I will get back in the nets.

It was a pair at Chelmsford that started my hot sequence. Now I have got back-to-back noughts, spread between the second innings at Trent Bridge and the first innings at Headingley.

Ten days, then. Ten days to get back on track.

South Africa 342 & 365, England 307 & 209. South Africa won by 191 runs

27 August

Two Test matches: one score, three failures, two of them noughts. After two back-to-back Tests, England finally have a week off. It is inevitable that I should be tired. But I am also short of runs, and if Kent had a championship game I would ask to play in it, tiredness notwithstanding. But Kent have a strange gap in their fixture list. Between the end of the fourth Test and the start of the fifth (a full ten days), we have only a single one-day match, one innings to get back on track.

Gloucestershire have been the country's best one-day side over the past decade. Well drilled, well led, disciplined with the ball, good in the field. Not many sides come to Bristol and win. The pitch looks poor and it is a day–night game. Translation: good luck the batters.

It has been odd being back among my Kent team mates for just two days. Murali, whom I know the least well, drove me here late last night. I hoped to avoid talking about England too much.

'Just a sixty or seventy in the last Test will be enough for you to get on the tour to Sri Lanka. We'll have dinner at my house with Freddie [Murali and Freddie were close friends at Lancashire]. It's a gorgeous country. You'll love it.' Sri Lankans have a special ability to make you feel they care about you. 'But in case you do tour, I'm not bowling at you in the nets any more,' Murali added with the broadest of happy smiles. 'I don't want you to start knowing my tricks.' Clever too.

A couple of hours before the game, I had lunch with Dave Fulton, Ian Brayshaw and Martyn Sigley – captain, coach and physio. I wanted to catch up on Kent news and they wanted to get a sense of my state of mind. I was honest about the England games, but minimalist: I spend enough time thinking about England without spending the rest of the time talking about it. I was genuinely keener to talk about Kent.

As we got up to leave, a few minutes before beginning warm-ups,

Dave said in a neutral tone of voice, 'It's very simple really, Ed. Get runs in the fifth Test and you'll be picked for two tours, on which you've a good chance of doing well. You could be established inside sixth months. Fail and, given that you were picked in good form, you might never play again.'

I hope my face stayed the same, but my mind froze. He had said nothing I didn't already know. Nor did he say it at all unpleasantly. Dave and I are both straight-shooters and we have said plenty of tough things to each other over the years. But the starkness of the words, coming from someone else's mouth, not from my inner voice, hit home. 'Fail and you might never play again.'

We won the toss and batted – always sensible in day–nighters – but I was hurried in my preparation. Just before going out to bat, I had been trying to tape over the England badge on my helmet. It was a Kent game today and I believe these things matter. 'Don't worry about it – no one cares,' a couple of players said in the dressing room as they watched me rushing to get ready. But I cared. I wanted to avoid the impression that my mind was still with the England team.

My mind may not have been with the England team, but it was certainly all over the place. I haven't been so poor mentally for a long time. 'Fail and you might never play again.' Those words kept coming back. My strong voice, the voice that I wrote about at the Oval, couldn't drown them out. I was angry at myself – but not with Dave – for not winning the battle of my two voices.

The Gloucestershire players may have sensed it, too. As I scratched around, taking over twenty balls to get into double figures, they passed asides around the infield. 'He only plays this badly in his England helmet.' Then, while I still couldn't accelerate even when I'd got the pace of the wicket, they changed tack. 'Doesn't care about the team, does he – more worried about his place in the England team.'

Today was another televised game, so Sky Sports have brought with them their vast replay screen for the crowd to enjoy. As I batted from the Pavilion end, it was just to the left of mid-on. I could still see myself – if I was weak enough to look (and today

I was) – as I settled in my stance. Every time I looked up to the screen I saw close-ups of my footwork, my Test match average, my county average – in the spotlight again, even playing for Kent. I imagined the commentary, predicted the criticisms, contradicted them in my mind. I was, in truth, feeling the pressure.

With Rob Key and Andrew Symonds out for single-figure scores, Matt Walker and I rebuilt. Matt is playing well at the moment, so I had faith that he would score quickly at one end. Still, the runs wouldn't come at mine. When I had 12 off 40 balls, I thought about having a slog – it might break the shackles, and if I got out, at least the ordeal would be over.

It was then that I heard my strong voice for the first time: 'If you throw it away now, you may as well throw the cricket away, you weak bastard! You should be ashamed of yourself. Show some fight. Weather the storm. Be here for a while. It will get easier.' I smiled for the first time all day and felt confident that I would make a contribution.

Rob Key once told me that good one-day players always do two things. First, once they make a decision, they do it one hundred per cent, with no 'what ifs' or half-heartedness. Secondly, they always know who has to bowl next and how hard it will be. I remembered his advice today. Mike Smith and Ian Harvey are probably the most accurate opening pair in county cricket. Smith, in particular, bowls gun-barrel straight: he skids the ball up to the bat without any width, demanding that you take risks against balls that will hit the stumps.

I decided in his sixth over that I would play him out, even if that meant facing three maidens. After Smith would come the right-handed Mark Alleyne and the off-spinner Martyn Ball – both successful one-day bowlers, but I reckoned they would be easier on this wicket. When Smith bowled out his nine overs for just 16, I had made a painstakingly slow 20.

While merely surviving against Smith, I had decided to attack Ball's off-spin from the first ball. Now Ball was coming on, I used my inward promise as a test of mental strength. 'If you don't go for it first ball,' I said to myself, 'you were nothing more than a coward, making excuses earlier.' I went down the wicket, hit it very hard but straight along the ground to Ball. It was a similar shot, though in opposite circumstances, to my attempted six off the fourth ball of Kevin Pietersen's last over before lunch at Maidstone.

A few years ago, having decided to hit over the top and failed first time, I would have retreated. Today, I went again second ball. This one I got clean and hit a low-trajectory six into the sight-screen at the Pavilion end. I saw my team mates clap from the dressing room, and wondered – before my good voice drowned out the distraction – what they might have been saying during my interminably slow start. In Ball's next over, I hit another six, this time a pick-up over wide mid-on. I was finally away, free from fears and distractions, and batting properly.

Through this inner turmoil, which I hadn't articulated outside my own mind, Matt Walker had said all the right things. 'Just hang in there,' he said at the end of every over, 'it will get easier – I'll take the risks, just hang in there.' I am not sure what I would have done had he been saying, 'What the hell are you doing out here?'

I was out with the score at 172 for 3, having made 59 and shared in a stand of 152 with Matt. It provided the perfect platform for our big hitters to express themselves. As I walked off the pitch, given the poor wicket, and the fact that Gloucestershire had to bat second under floodlights, I felt almost certain that we would win.

We did. The middle order struck the ball brutally. In the field, as dew settled and the lights brightened, Amjad Khan and Martin Saggers bowled briskly. It will do Saggs no harm to have bowled quickly on TV. Rightly or not, England seem to like bowlers with an extra yard of pace.

Then there was Murali, rarely less than brilliant. It is an odd feeling to throw him the ball with the game in the balance and be almost certain that we will win it. With Murali in the side, behind is level, level is ahead, ahead is home and dry. We haven't been far enough behind to lose yet.

He drove me home after the game. He is quick, eccentric and easily amused. Between the laughs, I asked some serious questions about Sri Lanka – its politics, religions, ethnic tensions. He didn't mind, but added, 'When you tour, there'll be people who know the answers better than me.'

We got to my house at 2 a.m. He looked down the drive, lit weakly by moonlight. 'All alone here with no wife? Aren't you scared of ghosts?'

It will look like a normal day at the office – a scratchy but important 59 in a one-day game. No one, until they read this, will ever know the truth. I will go to sleep more happily and quickly tonight, with some self-respect salvaged.

Kent 251/7, Gloucestershire 215. Kent won by 36 runs

31 August

At the end of the 2001 season, I very much wanted to be selected on the inaugural intake of the National Academy in Adelaide. That year, and again the following season, others got the nod ahead of me. That left me with only one means of getting into the Test team: simple weight of runs in county cricket. The first and most important reason why I wanted to get into the Academy was because I thought it might help me to become a better athlete, a more experienced team player and simply better at batting. In the new year of 2002, several hundred miles west of the Academy camp in Adelaide, I was running, swimming and practising in Hale School in Perth, trying to re-create the Academy on a smaller scale.

The second reason why I wanted to get into the Academy was more complicated. I sensed widespread support for the Academy in the media, a belief that it would replace county cricket as a feeder for the national side. As well as relishing the up-side of being in the Academy, I feared the down-side of being outside it.

Even back in 2001, though it sounds arrogant to say so, I thought it quite likely that at some point in the next two or three seasons I would score enough runs to put myself in contention for the Test team. If that happened to me as 'just a county pro' – simple labels only, please – I knew there would be a certain reluctance (not necessarily by the selectors, but among other voices) to endorse my selection. I would not only have to leapfrog the academicians, I would also have less time at the top table – if I reached it – to prove myself. Being a county pro was unfashionable, and many voices in English cricket have become quite swayed by fashion.

The backlash (if that is not too strong a term) against my selection that followed the defeat at Headingley has borne out my prediction. Several people have written articles saying my failure at Leeds – one game, played on one of the worst wickets I have ever seen – should end 'the experiment with picking county pros'. According to an article in the *Daily Telegraph* by Simon Briggs – who wrote a very generous piece about me in the lead-up to my debut at Trent Bridge – Michael Vaughan now sees it that way, too.

So, what is a county pro, and am I one? Well, quite literally, yes, I must be. I draw a salary from Kent C.C.C., and have done since 1996, and that (until two weeks ago) was the highest level of cricket I have ever played at. I am proud of playing for Kent and never apologize for it.

But do I have any characteristics of the stereotypical county pro, the straw man set up by angry sports columnists to explain the failings of English cricket? This county pro lacks ambition, preferring to sit in his sponsored car, counting his £50,000 salary. This county pro would like to play for England, but not if it means making sacrifices and restructuring his life to achieve that ambition. Rather than look inwards to explain failure, this county pro is too quick to blame bad luck. This county pro has a jokey exterior that conceals a desperate determination to cling on to his contract. This county pro wants to succeed, but not as much as he wants a benefit year.

Now, I may have many flaws, but those five are not among them. In fact, I am one player – going back a few years – who could have done with a splash of county pro-ness. 'Only a game, Ed, don't beat yourself up too much, the sun still comes up tomorrow, have a drink.' I needed some of that when I was twenty, not 'Prove to me that you really, really want it, kiddo.' I wanted it too much.

As for benefit years, though I would think twice before turning down £200,000 tax free, the chances of me 'hanging on for a benefit' are about as likely as Andrew Symonds taking up ballet and living happily ever after in the 16th arrondissement in Paris.

I have read fewer cricket reports than normal during the last fortnight, and none at all during the Test matches. But people tell me – even show me – what is written. I am far too young and optimistic to become bitter about a handful of newspaper reports that may not have much real significance. But it intrigues me that someone who is twenty-six years and one month old should be considered a fully, and unchangeably, formed player, stuck in his 'county ways' and unprepared to leave his 'comfort zone'. To borrow from Bob Dylan: 'No, no, no, it ain't me, babe.'

Most batsmen are at their best in their early thirties. Exactly what is stopping this 'county pro' from continuing to get better?

September 2003

'I will make a difference.' That is what we say to ourselves. All those years of thinking about playing for England, all those hours spent watching Test matches on television, all those dreams of wearing an England cap – all the time thinking, 'I will make a difference when I get out there.'

So I will never forget the crashing reality of this afternoon. The Oval was full, with 20,000 England fans. It was an unusually hot and sunny September afternoon. South Africa were 300 for 2, with Herschelle Gibbs, well past a hundred, stroking it all over the ground. Some sections of the crowd had turned against the England bowlers, others had turned against England full stop. I was fielding on the boundary, trying to anticipate where Gibbs was going to hit his cover drives, unable to close my ears to the jeers of our own crowd. We were being whipped. It was as simple as that.

The little I could do was to shout encouragement, give bowlers a pat whenever they had finished a good over or spell, think and act positively, and let it hurt. That sounds worthy. But it was what I did. All fielders, if pushed, will admit that they have sessions when they are less engaged, other sessions when they are more fully involved. Today, in the last Test of an unbelievably fluctuating summer, there seemed nothing around the corner worth preserving energy for.

An hour or two later, in early evening, with long shadows on the outfield, Jimmy Anderson found the edge of Neil McKenzie's bat with the very last ball of the day. After such a pounding all day, going off with our mood lifted by a late wicket felt significant. I was as happy about us getting this fourth wicket (leaving the South African 'collapse' at 362 for 4) as the wickets that led to the win at

Trent Bridge. I kept saying 'Brilliant, Jimmy, brilliant!' as we walked off the field.

It had been a hard day until that moment. South Africa had 100 up within 25 overs (for the loss of only one wicket – a run-out by Michael Vaughan); 111 for 1 at lunch; 230 for 1 at tea. Michael Vaughan turned to the spin option of Ashley Giles within the first hour, threw the ball to Mark Butcher in the afternoon, and opened the bowling with himself after tea. The front-line bowlers swapped ends and bowled in different combinations. Nothing changed the fact that South Africa were dominant.

The destroyer-in-chief was Herschelle Gibbs. He has been quiet for the last couple of Tests. A flat Oval wicket was just what he was looking for. He started as he continued – with a series of lightning off drives. It didn't seem to matter where the off-side fielders stood. He hit the gaps. He hit the ball so sweetly that even sweepers on the off-side boundary didn't make much difference. I was at deep cover in the over after he reached a hundred. He hit three off-side boundaries – two drives and a cut – as if to confirm he was moving up a gear.

Apart from the run-out, the first two wickets went to Ashley Giles. First Gary Kirsten swept and missed and was lbw for 90. Then Gibbs, aiming just over my left shoulder at short leg, tried to hit one out of Kennington, and was bowled out of the rough. It is a measure of how well he played that when he walked off with 183, we sensed it could have been a lot worse.

James Anderson and Steve Harmison took the new ball after 83 overs. The next seven overs, the last seven of the day, cost only 7 runs and ended with the wicket of McKenzie. For the first time in the day, we had control. The day was still South Africa's. But it was a small but highly significant momentum shift to England.

The coaching staff felt the same. They were waiting at the top of the stairs, patting us each on the back as we walked in. Duncan, who doesn't throw praise around idly, said, 'Well done, big Ed – good lad' as I passed him.

I spoke briefly to my dad outside the pavilion. 'You're going to think I'm mad, but I think we've got a real chance of winning,' I told him. He is used to my optimism, but he let me finish. 'Sri Lanka beat England here in 1998. England batted first on a flat wicket, made 400-odd. Sri Lanka made 600 in the middle, then bowled us out cheaply in the third innings. I know they had Murali. But it's not impossible from here.'

I am more tired than I have been after any of my eleven days' Test cricket.

South Africa 362/4

5 September

At Trent Bridge we bowled really well at the end of the second day, then got our reward with early wickets the next morning. The same happened today. Martin Bicknell, settling into his usual home-ground rhythm, trapped Jacques Rudolph lbw for nought in the first over. That set the tone. In the morning session, we took five wickets for 67 runs. Boucher edged to Alec Stewart, Kallis was unluckily run out at the bowler's end, Hall was lbw to Freddie, then Mark Butcher ran out Paul Adams from deep extra cover. That was the last ball of the morning session – so again we walked off for a break with smiles on our faces. South Africa had collapsed from 344 for 2 to 432 for 9. It was a level game again, and the crowd were right back with us.

Pollock, this time in partnership with number eleven Ntini, again counter-attacked. The tenth-wicket partnership – that most irritating phenomenon – added 52 runs. But that could take only a little of the shine off a wonderful fight back by us. If offered 484 all out yesterday afternoon, we not only would have taken it; we would have called it a miracle.

Michael Vaughan started our innings with three glorious drives, hit between straight mid-off and cover point. Along with the pull shot, they are his trademark shots. No one plays them better. Just when he was threatening to build a really big innings, he nicked Shaun Pollock to slip on 23, giving Pollock his 300th Test wicket.

I go through the usual routine of being two away from being in. I put on my thigh pads and cricket shoes, and leave my pads propped up in my corner of the dressing room. I have played well at the Oval this year. I like batting here. It is another good wicket, very similar to the one I scored a hundred on in early July – the ton that started the sequence. I sit, like I usually do, on the last seat nearest the stairs down to the pitch, watching every ball.

Mark Butcher carried on where Michael Vaughan left off. Butch is probably in the best form of any England batter, and this is a pitch he has played on throughout his career. Most Surrey batters, having played for years on wickets with true bounce at the Oval, play with great freedom outside the off stump. Sometimes they don't fret about whether it is a front-foot or a back-foot drive. They just get a solid base with their feet, then throw their hands through the ball – the Surrey launch.

But having made 32 off just 33 balls, Butch is hit in front by a Hall inswinger and given out lbw. While I put on my pads, and put my gloves inside my helmet in the way I always do, Graham Thorpe leaves the dressing room to play his international come-back innings on his home ground. Over the last year, he has been through a fractious and public separation from his wife, withdrawn from the Ashes tour last winter, played a season of county cricket for Surrey, and now returned to the Test arena. The crowd give him a huge ovation, some standing and applauding as he walks down the steps through the crowd and on to the outfield. It is an emotional moment. I am now next in, and my nerves are more acute.

I am nearly in straight away. First ball hits him on the pad but is missing leg stump. He is off the mark next ball, nudging a typical single off his legs.

The last session is England's. Again a long partnership develops for the third wicket, with our two left-handers playing better and better. With about half an hour to go, while I am sitting next to the captain and coach, the issue of a night watchman comes up.

Do I want one? 'No, it's fine, having waited for so long, I'd rather get out there tonight if a wicket falls.'

It was academic. I had yet more waiting to do. At close of play, England were 165 for 2, with Thorpe on 28 and Trescothick on 64, in reply to South Africa's 484. This Test match could not be better placed. I am next in. It may be the most important innings I've ever played.

South Africa 484, England 165/2

6 September

It all happened today: fairy tales, nightmares, glorious returns and anxious exits. Sadly, I was on the wrong end of it all.

While I sat with my pads on all morning, watching every ball while waiting to bat, Marcus Trescothick and Graham Thorpe added 106 scintillating runs. At lunch, they had 103 and 86 respectively, and England were in the box seat at 271 for 2. I could eat a small lunch, then take a psychological rest for twenty minutes. Waiting and watching is tiring. Especially in these circumstances.

The circumstances were extraordinarily intense. England are trying to complete one of the greatest ever comebacks, win a vital Test match and level the series. I am batting for my immediate Test career, which is under threat.

The old truism is that cricket is a team game played by individuals. That guarantees mixed emotions and complicated scenarios. Coming off the back of three consecutive failures, I may need to play well here in order to secure a place on the winter tours. But my form may not be the only determining factor. It may come down to either me or Graham Thorpe, who is batting immediately ahead of me.

The standard practice is to lie about such things. That it never came into your head. That it is a straightforward business, simply wanting the best for yourself and your team mates. It might be a good idea to try to think like that. But it is hard not to think about the future and how it is being influenced by other people.

So as I watched Graham move towards his hundred, I had several different emotions. First, it was obviously good for England, and we needed it. Secondly, it was a great story in itself – he has been through huge trauma, and now cricket was providing a glorious moment of celebration. Thirdly, I knew the equation for me was getting simpler with every minute and every run.

As England moved nearer to South Africa's total, the chances of us batting for a long time in the second innings decreased. Assuming we go on to make a huge first-innings total, the game looks likely to progress in one of two ways. Either South Africa will bat well in their second innings, leave us no time to bat again, and it will be a boring draw. Or South Africa will be bowled out for a small total, leaving us few runs to get, batting fourth. The fall-out for me is that I may well not bat in the second innings. Result: this innings is it.

So with Graham moving closer to securing a touring place, and the likelihood of me getting two innings here decreasing, it was becoming simpler and simpler. One chance: runs needed.

Graham got his hundred. I didn't. He lifted both arms aloft while his home crowd saluted the return of the prodigal son. I made 16. My walk off was greeted with sympathetic applause. But that was soon drowned out by a huge standing ovation for Alec Stewart's farewell. I was the failure between two emotional Surrey ovations.

That is plenty of drama for one Test match. It all happened within an hour. First, in the early afternoon, Graham knocked a two off Ntini and reached his hundred. The crowd erupted, the dressing room cheered, up went his arms. Even to me, it seemed appropriate and inspiring: that sport can give second chances, that no one is ever finished, that fairy tales happen, that someone can look so happy on a cricket field. I will never forget it.

When we passed each other on the stairs a few minutes later, I had to block out all the emotion of what had gone before. This was my moment of truth and I refused to get caught up in the broader drama. I hit my first ball, from Kallis, perfectly off my hip for four. I had been waiting to bat for the best part of a day. 'Great start, Ed, great start,' Marcus Trescothick, well past his own century, said between overs.

The next over, I played two solid defensive shots off Andrew Hall, enough to realize that it is a belter of a wicket. Then light drizzle started, and we walked off for tea with Marcus on 137 and me on 5. Already, in just three balls, I felt I had made a real start. I had blocked everything out and played my own game.

After tea, I played straighter and more solidly than in any of my other innings this series. I left anything wide and defended straight. If I could just get a platform on this wicket, I would score more than quickly enough when I got going.

At the other end, Marcus reached his 150. Until then, I had only been in the middle while one milestone of a hundred or more had been reached. That was Nasser's hundred at Trent Bridge. This felt even louder. Enough to remind me how desperately I would like it to be me one day.

I played out three maidens, one from Pollock, two from Kallis. A tiny but noisy section of the crowd, having enjoyed the day's carnival of batting and a few drinks too, became restless at my circumspection. 'Run him out, Tresco!' shouted one wag.

A few balls later, after I hit two consecutive fours off Pollock, a straight drive to the pavilion and then a pull wide of mid-on – two favourite shots – the same section of the crowd started singing, 'We love you, Eddie, we do, we love you, Eddie, we do – oh Eddie, we love you.' I didn't care about either the heckling or the swift turn-around.

In the next over, the first I faced from Andrew Hall in this session, he bowled one just back of a length, bouncing about thigh high. On true, bouncy wickets, I often hit those through midwicket. It is a shot that I play naturally and instinctively. It has brought lots of runs this and every season. But I missed this one and there was a huge appeal. I thought straight away, 'Not out, going over.' After a longish wait, the finger went up.

There is disappointment, and there is acute disappointment. I have never felt quite so bad walking off any field. Regret, rage and helplessness swirled around in my head. I had been given the chance to secure what I have always wanted – an England spot – and I had failed. My primary thought as I walked off was, 'This cannot be it, this cannot be it, this simply cannot be it!' That and, 'It wasn't out, it wasn't out!'

It wasn't. Television replays showed it clearly going over the top of the stumps.

While I threw down my bat in despair, Alec Stewart was being cheered all the way to the middle. The South Africans formed a tunnel to salute him in his last game. History had taken over.

But there was only to be one fairy tale today. Alec played some dazzling shots in his 38. And when he was dropped by McKenzie, a straightforward chance at extra cover, it seemed destiny was on Alec's side. 'They've read the script,' we all said about the drop in the dressing room. After a hundred in his hundredth Test, three years ago, no one in the ground would have bet against a farewell ton as well. But three overs later, he was lbw to Pollock. 38 and no dream swansong. He joined me in disappointment on the balcony. Two men at opposite moments in their careers, who had both hoped for much, much more from today.

That started a mini-collapse. Marcus Trescothick eventually skied a hook on 219. It has been the most comprehensive return to form imaginable. He started his innings slowly, then gradually moved through the gears, and he spent much of the last two hours at the top of his game. He worked relentlessly in the nets in the two practice days before the Test. His reward was a thrilling double hundred.

We ended on 502 for 7. But Freddie is still in on 10. England are still on top. And I have a lot to think about. Not that it will make any difference what I think.

When the replay of my lbw came on to the TV in the dressing room, Michael Vaughan said, 'That was bad luck, that one.'

Bad timing to have bad luck.

South Africa 484, England 502/7

7 September

An hour of Flintoff – that was what we all hoped for today. A fun, brutal innings to deflate South Africa and ignite us. Freddie gave us ninety minutes instead. It was marvellous. In this instance, there really is no way of avoiding comparisons with Botham. It was some of the best hitting I have ever seen.

The ninth-wicket stand with Steve Harmison was worth 99. Freddie batted like he did at Canterbury in May. It was simple, uncomplicated brilliance. He hit back-foot straight-batted pulls over mid-on. He hit slog sweeps out of the ground. He hit cuts over point. He hit a straight-drive off Ntini over straight long-off. That one hit the reinforced glass in front of the players' dressing room, about three feet from where I was sitting. He hit it with such a compact swing that none of the England players moved until it nearly hit us. It couldn't reach all the way up here, not with just a check drive against a fast bowler, not all the way up here, surely? It did, and it smashed the glass.

There was a special atmosphere in the ground this morning. It has already been an extraordinary game. But I think everyone in the Oval sensed that Freddie had the chance to do something memorable today. They couldn't have asked for more. The fans were probably having chats in the stands similar to the ones we were having on the balcony. 'Where's he going to hit the next one?' 'Over the Vodafone boundary board at long-on.' 'No – more towards the pavilion.' So it went on, sixes in the middle, roars from the crowd, smiles in the dressing room.

The fall-out from Freddie's breath-taking innings was threefold. First, it meant that we had enough of a lead to attack when we bowled. Secondly, it changed the whole atmosphere of the ground and the Test match. Thirdly, it depressed South Africa and inspired us in equal measure.

Freddie was finally out for 95, trying to get his hundred with another six off Adams. He had played like everyone dreams of playing in a Test match: with uninhibited self-expression.

He set up another great day. We declared, nine down, with a lead of 120. For the next four hours the extraordinary emotional atmosphere of the game rarely levelled to normality. We kept taking wickets, usually in mini-collapses of two at a time. The crowd never drifted out of the game. It was one of those enthralling days only Test cricket can produce.

It started when Gibbs nicked a wide one off James Anderson. Then Martin Bicknell trapped Smith lbw in the tenth over. Steve Harmison, bowling fast and accurately, removed Kirtsten and Kallis in consecutive overs, reducing South Africa to 93 for 4. Bickers then produced a three-card trick to remove Rudolph: away-swinger, away-swinger, inswinger. Rudolph left it and lost his off bail.

McKenzie and Boucher, who have often stuck around together this series, stopped the collapse. But McKenzie was given out lbw for 38 off Freddie. Having bemoaned my bad luck yesterday, I should add that replays showed he clearly nicked it on to his pad.

Shaun Pollock hit his first ball to my left hand at short leg, toppled a little out of his crease, and I hit the stumps with an under-arm flick. It was referred to the third umpire. If I celebrated loudly when I ran out Darren Robinson at Chelmsford in May, I probably would have broken someone's eardrum had Pollock been given out today. But he had grounded his bat and was safe.

After surviving ten overs, Pollock and Boucher were eventually offered the light and inevitably accepted. But with South Africa 185 for 6, leading by just 65, we walked off tonight knowing that only rain or miraculous batting tomorrow will prevent us from winning one of the greatest comebacks in recent history.

The tour party for this winter is picked immediately after the end of the game tomorrow. Like any normal human being, I cannot help thinking about my future and whether I will be given the chance to cement a place in the England team in Bangladesh or be left to fight my way back at another time. But it is a lot easier to put that out of your mind, to have moments of full absorption in something else, when you are in the middle of a truly wonderful Test match.

There is no other word than 'electric'. Several people I knew in the crowd, who have played and watched a lot of cricket, said it was the best day's play they had ever seen. The first over was South Africa's. The rest was ours.

South Africa 484 & 185/6, England 604/9 declared

8 September

Tickets were reduced to £10 today and under-17s were let in free. 20,000 turned up, which means that 100,000 have watched this game over the five days. They came to see England win.

At 10.15 this morning, five minutes before the start of play, Alec led us on to the field. We waited for a minute at the top of the stairs, allowing him to accept the standing ovation on his own. How much better to say farewell in a 'live' game, with the crowd there to savour something still undecided, not simply loyally turning up at the end of a boring draw. It couldn't have worked out better: a packed Oval crowd, desperate to see England win a great Test match, applauding the most capped English cricketer.

We have taken to having huddles near the edge of the outfield before every session of play. Michael Vaughan said a few words, then handed over to Alec. 'Each of us here has always dreamed of being a hero,' he said. 'Well, this morning all eleven of us have the chance to be heroes.'

It went according to his script. The worry was that South Africa would get just far enough ahead to make it a nervy run-chase. Boucher, Pollock and Hall have all turned games around in this series. The fourth over of the day got rid of two of them. Boucher nicked Bickers to Alec. Then, first ball, Hall flicked straight to me at midwicket. We talk of premonitions in cricket (another weird irrationality): the strange feeling that a wicket is just around the corner. I have never had a stronger premonition that a batsman would be out first ball. That may be why I didn't celebrate wildly when I caught it. I tossed the ball to the umpire and jogged towards Bickers.

At 193 for 8, only Pollock could now ruin our day. So there was relief as well as joy in the huge cheer that followed Graham Thorpe's catching him at deep gully off Steve Harmison. Four overs later, again off Harmison, Ntini shovelled a kind of paddle hook shot over my left shoulder at short leg. I reached out my left hand, and dived left and slightly backwards. The ball hit the perfect catching area – just below where your first two fingers meet the palm of your hand. My fingers closed around the ball as I fell. As I lay on the grass, having worried that the ball might pop out when I hit the ground, I thought, 'It's still there!'

I celebrated that one. I ran towards Steve Harmison. He has bowled like we all know he can: fast, back of a length, bouncy, awkward to face. Soon the whole England team surrounded us, shouting congratulations at Steve and banging the top of my helmet. That was the tenth wicket. We had bowled out South Africa for 229, leaving us 110 to win. There is no sign of the rain that was forecast. We have more than enough time. The wicket is still flat. We left the field in euphoria.

The four South African wickets that fell today were: caught Stewart, bowled Bicknell; caught Smith, bowled Bicknell; caught Thorpe, bowled Harmison; caught Smith, bowled Harmison. Nearly ten years separate Steve and me from Graham and Bickers; fifteen separate us from Alec. Beneath the gripping central drama, this Test match is full of contrasts and ironies.

Back in the dressing room, Duncan greeted every player with a pat on the back and a word of praise. While the tenth wicket was replayed on the dressing-room TV, Nasser Hussain, out of the side with a broken toe – who has turned up to watch – said, 'Good snaffling, Jazzer!'

110 on a flat wicket. At the back of most people's minds was, 'Will Alec get another chance to bat?' At the front of my mind was 'Will I?' Neither of us did. Michael Vaughan's was the only wicket to fall. When Mark Butcher joined Marcus Trescothick in the middle, Ashley Giles turned to me on the balcony. 'I think we're

going to see some serious shots here!' Butch is in great form, Marcus already has a double hundred in the match. They didn't disappoint. We won in style, a luxury no one would have dared dream about for most of this astonishing Test match.

The celebrations started in the dressing room, then moved on to the outfield for the presentations: Marcus Trescothick, Man of the Match, Graeme Smith and Andrew Flintoff, Men of the Series. Michael Vaughan and Graeme Smith spoke about a series that has been both closely fought and played in a decent spirit. Master of Ceremonies Dermot Reeve introduced us all as we collected our individual medals. 'And number five, who took that brilliant catch today, Ed Smith.' I would rather I had been introduced as a first-innings centurion, but it was better than nothing.

After the ceremony, the team did a lap of honour around the outfield, thanking the crowd for being so central to the atmosphere of the Test match. Freddie had the idea of carrying Alec as we went. So the most capped Englishman spent his last few minutes in an England shirt draped in the flag of St George and being carried around his home ground on the shoulders of Freddie Flintoff and Steve Harmison. Even the coolest of rational minds would find it hard to deny that destiny was having her say.

But if the moment belonged to Alec, the day pointed forward not back, to the men doing the carrying. Freddie can reflect that his summer has been all about performance, not potential – something confirmed by being named Man of the Series. We have always known he is capable of winning five-day games. Now he is winning them. Steve Harmison, who bowled in the same mould as Courtney Walsh this game, will also now know he can do it – which is different from thinking you can do it.

For me, the next twenty-four fours will be strange, a weird mixture of joy and concern. Most of this eleven can be certain of a touring place. I am not. After the lap of the outfield, Radio 4's 'Test Match Special' programme interviewed me and awarded me the day's 'champagne moment' for the catch. Standing below the famous red-brick Oval pavilion, with a magnum of champagne in my hands and an uncertain future, I tried to get the right balance between celebrating a wonderful game and being honest about my own emotions.

My own emotions are mixed. How could they not be? But they should not stop me – still less anyone else – from revelling in something very special.

The huge team bath tub in the shower room has been filled. Soon it will flow with bubbles from Epernay. The singing has begun. There is a case of champagne to drink, a match to re-live, a private and more joyous victory ceremony to conduct. We have done something rare and inspiring here. This is a moment to savour. Personal concerns will not ruin it.

South Africa 484 & 229, England 604/9 declared & 110/1. England won by 9 wickets

9 September

Jimmy Anderson was still asleep this morning while I packed my bags and cleared out of the Grange City Hotel. I wasn't fully conscious as I went through the practical steps of getting ready to leave. Like a zombie, I moved slowly and on auto-pilot. The hotel concierge drove my car to the front door for me. I won't be getting that kind of service in the Hilton at Leicester, where I rejoin the Kent team tonight.

Between the drama of yesterday's win, the alcohol of last night's celebrations, and the uncertainty about my future in an England cap, I have run out of psychological energy. I am numb and tired, both elated and concerned. I crossed Tower Bridge with bright autumn sunshine lighting up the illusionist David Blaine's isolated Perspex box. I, too, feel I have been living in a goldfish bowl.

Today was the most ludicrous day of the season. Little sleep, a drive from London to Wye, a load of washing and a change of kit – from England lions to Kent horse – and then back in a car to Leicester. I am played out.

Martin Saggers drove me to Leicester. He sensitively allowed me to spend the afternoon at home – home? I think I remember what it's like – and waited until seven o'clock before picking me up. He has strong ambitions to play for England himself and might easily have pumped me for the inside track. He didn't, allowing me to oscillate between light chat and rest.

All the time, while we were stopped at one of those horrific service stations, while we were banging up the cricketer's most hated motorway, I wondered: will I get the telephone call? If I do, am I in or out? Will my ability to pick up the vibes tell me from the first introductory pleasantries?

'Ed? It's Grav [David Graveney]. Could you call me on this number? Thanks.'

It was an answerphone message. I somehow missed the call. A kind but weary tone of voice. I am out. But I am shaking a little anyway when I call back.

'It's Ed Smith.'

'Hi, Ed. How was your evening last night?'

Definitely out. Oh God, let's get this over with. I hate prolonging someone else's discomfort.

What David Graveney said is private and should remain so. He had some positive and encouraging things to say to me alongside the bad news. I had no intention of pushing for more information about why I wasn't picked. Some players like to know the ins and outs of selection, the shifts in opinion and favour. I think it is the right of selectors to keep it to themselves.

I wanted no appeasing, no softening of the blow. There it was – *not going* – and no words could change it. I left Grav to the rest of his phone calls, happy and sad, and he left me to the rest of my journey.

Martin said simply, 'I don't know what to say.'

'Oh, nothing is fine. Just a bit of quiet for a while.'

12 September

It won't surprise anyone that there is only one entry for this game. I am tired and we were stuffed. Nor did it count towards very much – Leicester are already relegated, Kent can neither win the championship nor be relegated. I made only 21 and 30.

I haven't played a championship match and failed to score a hundred since June. That is five games ago. They are the bare facts. The casual observer might assume I have thrown in the towel.

The truth is very different. Before the start of play on Wednesday, our coach Ian Brayshaw walked with me to look at the wicket. 'You're back on this stage now,' he said. 'People will be watching carefully to see if you still care.' He needn't have bothered. Between that phone call from David Graveney on Tuesday night and my first ball on Wednesday morning, I gave myself one of the severest self-lectures of the season.

So many players come back to county cricket from England psychologically damaged. The media scrutiny has scarred their self-belief; the step down in glamour defuses their competitive fire. I was determined I wouldn't join the list. I decided that I would play every county match from now on like a Test match. Practising is the best way to become good at something – so why not practise your psychological state just as you practise your off drive? I would give myself no easy outs; no 'Well, how can I get up for this – it's only a county game'; I would be tougher on myself than ever before. There was, in my mind, no reason why I shouldn't be better now than when I had been picked in the first place. Privately, I expected to get a big score.

I didn't get one. But I was in good form mentally. It was a damp, seaming wicket. My combined total of 51 was close to being the highest match total for any Kent player. It was, I reckoned, worth a hundred in normal circumstances.

I have never felt clearer than now. Having been exposed to Test cricket, I desperately want more. The way to become better equipped to play for England is to practise getting into that good mental state. The way to practise that good mental state – balanced, relentless, calm – is also the best way of scoring big runs for Kent. All paths lead towards performance, only performance. Everything else is peripheral. I don't have the energy for peripheral. I just need a decent wicket.

Though I have enjoyed being back among my Kent colleagues, I am a little worried that they may misread my no-frills outlook as ex-England loftiness. Nothing could be further from the truth. It is simply a question of emotional energy. I almost feel I have to choose between laughing and joking on the one hand, and scoring runs on the other. Normally I can do both. But the tank is running dry and I need every last drop for the last few days of the season.

Even Murali couldn't make me laugh. He kept saying, 'You're bloody useless, you are! What were you doing playing across a straight ball in the fifth Test? You threw away an easy 70! Absolutely useless! Now we can't have dinner in Sri Lanka. Useless!' I am pretty thick-skinned, and it was meant affectionately, but some other sportsmen might have found this ever so slightly wearing.

We have one championship game left and two big games left to win in the Sunday league, one of them this Sunday against Leicester.

The good news this week is that Geraint Jones has been picked on the England tour to Bangladesh and Sri Lanka. He is a no-nonsense wicketkeeper, a very decent person, and a fine, attacking batsman. It has been a wonderful first season for him. I was glad it wasn't all bad news for Kent players on the England front.

Leicestershire 295 & 5/0, Kent 130 & 169. Leicestershire won by 10 wickets

14 September

This was a crucial game. Both Leicester and we needed to win in order to survive in the First Division of the National League. What could stop it being a good game? A bad wicket. I was amazed that the pitch was covered when Kent practised at the ground yesterday. Today the wicket was still damp. Batting first was a lottery.

Leicester lost the toss and we put them in. We had them 37 for 4, 50 for 5 and all out for 98. Amjad Khan bowled fast and straight, and deserved his figures of 4 for 26. But batting looked almost impossible at times. When the ball is moving dramatically off the seam at 90 m.p.h., survival is hard enough, let alone the self-expression that one-day cricket demands.

The sun had baked off some of the moisture by the time we batted. I only got 1, but we cruised to 101 off only 19 overs, with Rob Key making 44 and Symmo getting 45. If we had started the game at four in the afternoon, it might have been worth watching.

But I am not really in the mood to think or write about bad county wickets. We got the points and still have a chance of staying in the First Division if we win next week.

Leicestershire 98, Kent 101/2. Kent won by 8 wickets

15 September

I have agreed to appear in the first programme of a new series of the TV comedy game show *They Think It's All Over*. It is recorded tonight and screened on BBC1 tomorrow.

Two months ago, during the championship game at the Oval, I appeared on a radio show in the same BBC Centre at White City. That night I arrived in anonymity, waited for a few minutes in the foyer, went upstairs, then sat down in the studio and recorded the programme.

Tonight, I was met in reception by someone called a 'celebrity booker', who whisked me to a private changing room. 'But I'm wearing what I've got on now,' I explained.

'Maybe – we'll ask the costume department if it's OK.'

Over the next few minutes, there were several knocks on the

dressing-room door from various BBC assistants. 'Hi, Ed, I'm Sandra/Catherine/Louise – I'm here to look after your clothes/make-up/food. Just shout if you need anything.'

My team consists of David Seaman, the comedian Rory McGrath and me; our opponents are Phil Tufnell, Jonathan Ross and Graeme Le Saux. The first problem was my shirt. It 'jumped,' apparently, meaning the very small check did funny things to the TV monitor. They swapped it for a navy linen shirt, which I happened to like, though I got the strong impression that my taste was not particularly central to the decision.

'So, obviously we've seen the show, Ed?' asked Nick Hancock, the show's witty host.

Having paused guiltily, I decided it was too late to lie, and said, 'Not really.'

'That's a good effort – never even seen it! – I'll talk you through it.'

First, we sat in our teams and went through the running order in the studio; then we broke up into separate teams to have dinner and plot how we were going to outwit the other side; then we recorded the show in front of a studio audience. The whole process takes about six hours, out of which they get thirty minutes' TV.

You quickly work out that one of your main jobs on *They Think It's All Over* is to be the uncomplaining butt of jokes made by the professional comedians. That's fine by me. It is, however, tough on the jaw muscles. By the end of the six hours, I felt like I'd been through a marathon diplomatic party: I didn't have a single smile left in me.

I only told one longish story, about Phil Tufnell bowling at me when I was a nineteen-year-old undergraduate at Fenner's. He objected very strongly to my voice when I called Yes, No or Wait from the non-striker's end. Talking gave me a nice break from smiling, and I'm pretty sure they'll use my story in the final take.

We all had a drink in the BBC's red room afterwards. But I wasn't in the mood for hob-nobbing with celebrities, and I left after saying thanks to the people who had made it an easy day for me.

I was chauffeured back to Wye by about eleven. I will watch tomorrow with that helpless feeling of not knowing what is in and what has been edited.

16 September

Over the past few weeks I have been thinking about the influence character has on your batting, and how batting influences your character.

Next time you hear a great batsman talking, listen carefully to how little he gives away, the caginess with which he discusses his craft, how he says less than he might, how his tone is: 'Yes, today was good, but hard times are rarely far away.' They aren't all like that. Some great batsmen have broad and innocent smiles, full of simple enjoyment of the game. But not many. The innocent ones don't tend to make it, and if they do it probably is more down to talent than persistence.

More typical of the great batter is caginess and cunning – either an innate, streetwise cunning (Javed Miandad), or a more studied caginess, deflected by layers of social charm (Colin Cowdrey). But the same thread of watchfulness runs through not only the play of great batsmen but their character too. Not many are gullible: imagine trying to pull the wool over Bradman's eyes – or Steve Waugh's.

Why do they – we – end up with that hunted, defiant look? Because we *are* hunted. Bowlers, bad pitches, poor umpires: they are all out to get us, or so it seems. Bowlers are the pack of hounds (admittedly only a pack of four or five, of whom only two run at the front during any one phase of the hunt), and we are the fox. Is the fox quick enough, wily enough, patient enough, lucky enough, resolute enough, determined enough to survive?

The same questions are asked of the batter. That is the nature of his examination. Some days he is overpowered (and would have been, no matter what he had done), some days he cannot take the pressure and capitulates, some days he is plain out of luck. Other days, one in three perhaps, the batter–fox endures and watches a tiring pack pant and wheeze its way to exhaustion in fruitless pursuit. His victory is rarely a moment (unlike bowler–hounds, who have the moment of death to celebrate) but a gradual drawing away into safety. The batter does not taste blood in victory, but witnesses the enemy's exhaustion. Batter–foxes must be in for the long haul. Those backward glances at tired-limbed and self-pitying hounds barking recriminations at each other are among the most joyous of a batter–fox's life.

But he also knows that the next hunt, in which the odds may be differently stacked, is not far away. Yes, he can let his guard down for a while. But the hounds will all the time be resting, eating, moaning and plotting. He must stay sharp because their pride will be hurt. The better at escape the batter–fox becomes, the more his scalp will be prized. His own success just adds value to the price offered for his life.

Don't like feeling chased, hunted, isolated, pressured, pursued, examined, hunted? Don't become a batsman.

17 September

There is a CD player in our dressing room which a few of us fight over: Michael Carberry likes rap, Andrew Symonds likes a CD called *Good Old Aussie Drinking Songs*, the rest of us are somewhere in between. I was first in this morning and put on James Taylor's 1970s classic 'Fire and Rain'. I heard Matt Walker's steps coming up the stairs. 'What a song!' he called out from the corridor. 'One of my top ten all-time tracks,' he continued. 'Who put that on?'

By the time Rob Key arrived, I had put on Bob Dylan's 'Most of the Time'. I said, 'Name the movie . . .'

'*High Fidelity* – starring John Cusack, from the Nick Hornby book,' Rob answered wearily. 'Any chance of a challenging question?'

So, in a sense, the season has ended how it began, with me, Rob and Matt talking about music and lists of great songs, albums and movies – the ties, as Bruce Springsteen put it, that bind.

Once warm-ups start, I don't want to practise too much, don't want to talk or be talked at unnecessarily, don't want to waste any competitive fire or psychological energy. I know what I have to do when the game starts and I want to get on with doing it.

This is a dead game, that is to say both Kent and Warwickshire will stay in the First Division next year, but neither of us can win any prize money or honours this year. It is the last game of the championship season, the sixteenth game of an arduous and exhausting season. It will inevitably have an end-of-term feel. But there is no reason why I should play as if it is the end of term.

I remember last year, when I was about to bat in a 'dead' fourth innings of a drawn game, Steve Waugh saying, 'This is when you practise it, this is when you practise mental strength; anyone can get up for big games, but this is where you get *good* at big games.' That is what I tried to say about that irrelevant fixture at the Bombay Gym in January. When it doesn't matter – *make it matter*.

I went in about half an hour before lunch at 95 for 1. As a number three, you have to be prepared to bat any time. It could be 11.01 a.m. or 6.25 p.m. You learn to feel neutral about timing. But, truth to tell, if I was asked to write a score and a time to go in, 95 for 1 half an hour before lunch would be about perfect. The day is not yet fully formed – it is still to be shaped – but the innings is off to a good start.

'Come on, let's hit these big pads straight away,' Ian Bell said before I took first ball, referring to my two lbw dismissals in the Tests. Dougie Brown bowled three off-side balls, then a straighter ball – meant to hit those big pads – which I clipped for a couple on the leg side. 'Come on, let's hit these pads bang in front,' I heard from somewhere. A few balls later, Dougie bowled another on about middle and leg, which I hit for four. That was greeted from behind the wicket by sighs and 'Ooohs' as if to say, 'Well, he can't keep on doing that.'

Players are vulnerable when they come back from England games. The whole professional community has been watching their examination on television. Their county opponents have been listening as their techniques have been picked apart. I remember playing against Surrey in September 2001, just after Ian Ward had played an unsuccessful series against Australia. We all knew everything that had been said, the minutiae of his preliminary movements, the way his bat sat in his grip, the fact that the Aussies had success bowling round the wicket. We felt we knew what to do to get him out and said so. Martin Saggers bowled round the wicket and got him out cheaply. (Ward got his revenge the next year with a brilliant, undefeated 150 that ruined our challenge against Surrey for the championship.)

Everyone wants to play for England. When you do, and others don't – no matter how sincere the generalized well-wishing for England victories – there is added spice in the contest when you get back to county cricket. Many people think it should have been them, or their friends, and that you fell short, or don't have it – whatever. You see it in their eyes. It is an extra pressure that it takes a while to recover from. I am absolutely determined both to acknowledge that extra degree of competitiveness as part of human nature and also to play as if I don't care what people think. I have been on both sides: a frustrated county player, and now a recently returned England player.

As for my innings today, I can now write words that I have often been told I should do more often: I played averagely and got a hundred. Coaches have said to me all my life, 'Learn to get runs when you're not playing well.' *Winning Ugly*, as Brad Gilbert called his book about tennis, is central to the whole concept of mental toughness. A surprisingly large number of players are capable, on their day, of batting brilliantly. Mark Wagh, who bowled a long spell against me today, can do it; Matt Walker, who was batting at the other end today, can do it. That is to be celebrated when it happens, but it's nowhere near the whole story. If I am to be as good as I want to be – and need to be for my private sense of well-being – I need not only to bat sometimes at the top of my game (like at Maidstone this July) but also to win games and bat for long periods when I am just moderate. Moderate, when you are twenty-six years old and in good form and thinking clearly and concentrating, should be enough to get the job done. You shouldn't be satisfied with it. But you should still make it count.

Today I was moderate for 121 not out at stumps. I felt short of rhythm, short of timing, low on energy, disappointed with my shot execution. Of the 13 fours I hit, none was memorable. My bat sounded cracked – in fact, it is cracked, but I chose not to change it. It felt peripheral that it was broken.

I also felt secure at the crease, unlikely to get out, settled and balanced. I made mistakes – you always do – but not stupid ones. I didn't play many big air-shots outside off stump. When I felt I was getting bogged down, I knocked a single. I was happy to be becalmed after my hundred, unbothered that I wasn't entertaining or fluent. There wasn't much joy in my batting today, just quiet relentlessness, which gives a different kind of satisfaction. I want to live more in this zone.

Despite the absence of external pressures, I found today more tiring than any innings this year – perhaps because I started the day drained, perhaps because it has been an emotional spell, perhaps because I turned today into a significant psychological test for myself. I just sat down in my corner at the end of play and felt happily empty.

As I have said in this diary, I am suspicious of some of the claims of sports psychologists. But in one area they are absolutely right. You can to some extent control your physical mood by acting the part. If you are tired and you act tired, you become more tired. If you are tired and you act alert (without expending unnecessary energy that you will need later when it counts), you feel less tired. If you are anxious and you act quietly assured, you become less anxious. Psychologists have proved that even your facial expressions have an effect on your physical state. If you can master masterful expression, you are one step closer to batting master-fully.

Playing sport when you are drained/nervous/below par thus becomes a form of method acting. The act becomes the show, the mask the man. But the act must be authentic. It cannot be so far beyond your psychological range that your body rebels and says, 'That's just not me, least of all now – I'm exhausted.' You must act yourself, but yourself at the fullest and best you can be. You perform best when you are the most you.

If that method acting has a positive effect on you, it has a negative effect on the opponents who witness it. I am not talking about banal bravado around opponents. But the way you walk up the stairs after a long day in the field, the way you look at lunch during an innings, the way you come across during the preparation for the day's play: it all affects your opponents' view of you. You can use them to your advantage. I am always amazed at how prepared cricketers are to give away weaknesses or worries to opponents – not only in what they say but also in the way they act.

Today I wanted to act the following outlook: I am in for the long haul, I am here all day. I was and now I am exhausted. I have the same ambition tomorrow.

Kent 379/3

18 September

This morning I felt exactly the same as yesterday – unrested, lethargic, drained, exhausted. I was exactly the same in warm-ups – quiet, not fully present, looking ahead. I also batted the same as yesterday. I played few memorable shots, never got into top gear, batted briskly but pragmatically, wasted no energy, pared down unnecessary thoughts and movements. Again, though far from being thrilling, I felt as focused and secure as I ever have.

When I had about 160, Warwickshire captain Michael Powell

said, 'Getting bored yet, Ed?' When I said no, he added, 'No, I didn't think so.' At lunch I had exactly 200.

Alex Loudon, who knows my game well and was watching as twelfth man, brought me lunch in the dressing room. He said, 'Well done,' then looked as if he had more to say. 'Well . . . I probably shouldn't be critical when you've got 200 . . .'

'No – that's exactly the time to be critical.'

'Well, it's just I've never seen you time the ball so badly for such a long period of time.'

That's what I was trying to say about yesterday.

I eventually had a slog at Jonathan Trott's part-time seamers after lunch. My 213 came off 343 balls with 26 fours. I batted for 7 hours and 9 minutes. They are all personal bests.

At the other end, Matt Walker passed a more important milestone. Just before reaching a hundred of his own, he hit his thousandth first-class run of the season. He looked rightly thrilled.

Inevitably when a side makes a huge total (594), there was much discussion by the fielding side about the impossibly flat nature of the pitch. I am not so sure – not because I am trying to turn my innings into something better than it was, but because the wicket continued to offer both lateral movement and variable bounce all the way through my knock. Not much, but enough.

But Warwickshire made it to 200 for 3 at stumps. We still have a great deal to do tomorrow. The quicker we can win this game the better – then we will have more time to focus on Sunday's one-dayer. We have to win that to stay up in the First Division.

There's not much left in this tank – and I'm sure I'm not alone.

Kent 594, Warwickshire 200/3

19 September

It couldn't have worked out much better than this: 17 wickets needed in two days; 17 wickets taken today; rest day tomorrow before the crucial National League game.

Warwickshire resumed their first innings on 200 for 3. But that became 267 all out as Mark Ealham bowled a great spell of away-swing bowling, taking 6 for 35. I think he bowled a bit quicker than normal today, without losing any of his away swing and accuracy.

Warwickshire followed on. And though their captain Michael Powell made a counter-attacking hundred, the second innings belonged to our two young spinners, Rob Ferley and James Tredwell. They shared five wickets as Warwickshire collapsed for the second time in the day, this time for 257.

There was relief and satisfaction. We have played well all game and have overcome late-season weariness of mind and body. Losing by an innings at Leicester last week was out of character. We were glad to bounce back well here. The way you finish a season affects the way you feel in the winter, while you look forward to the next one.

But no one will remember this if we lose on Sunday. It couldn't be simpler: one must-win game remains.

Kent 594, Warwickshire 267 & 257. Kent won by 70 runs

20 September

Tomorrow, that's all. One day left, one day left! I just need to find one last bit of energy and (more important) concentration. My double hundred this week required me to dip into the last of my psychological reserves. I have been feeling shattered ever since.

Even though we won the championship game inside three days,

we practised today on what would have been the fourth day. Dave Fulton is determined we will be fully drilled for tomorrow's game: it will most likely decide whether Kent will be relegated in the National League. If we win tomorrow – and we survive in the top flight – we will exit the season with pride intact. Given all the crises and challenges we have faced, staying in the First Division of both competitions would be a quiet triumph.

I am beyond daytime sleep. This isn't the kind of tiredness that can be cured by an afternoon nap. In fact, I would rather some distraction, something different, a new perspective to refresh my mind.

Two friends of mine from Boston are visiting England and have broken their journey to come and watch tomorrow's game. They have never seen a cricket match. So you can imagine my anxieties tomorrow: that it will be a miserable September weekend and a dreary on–off game full of rain breaks; that I will fail with the bat and we will lose; that they won't have any idea what is going on out there.

Today, as we sat in my garden on a high summer's day in mid-September, I find myself explaining not only cricket, and the significance of tomorrow, but also what I have been through over the whole season, the frustrations and despair and moments of private victory. I doubt I have spoken to anyone so fully about the broad sweep of the summer. How strange: rather than talk to those closest to us, it is sometimes easier to confess to people we don't know so well or see so often.

It was a cathartic conversation, looking both back on this summer and forward to the autumn, when I will be spending some time at Harvard.

I drove off to have dinner with my parents, looking forward to one last push tomorrow.

21 September

I have reserved a corporate box in the Les Ames stand at Canterbury for today's game. It is a favour from the club. I asked for just the box (no food or drink – I didn't want to push my leverage in the club after a hundred or two) – so this morning I was nearly late for warm-ups while I drove to the other side of the ground and emptied the contents of my kitchen into Box I. I am not sure what the likelihood is of my assorted friends (a) catching the right trains from London, (b) having a hope of finding this box, (c) understanding cricket, or (d) liking one another. The temptation to glance up to Box I when I am fielding will be enormous.

For my mental outlook before today's game, re-read my thoughts before the first day of this championship game – only this time I am even more tired and burnt out. I did my usual practice routine with coach Ian Brayshaw before the game. I have never hit the ball worse. 'This is a waste of time – if I'm not ready to play today's game now, I won't be any better off after crunching a few off drives.' That's the first time I've ever quit on bad practice – and I know it will make no difference at all either way.

I had only one last thing to say to myself before today's innings: you have always wanted to play in a Cup Final at Lord's; make this match a must-win game with no second place or second chances, a Cup Final in your mind; imagine that staying up in the First Division is like winning a trophy.

More Kent fans wished me good luck – 'We just can't get relegated, Ed!' – than ever before. We are one of the best supported counties, and they are very proud of our tradition of always being in the First Division.

It is, unbelievably, yet another perfect day. Too perfect, maybe – I wouldn't mind if it was fresher, then I would feel more awake and alert. Kent won the toss and decided to bat. Rather eccentrically, before walking out to bat, Rob Key and I listened to Bob Dylan's 'Not Dark Yet', a meditation on death and dying, recently likened to Keats by literary critic Christopher Ricks. *That* I can't explain. Anyway, it was Rob's idea.

Warwickshire's overseas pro Waqar Younis, the great Pakistani fast bowler, did not play in this week's championship game. But he is playing today, and he bowled the first over against me. After a wide first up, I cut the second for four. There was loud applause from a packed Canterbury crowd, more than you normally get for an early boundary. They really are nervous! The tense atmosphere in the ground receded a bit.

I hit four early boundaries and we got off to a quick start. I did not feel in great form. The early boundaries were just there to hit, and I got them between fielders. But with my score in the high teens, the boundaries dried up. Rob was playing well at the other end, but I was struggling both to pierce the field and to get singles. Rob would get a single early in the over, then I would use up much of the rest of it without scoring.

I was physically lethargic and technically short of timing and rhythm. It was hot, but my tiredness was disproportionate: I have batted in much hotter weather and felt fine. I think I was simply played out. Sitting on my haunches at the non-striker's end at the end of one over, my 'bad voice' even wondered if I might be better leaving it to other batters in a sharper frame of mind and with fresher legs.

What about that Cup Final mentality, I countered. What a time to leave it to others. After such a season – after being so determined not to leave it to other people. I reminded myself that the wicket was awkward and uneven-paced. It was difficult to bat fluently. Which meant it would be harder still for any new batsmen who weren't used to it. If I could stay in until the last ten overs, the big hitters in the middle order would be able to hit with freedom.

When Rob Key was out for 28, Andrew Symonds walked to the wicket so fast and intently that I feared he might be in a 'six, four or out' mood. 'You're swinging too hard at the ball, Ed,' he said as he walked past me. 'Bunt the ball for singles and get off strike.' I followed him towards the striker's end, saying, 'Good luck, give yourself a chance to get in – it's not an easy wicket to play big shots.' Symmo's first ball: Whoosh! Miss. Stretch. Scratch of the guard. Glad we got that one out of the way.

He was, however, absolutely right about me. I found a little bit more rhythm, and hit more singles. I started to get into the contest. Again, there was plenty of spice in the contest – and no end-of-term feeling. Warwickshire keeper Keith Piper and Symmo were engaged in a private battle; Dougie Brown explained why he had had more than enough of me for one week.

Gradually, our stand moved from promising to significant. The difference between winning one-day games easily and having to scrap all the way is often one big partnership. As I learned in the years when I often watched one-day cricket from the side-lines, 100 for 1 or 2 is a start – but if it turns into 120 for 4, it wasn't worth that much. 180 for 1 or 2, on the other hand, might well be match-defining. It takes the pressure off the middle order. They can hit out without fear. That middle period of the innings has got a lot to do with simply carrying on and taking the right options – unglamorous, nuts-and-bolts cricket.

Some overseas pros just turn up and play for a county, then leave without much sense of belonging. Symmo is different. He considers Kent his second home and is passionate about us winning. He needed no second invitation to fire up and get involved today. We have shared some big stands over the years – the best one being 200 at Leicester two years ago when we chased over 400 in two sessions to win a championship game. We also batted throughout the middle period of the one-day game this year at Maidstone when we beat Glamorgan.

In today's chats between overs, I kept saying, 'Just like Leicester,' or 'Just like Maidstone.'

'Keep running hard!' Symmo would shout as he set off for two. I was struggling a bit and erred on the side of conservatism. Symmo always scores very fast. I got going too, hitting a straight drive and a clip off my hip for two boundaries off Waqar. In the fifties and sixties, I was hitting boundaries again, but I still felt physically short of hustle. I reasoned – and this time it was a sensible voice, not my bad voice – that now we had an excellent platform, I was better off looking for boundaries. Our strong middle order was stacked with batting. I could afford a risk or two.

With Kent on 159 and my score on 74, I skied a lofted drive and was caught and bowled by Alan Richardson. I walked off at Canterbury for the last time in 2003, pouring with sweat and utterly drained. I looked up and saw I was getting a standing ovation from the Frank Woolley Stand. Some of the applause, I think, was for the season that led up to today, not just the 74.

'You look awful,' a couple of people said to me. In the mirror I saw a very red, puffy face staring back at me. Our physio ran a cold bath and suggested I take some dehydration powder. I sat in my corner in the dressing room, drinking as much as I could, refuelling on bananas and watching Matt Walker get straight into fifth gear with some great shots. The twelfth man, who took Symmo a drink when I was out, told me Symmo was furious with me for giving it away.

A couple of overs later, Symmo was out for 49. He walked off as quickly as he had walked on. That worried me. He stared at me as he stormed into the dressing room, then threw his pads into his kit bag. His added 'What's the point!' was aimed in my direction. But there was no point having the conversation now. I was very confident Kent would both make a big score and win the game.

Thanks to some great hitting from Matt Walker and Mark Ealham, we ended up with 267. As I watched them hit four huge sixes, I reflected that – for once – it might be better that someone else was out there, not me. I am not, however, going to make a habit of thinking like that.

We started brilliantly with the ball. Amjad Khan, again bowling fast and straight, got three early wickets, including Warwickshire's danger-man, Nick Knight. Amjad won us last week's game at Leicester. When he is in this kind of form, he is as likely to take wickets as anyone in the country.

We never looked seriously threatened at any stage. But Dave Fulton, who has lived this difficult season so intensely, kept urging us to stay sharp and not take anything for granted. Symmo, who took two wickets to go with his 49, looked like he might murder anyone who appeared to be relaxing before the tenth.

When it came, the tenth wicket, a lofted drive to long-off by Waqar Younis off James Tredwell, landed straight in my hands on the boundary. I was fielding a few feet away from the box full of my friends and family. I glanced up and saw a few of them leaning out to get a better view. I try to avoid sentimentality, but that was a nice moment.

While the players all congratulated one another, I shook Dave Fulton's hand. What a journey he has been on. At least there has been an acceptably happy ending. He will not spend the winter living with the disappointment of being relegated. We are in fact the only team that has never played outside Division One in either championship.

The crowd reacted as if we had won a cup final, rushing on to the pitch, demanding autographs and surplus pieces of kit to take home. I eventually made it off the outfield, after signing more autographs than normal. Up on the balcony, waiting for the end of match ceremonies, most of the players threw old caps, gloves and shirts into the hands of the kids below.

I was a long way short of elation, but I didn't want the moment to pass too quickly. I looked across the outfield, pale and parched after a dry summer. The light, reminding us of autumn's arrival, was fading more quickly than I felt it should after such a hot day. My team mates, free from anxiety for the first time since April, were smiling and opening bottles of beer. I saw my group from Box 1 chatting in a circle on the outfield.

I moved my focus to various random faces in the crowd. How much happier their car journeys back home will be after a win, particularly this win. I remember. I did it plenty of times, after wins and losses, as a child. It is a strange thing, allegiance to a team. I looked at the faces looking up at me, for the last time in 2003. We players are the temporary custodians of our club and our game. How lucky we are.

Kent 267/7, Warwickshire 163. Kent won by 104 runs

22 *September*

Tonight was the P.C.A. Awards evening, a glitzy black-tie dinner in Park Lane to celebrate the highlights of the summer and to present trophies to the players of the year. Most pros, including me, turn up and say goodbye to another season.

The P.C.A. telephoned me a few days ago to make sure I was going – they want to take a photo of me with a player-of-the-month award from July. But the six monthly awards – all already announced – are peripheral to the main prizes. I confirmed I was going and thought no more of the call.

Under the stewardship of David Graveney and Richard Bevan, the P.C.A. has become increasingly professional and influential. They offer help to players on insurance, legal matters, education, cars, accountancy and investment. They have also set up a charitable fund that looks after ex-players who have fallen upon hard times.

Even the dinner is a testament to the P.C.A. It is fast-paced, slick and brilliantly organized – complete with live bands, professional comperes, TV cameras and huge video screens. Before the awards were presented, a video was shown of the season's narrative – the story of county and Test cricket in 2003, the resignations and debuts, the retirements and appointments, the nadirs and celebrations, the whole story and its cast of characters, a collage of memories set to a variety of famous pop songs.

When I appeared on the vast video screens from time to time, spliced into the narrative to accompany the beats of a rap song, I felt the curious sensation of watching myself being watched. A thousand eyes, many belonging to people who play cricket for a living, were watching me celebrate my 203 at Blackpool and then my fifty at Trent Bridge.

Ah, the sporting montage! The highest of highlights – without a boring second or flat emotion – played alongside the danciest of dance music. How easily we are manipulated into rapt attention. Sporting montage appeals to our deepest sporting fantasies: heroism without the boring bits, set to catchy tunes. It is hard not to surrender, hard not to love it.

As a ten-year-old, I had a whole video of sporting montages that I had recorded from the television one after the other. It began with a four-minute summary of the 1986–7 Ashes victory, Botham's sixes and Broad's centuries and everyone else's diving catches (song: 'I'm walking on sunshine, yeah yeah, I'm trying to feel good . . . I'm walking on sunshine . . .'). That was followed by a few minutes of highlights from the 1986 Commonwealth Games – the sprint relays, the tearful withdrawals, the joy on the podium (song: Bruce Hornsby and The Range's 'That's the Way It Is'). Hot on Roger Black's heels came Magic Johnson and Michael Jordan slam-dunking across America's basketball courts in the NBA, while MC Hammer rapped 'You Can't Touch This'.

Even now, sixteen years on, I can recall the details without straining a memory muscle. I watched that video over and over until the VHS film wore out. It was the prompt for sporting fantasies of my own: playing for England, thrilling a crowd, winning the Ashes. I didn't flirt with dreams of playing sport professionally. I created a complete picture of what it would be like and knew it intimately. I internalized the music and the images of those sporting montages into my private world of sporting ambition – a world in which I spent a huge amount of time when I was growing up.

But tonight, when it was some of my fours and sixes that swung to the beat, I was struck by the huge difference between sport as it is lived and sport as it is consumed. That day in Blackpool, from which several shots were used tonight, I remember not elation nor adrenalin but a kind of concentrated blankness. It was fun, of course it was. But it was a calm kind of fun, a million miles away from the pumped-up adrenalin-fuelled experience that the sporting montage suggested. So much of the time we sportsmen are trying to stay calm, to rev at a lower intensity; the editor of the highlights package wants to create the illusion that it is all macho thrills and hot-blooded drama. The truth, I reflected as I watched tonight's video, is so, so different.

The first major award was the Young Player of the Year, which Kabir Ali won ahead of James Anderson. Next was the Sheer Instinct Award. Charles Colville said it is given for an outstanding moment, 'the player who does something that stands out, something really special'. A moment? My heart didn't speed up at all. Until, that is, Chris Adams read out from his card, 'The winner of the Slazenger Sheer Instinct Award, for his four consecutive first-class hundreds in July, is Ed Smith.'

The spotlight beam picked me out at the Kent table and followed me to the stage, where Chris gave me the award and Charles Colville told me to stay for a quick interview. Given that the selectors had made the terrible mistake of leaving me out of the tour party, he joked, would I be spending the winter writing in America or playing cricket in the southern hemisphere? A bit of both, I said. What about the Test matches, he went on, what terrible wickets! I said something about that all being part of Test cricket and what an honour it had been to play in Alec's last game and such a wonderful finale at the Oval.

It went OK, but, truth to tell, I was shocked to win something and unprepared to say anything. Walking back to the Kent table, I looked out at the array of professional cricketers in front of me, from nineteen-year-olds yet to make their debuts to veteran warhorses near the end. Several of them, like Alec Stewart and Matt Maynard, had given me such pleasure as a fan long before I ever met them as opponents or colleagues. There was a lot of talent in that room, and I felt humble and proud to have won something in that company.

I was one of the four players nominated for Player of the Year – *more* sporting montage – but Mushtaq Ahmed rightly won it. The rest of the evening was a farewell to Alec Stewart, who looked as chipper and forward-looking as ever, as if another twenty years at the top might not be beyond him.

After dinner, while the bands tuned up and the tables were cleared, I wandered aimlessly, chatting with whoever I bumped into. Some were keen to avoid cricket – a cross they no longer had to bear – others were happy to replay the highlights and low

moments. Marcus Trescothick was standing next to me when the
P.C.A. photographer took a picture of me. The last time we
had spoken properly, we were driving back to the hotel after an
unbelievably happy team sing-song at the Oval. Like when I
bumped into him in the foyer of the hotel before my first day with
the England team, I didn't want Marcus to feel obliged to
go through the motions of saying, 'Bad luck on missing out.' I
moved on.

I saw Dean Cosker of Glamorgan, who played with me for
England Under 19s. 'How was the summer?' I asked. (Stupid
question – if you don't know yourself, there's a good chance the
other person won't want to talk about it.) 'Much the same as when
we spoke two weeks ago, Ed.'

Paul Havell was keener to talk cricket. On a freezing cold
morning in March, when Paul was trialling with Kent after being
sacked at Sussex, we had been in adjacent baths in the dressing
room at Canterbury. He was trying to resuscitate his career, the
long and lonely process of being a triallist: a soul-destroying round
of bed-and-breakfasts and £26 a day plus travel expenses and
weary clichés from coaches saying, 'Sorry, son, no luck here.' That
morning he had just finished bowling at me in the nets. 'I can bowl
better than that,' he said. 'There's another gear, I just can't quite
get there at the moment. There's another gear. I can bowl better
than that. There's another gear.' We didn't offer him a contract
and I haven't seen him since. Tonight, he was as happy as any
prize-winner. Derby had just given him a two-year contract and
he was back in the professional community. 'Well done, Ed –
brilliant!'

'Well done yourself.'

Alec Stewart had rather more conversations to deal with, no
doubt, so I didn't keep him long. He'd had some little batting tips
for me at the Oval Test – perhaps we could meet up in the winter
and discuss them properly? 'I'd like that, Ed.'

Kent's two games against Sussex this year were in May and June
– some seriously unhappy memories! – so since I last saw Robin
Martin-Jenkins I have played three times for England and he has

won the championship. Back in January, on a potentially lonely practice trip to Bombay, Robin had been brilliant company – curious about a new culture, and amused by the mini-dramas and eccentricities of life in India. There was a lot to talk about – too much, in fact, to fit into a semi-drunken chat that was constantly interrupted by others.

As the drink loosened the politeness and cautiousness, I could have stayed to the bitter end, being congratulated and congratulating others, consoling and being consoled. I was touched by the warmth and respect of what many people said. But I felt tired and couldn't face going over the same old ground too many times. I slipped out early, with a trophy under my arm and a bitter-sweet feeling.

Waiting outside the hotel for a taxi, when a voice shouted, 'Are you still talking to me, now you're a prize-winner?!' It was Will House, formerly of Cambridge, Kent and Sussex, now retired from cricket and working in London. Between the ages of thirteen and twenty-three, Will waited to bat after me or with me literally hundreds of times. We grew up ten minutes apart from each other in Kent, attended rival local schools, and played dozens of games together for our club, Sevenoaks Vine. Having played for years as Kent juniors, we made our full Kent debuts in the same week of 1996 – me in the championship, Will in the Sunday league. We were exact contemporaries at Cambridge, where we both studied history and played three years in the cricket team. For a while we even went out with two girls from the same college.

Now Will has retired from cricket, the present is free from direct comparisons, but the past remains full of shared experiences. He was pleased to catch up tonight, and I wished him luck for his wedding in Cambridge next week. I will be there – another homecoming of sorts – watching Will marry his Cambridge girlfriend, while my thoughts turn towards America, where I will be spending most of October and November at Harvard.

Epilogue

What a year, a season of chaotic swings and yet uncanny symmetry. It started in India this January, in the heat and the dust and the search for a giant leap forward; next January, I will be back in the subcontinent, this time on the England 'A' tour, under the tutelage of Rodney Marsh. As for the present, I write from Harvard, where, again exactly a year ago, in autumn 2002, *The Times* sent me to write an article about the Harvard–Yale football game and the differing cultures of university sport in Britain and America. Now, as was the case a year ago, I am not in the England side.

But between India and India, Harvard and Harvard, not being in the England side and not being in the England side once again, lies a season of freaky extremes, ducks and double hundreds, call-ups and let-downs, three England caps, some personal trophies, and a run-scoring record or two. But anyone could have read all that in the papers.

It has also been a year of ambition both sated and whetted – to play for England, achieved; to succeed for England, awaited; a year of personal tragedy (for David Fulton) and personal frustration, then elation (for me); a year which started with the longest period of reflective introspection of my life and ends with me looking forward plainly and jauntily. It is also perhaps the only year of the last six that I will end less eccentric than I began it. Perhaps it is failure, not success, that sends us in unusual directions.

This year has brought me a new house, home and lifestyle, one that threatened to be solitary and turned out warmly social. This season brought a new attitude to the game I love. The player in me, in short, caught up with my personality. A breakthrough year indeed. How glad I am that Steve Waugh told me so many times that I had to write a diary, and that months later, having forgotten the project, I bumped into a Penguin editor at a books party who was prepared to take a risk that I might come good. If I did, imperfectly and intermittently, I owe it partly to the long list of people who either never doubted that I would or who found ways of contorting their tone of voice to make it sound like they still believed.

A year ago I wondered what I had to do to play – and play well – for England. Now I think I know, and I want to get on with doing it. To that extent, this year has been a process of glorious simplification, a mass of advice and differing approaches whittled down to a stark phrase: you know how to get runs, just do so, today, tomorrow, the next day, on and on, relentlessly. If you can't, now you know how, it's time to move on. But as a historian of the past, I think the sequence looks good for the future. The 213 in September proved that July was not the high point but the starting point. That was why I was so keen to get runs in the last game.

So much for the historian in me. The sportsman, too, feels what the historian thinks. There is a lot of unfinished business and I am going to get it done.